D1236615

COMPETITION, GROWTH STRATEGIES AND THE GLOBALIZATION OF SERVICES

Competition, Growth Strategies and the Globalization of Services examines the international growth and diversification of real estate advisory services in the United States, the United Kingdom, Germany and Japan since 1960. The book explains how successful firms develop competitive advantages in the global marketplace.

An evaluation of forty prominent firms (ten from each country) provides a comparative reference for a detailed analysis of the growth and internationalization of four major real estate advisory service firms (one from each country). The firms have responded in many ways to changes in international real estate investment, and their fortunes have varied accordingly. This raises a number of important questions:

- What is the best growth strategy?
- What are the most effective market-entry strategies?
- Why do some companies make a successful transition to the international marketplace?
- Why do others fail?
- Which cultural differences affect international growth?
- Do successful companies grow organically or by using joint ventures, networks and strategic alliances?
- What is the importance of innovation and diversification for competitive advantage?

The analysis provides factual evidence demonstrating growth strategies that enable a firm to become a successful real estate advisory service in today's global economy.

Dr Terrence LaPier is the Entrepreneur-in-Residence at the Entrepreneurial Center at the Wharton School of the University of Pennsylvania. He leads a global research and consulting effort with CEOs focusing on entrepreneur-to-professional-management dilemmas.

ROUTLEDGE STUDIES IN INTERNATIONAL BUSINESS AND THE WORLD ECONOMY

COMPETITION, GROWTH STRATEGIES AND THE GLOBALIZATION OF SERVICES

Real estate advisory services in Japan, Europe and the United States

Terrence LaPier

London and New York

First published 1998
by Routledge
11 New Fetter Lane, London EC4P 4EE

Simultaneously published in the USA and Canada
by Routledge
29 West 35th Street, New York, NY 10001

Routledge is an imprint of the Taylor and Francis Group

Reprinted 1999

© 1998 Terrence LaPier

Typeset in Garamond by Routledge

Printed and bound in Great Britain by Biddles Ltd, Guildford and King's Lynn

British Library Cataloguing in Publication Data
A catalogue record for this book is available from the British Library

Library of Congress Cataloging in Publication Data
LaPier, Terrence, 1954–
Competition, growth strategies and the globalization of services:
real estate advisory services in Japan, Europe and the United
States / Terrence LaPier.
p. cm.
Includes bibliographical references and index.
1. Real estate business–Japan. 2. Real estate business–Europe.
3. Real estate business–United States. I. Title.
HD913.L36 1998
333.33–dc21
97–45903
CIP

ISBN 0–415–16924–0

CONTENTS

ILLUSTRATIONS

Figures

Tables

FOREWORD

Dr Ian MacMillan

Terrence LaPier's book is based on a carefully assembled and painstakingly detailed analysis of the globalization of real estate advisory service firms that spans both decades and continents. Thus no serious real estate professional who is concerned with international real estate business can afford to ignore this monumental and unique undertaking.

The fundamental insight that is the foundation for the book is the observation that, despite the globalization of this industry, real estate is ultimately a localized industry requiring expert knowledge of local property and investment markets, and that the firms' ultimate success in each competitive market depended on the combination of their local expertise, reputation and professional relationships. The dilemma for firms engaged in globalization is that the unit of real estate is illiquid and has unique properties largely dependent on local economic and property market conditions. Thus localization of the real estate advisory services was a necessary, but not sufficient condition for global success – there arose a need for a multinational organizational structure in response to the growth of international real estate service needs, primarily driven by the demands of clients who were multinational corporations making substantial cross-border direct investments in real estate as their multinational expansion took on global characteristics.

Thus LaPier shows us how globalization of real estate advisory services flowed from two major macro processes: first, from the development and opening of formerly national real estate markets and second, the subsequent pattern by which firm development marched to the cadence of cross border direct investment. The opening of national markets was accompanied by, and also pressured by, migration of real estate investments, investors and professional advisors, which then drove an expanding demand for advisory service products. Thus expanding rates of cross-border investment by and among global investors in globalizing financial markets (led by investments from corporations, financial institutions, securities and investment banks, pension and insurance funds) paved the way for real estate advisory firms to open offices and introduce innovative advisory service products.

In the absence of detailed and uniform government and industry data within the domestic markets and among the four countries of his study (US, UK, Germany and Japan) LaPier has painstakingly combined and interpreted cross-border direct investment statistics, general economic statistics and detailed case studies of leading firms based in each of the focal countries. He followed this up with personal interviews with industry and academic leaders, industry publications, professional journals and consultants' reports. This book is therefore a unique compilation of data with respect to the globalization of the industry. By reviewing fluctuations in cross-border direct investment in real estate in each of the four countries and documenting major trends and episodes in the foreign expansion of real estate advisory services in the four countries, his book reconciles specific national factors that shaped internationalization in local property services with global trends in real estate investment.

LaPier shows that the basic dynamic that drove the development of the advisory firms themselves was demand derived from the growing need to support the cross-border investment patterns. The book traces the patterns of cross-border investment by the major investor groups who tended to prevail in different national markets at different times. The internationalization of the advisory firms developed as they attempted to compete by attending to the differing circumstances they faced in the disparate countries. They did this by offering new services and new functions in foreign markets and to foreign investor clients in response to macroeconomic regional changes (such as the emergence of the Eurobond market after 1963 and deregulation in the 1980s in Europe and Japan).

At the heart of success for real estate advisory firms was their access to key clients, the best of whom placed high demand for only the best advisors. This put in place a virtuous cycle – the advisory firms' increasing ability to create innovative services to support a burgeoning volume of cross-border real estate investment activity expanded each national market's ability to attract superior investors, which in turn demanded even greater quality and variety of advisory skills which led to a further ability to continuously innovate by those advisory firms responding.

The book then turns to an in-depth analysis of the expansion strategies, product diversifications and shifts in forms of ownership and management structure of ten leading firms in each focal country, to explore and explain the market and organizational determinants of success in global expansion. The findings from this forty firm analysis provide the framework for the in-depth case analysis of four firms, each in one of the focal countries, that were deemed successful globalizers.

The in-depth case analysis of the four successful firms explores the major innovations in product and services that emerged through the 1963–1993 time period. The analysis attends to the evolution of these firms and how this evolution was shaped by the diverse traditions, cultures, national economic policies of the parent countries and allows us to distinguish the major determinants of successful real estate advisory service strategies.

Real estate advisory services represent a highly unregulated profession encompassing a number of professional disciplines: brokerage and agency activities, property management, appraisal and portfolio evaluation, development and construction management, real estate market research, real estate investment banking and portfolio investment management.

LaPier observes that under pressure from the rise of cross-border direct investment in their domestic markets and abroad each successful firm eventually invested substantial capital to diversify its original advisory services. In its own way, in response to its local cultural and national environment, each successful enterprise developed strategies that deepened the firm's penetration of the rapidly growing international corporate and investment markets initially at home and then increasingly abroad. Additionally, the emergence of formidable competition from professional service providers like accounting firms and from financial intermediaries like commercial and investment banks (who had a long history in real estate debt and equity instruments) pioneered innovations that were subsequently adopted by real estate advisory service firms.

LaPier concludes that success attended those globalizing real estate advisory service firms which first cultivated and achieved a substantial reputation in their parent country ahead of their international expansion. This was accomplished by conservative financial management strategies which husbanded and provided the funds needed to capitalize their product diversifications and their geographic expansions from retained earning, followed by judicious infusions of domestic and foreign capital from equity partners of shareholders. The expansion of the successful firms was accompanied by the parallel creation of multidepartmental structures integrating a centralized but entrepreneurial control system with localized operations management.

LaPier's Herculean analysis provides the basis for the following important conclusions. First, although the development of global real estate advisory service to a large extent paralleled the ebbs and flows of cross border direct investment, the major basis of competition of real estate advisory firms was, and will continue to be on the basis of three major and interrelated competitive forces: superior access to markets, capital and clients; reputation stemming from secure domestic and international sources; and internationalized professionalism resulting from aggressive investment in the best quality professional staff.

Second, firms based in free trade national markets had the benefit of being able to exploit international competition and an increased access to cross-border transfer of information which gave access to innovations, clients and capital superior to those of firms in restricted markets.

Third, the optimum organization structure accommodated the requirements for a global strategy integrated with local responsiveness. This called for a centralized, multiregional and multinational network of offices but with an autonomous but cooperative multidiscipled departmental system. Such multifunctional and multiregional practices were difficult and expensive to imitate.

Fourth, key to accelerated expansion was the ability to secure and retain multinational and foreign clients, such as property intensive enterprises like manufacturing firms moving internationally or large diversified investment funds seeking cross-border investments.

Fifth, to capture such clients, leading firms consistently invested corporate capital in recruiting, retaining and training well educated professionals whose professional quality directly affected reputation – the key to establishing value with clients. It appears that investment in and retention of trained professionals had greater long-term value in national and international competition among property advisory firms than did an abundance of capital.

Sixth, success was highly dependent on responsiveness in service diversification to client demand, which then led to an ability to thereby broaden access to other types of clients and to new sources of potential revenue. The tendency was to react to changes in markets and competition rather than to proactively invest in systematically researching and developing innovations.

Seventh, privately owned and operated firms tended to have the greatest flexibility to grow, contract or expand incrementally in response to shifts in property and investment markets.

Eighth, in the mid-1990s the trend was toward global consolidation in the industry through acquisitions and alliances, as the emphasis shifted from growth in staff to reduction in costs as profit margins decreased due to the increased competitive environment. The expectation is that those advisory firms that lead the process by acquiring rather than becoming the targets of acquisition will tend to prevail.

ACKNOWLEDGMENTS

Competition, Growth Strategies and the Globalization of Services is the product of my experience at the three particular institutions – Bechtel, the London School of Economics, and The Wharton School – crucial to my professional development. At each institution it was my good fortune to work with – and learn from – unique and distinguished colleagues. At Bechtel I developed the skills and knowledge necessary to conduct a successful international business; at the London School of Economics I developed the discipline necessary to study objectively what makes a global business successful; and at the Snider Entrepreneurial Center at Wharton I taught venturing courses on how to make such study useful to both worlds: business and academic.

As with all major undertakings, this book would not have been possible without the assistance and goodwill of the several individuals who contributed their knowledge and experience to my efforts over the past seven years, while researching and writing my doctoral thesis at the London School of Economics, and during the thesis transformation into this more broadly focused book. I am most grateful to Professor Leslie Hannah of the London School of Economics (LSE), my adviser for the PhD degree. Through countless discussions and his extensive and repeated comments, I gained an immense and wide-ranging understanding of international business and economics. Since I commenced research on the international services industry, he has inspired me to explore other creative and analytical avenues. I am indebted to Professor Hannah for the degree of flexibility he permitted me during those critical intellectual growth years.

I am especially indebted to Professor Ian MacMillan of the Sol C. Snider Entrepreneurial Center at The Wharton School of the University of Pennsylvania for his inspirational discussions about strategy research, and for the Center's generous financial support of this book. Professor MacMillan has been a special mentor to me as I further integrate my career with business, academic and government experience to better understand complicated dilemmas and create effective solutions. I have learned a great deal in general from him. For this book in particular, he took the time to review numerous drafts and provided many thoughtful suggestions, enabling me to refine and clarify my ideas with more careful analysis.

Two colleagues who share my interest in real estate played important roles in helping me finish this book: Dr Peter Linneman, the Director of the Real Estate Center of The Wharton School, and Dr Susan Wachter, the Chair of the Real Estate Department of The Wharton School. I want to thank them again for their help.

My research assistants, Michael Palys of the Real Estate Center of The Wharton School and Jackie McCafferty of the Sol C. Snider Entrepreneurial Center of The Wharton School, were a major help in providing greater detail to each section.

Throughout my research, I interacted with hundreds of real estate advisers, corporate managers, academics and investment bankers throughout the world. These individuals have forged many joint ventures, alliances and innovations for many of the latest competitive strategies for market-entry purposes. As an international businessman and academic, I have a renewed respect for individuals who, even as I record their problems and solutions, are searching for pragmatic responses to new and vexing organizational issues and dilemmas at the frontier of international management. Without their assistance and generosity, this book could not have been written.

A number of other individuals also contributed to my effort. I am especially grateful to Keith Steventon of Weatherall, Green & Smith; Dr Greg Marchildon of the London School of Economics and more recently of Johns Hopkins University's School for Advanced International Studies; Pierre Rolin of Credit Suisse in London; Wayne Kullman, formerly of Orix; Andrew Burt of Jones Lang Wootton; a number of key executives at Cushman & Wakefield; Stewart Forbes of Colliers International; several partners and professional staff members of Goldman Sachs and Morgan Stanley; and Ms Akiba of the Japan Desk at the US Library of Congress. John Rutter of the US Department of Commerce has provided invaluable assistance in identifying government data sources for each focal country and reviewing statistical data and analyses.

I extend sincere appreciation to the editorial staff at Routledge where, in particular, Dean Hanley and Alan Jarvis kept a watchful eye on the book.

Meredith, my wife, has continuously encouraged me through the rigorous research and writing process to strive for excellence. I appreciate her patience and perseverance during this time. Finally, I am deeply grateful to my parents and family for their constant and unsurpassed support, always encouraging me to achieve the goals for which I strive.

Winter 1997
Philadelphia, Pennsylvania

1

INTRODUCTION

Growth strategies that work

In order to understand the creation of competitive advantage for successful service firms, *Competition, Growth Strategies and the Globalization of Services* examines the international growth and diversification of real estate advisory services in the United States, the United Kingdom, Germany and Japan since 1960. These four countries were selected because they were the most active in cross-border direct investment (stock and portfolio) during this period. Their intricate economic interdependencies prompted the greatest advancements in innovative real estate advisory services. They also showed the widest variety in types of investment as well as economic and industrial cycles.

An evaluation of forty prominent firms – ten from each country – provided a comparative reference for a detailed analysis of the growth and internationalization of four major real estate advisory service firms – one from each country. The examination focused on the essential factors influencing international growth: the size of the firm, staff growth, domestic and foreign personnel, service diversification, property markets, cross-border real estate investment, and a client profile of fee revenues. The case studies present a comparative analysis of the international expansion strategies and the resulting corporate structures of four companies that were among the leading domestic real estate advisory firms to capitalize on the growth of both national and foreign real estate markets after 1960.

The case studies provide factual evidence for a number of growth strategies already tested in the real world. In order to become a successful real estate advisory service firm in today's global economy, a firm should follow the following strategies:

- Identify and follow the investment flows of capital for client and market-focus considerations.
- Use a tracking technique to monitor existing and potential clients' ongoing requirements.
- Develop a solid reputation for objective counsel and technical capability.

- Establish a reputation in an international market location such as London, Tokyo, New York, Hong Kong, Frankfurt, Paris, Berlin, Miami, Los Angeles, Sao Paulo or Buenos Aires.
- Establish a reputation with strong credentials and expertise in a particular market or technical service.
- Recruit skilled personnel; make sure they acquire a thorough knowledge of the local market; and continually train them in the latest technical, innovation and market developments.
- Introduce innovative services and techniques.
- Diversify into affiliated real estate services to broaden the range of potential clients.
- Develop a network of offices worldwide.
- Gain experience in foreign markets and the logistics of international expansion.
- Use a decentralized, multi-division organization in foreign expansion to take advantage of market and technical trends in a prompt and efficient manner.
- Gain competitive advantage by investing in service diversification and geographic expansion.

This book identifies and describes which firms executed these strategies most consistently in various markets around the world. Although many, if not all, of these strategies were crucial to the effective and efficient international growth of the most successful real estate advisory firms described, many firms neglected to follow them and consequently failed to achieve all of their goals.

By raising the key questions to be answered and identifying the main issues discussed, this chapter provides an overview of the entire book in the following sections:

- Questions for success
- The changing market
- Economic drivers: the determinants of international expansion
- Innovation and expansion
- Who should read this book
- How the book is organized

Questions for success

International real estate investment flows have undergone many changes over the past four decades; economic and industry-specific cycles have affected all of the firms and services involved globally in real estate. Real estate advisory service firms have responded in many ways, and their fortunes have varied accordingly. These developments raise a number of important questions that will be reviewed in this book:

- What is the best domestic and international expansion growth strategy for a company?
- What are the most effective local, national, and foreign market-entry strategies?
- How do small and medium-size service firms grow internationally?
- Why do some companies make a successful transition to the international marketplace? Why do others fail?
- Which cultural differences affect international growth?
- Do successful companies grow organically or by using joint ventures, networks and strategic alliances?
- What is the importance of innovation and diversification for competitive advantage?
- How can a firm grow globally in today's hypercompetitive marketplace?

In order to understand why some firms expand successfully while others do not, the book examines several dimensions of the economy affected by domestic and foreign investment in commercial real estate assets after 1960. For example, rising worldwide commercial property investment appeared to be an important factor in the following areas:

- The escalation of domestic and multinational corporate real estate values.
- The growth of construction industries and related service sectors.
- The changes in the net worth of major financial institutions and private investment groups.
- The creation of REITs and opportunity funds in the worldwide marketplace.
- The asset diversification of insurance, mutual fund and pension fund portfolios.

As part of this trend, the growth of international business and the rise in mergers and acquisitions also elevated cross-border direct investment activity in real estate as manufacturing-based and financial service firms expanded into industrialized and emerging markets. The book also identifies the relative impact of total cross-border real estate investment flows on employment levels in the commercial real estate sector in the US, UK, Germany and Japan.[1]

The changing market

Increasingly competitive and complex real estate markets required international investors to become more knowledgeable about the unique requirements of real estate assets. The demand for the *objective* counsel of property advisers with technical knowledge of functional areas and products appeared to rise incrementally with the expansion of commercial property investment. Real estate advisory services covered diverse disciplines within the real estate profession: the sale and leasing of property, real estate finance, institutional investment, property and asset management, portfolio investment management, and project management and construction. In light of the profession's broad scope, the firms studied included several types of organizations: full-service and fully diversified firms; "niche" firms with limited, specialized practices; and other professional service firms, such as accountants, attorneys, mortgage lenders and financial counselors, which began to introduce specific real estate advisory service capabilities in the late 1960s.[2]

A critical issue in an examination of international real estate advisory service firms is that real estate, in all its manifestations, is ultimately a localized industry that requires expert knowledge and understanding of local property and investment markets. Whether regional, national or international in their scope, real estate advisory firms reviewed in the course of this study succeeded or failed due to their collective local expertise, reputation and professional relationships. These twin, and often competing, requirements for local responsiveness and a multinational organizational structure define the broad outlines for evaluating the relevant factors that have prompted and sustained the growth of international real estate services since 1960. Unlike capital and securities markets, real estate lacked a centralized market mechanism; each market, large or small, was discrete and fiercely independent. Thus, to a greater extent than other financial services, real estate advisory services depended on both market mechanisms and the firm as a coordinating element.

The client market was also unstructured. Clients, typically the source of investment capital, commissioned real estate advisers for third-party counsel and for specialized expertise about particular property and financial markets. Most property service firms advised both real estate and non-real estate entities: individual investors, multinational corporations, commercial and merchant banks, building societies in the UK, savings and loan associations in the US, insurance and pension funds, universities, local governments, securitized investment and unit trusts, and international developers and construction firms.

The book explores the process by which property advisory services internationalized and gained an important role in the global service economy by counseling investors on the location and volume of investment activities, thereby influencing the international flow of real estate investment funds. It also examines whether real estate advisory firms gained competitive advantage over the period due to the presence of two basic conditions: first, an international network of property professionals; and, second, a diversified services practice – brokerage, property management, finance, facilities planning and development, and real estate sales and purchases.

By reviewing national fluctuations in cross-border direct investment in real estate, and periodic changes and major episodes in the foreign expansion of real estate advisory services, the book seeks to examine specific national factors that influenced effective internationalization in domestic property services. Basic principles of economic history provide the theoretical framework concerning competitive and comparative advantages among nations and particular organizations.

The subjects of discussion are not just a few notable successes, but those firms that experienced moderate international growth and those that failed both domestically and abroad. The focus of the analyses throughout is on the international expansion of firms, the mobility of firms in foreign markets, and service dissemination across national borders. Indeed, the industry structure and the sector's overall population were not much larger in 1997 than they were in 1960, as reviewed in Chapter 3. The countries studied were largely dominated by domestic firms with domestic practices in 1960; only those firms that existed in 1960 and attempted to expand abroad or actually internationalized were evaluated. There are various discussions regarding firms that evolved during the period between 1960 and the present, but do not conform to this study. Firms selected for evaluation in the collective profile in Chapter 4 and the case studies in Chapter 6 were specifically identified, based on both the firm's internationalization over the period and its size in 1990. The book devotes limited attention to analyzing local and regional firms and domestic professional property services. Several firms that failed in international expansion are reviewed in Chapter 4.

Economic drivers: the determinants of international expansion

Real estate markets in the US, UK, Germany and Japan experienced a dramatic restructuring between 1960 and the present, shifting from a predominantly local focus to a national and international orientation. The globalization of the real estate industry, which first emerged in the early 1960s and catapulted to international prominence in the 1980s, was driven by the rise in cross-border direct investment in real estate.[3] Certain professional services that internationalized concurrently with growing cross-border investment supported foreign investment activity by following capital and investors across international borders. A growing body of recent research indicates that market expansion, in turn, aided allied services to establish independent channels of global trade in banking, accounting, law, construction, securities, insurance and real estate advisory services.

In fact, a study sponsored by the Corporation of London with the London Business School focused on the interesting issue of a firm's home-base location and the important contribution a headquarters base in a city such as London – an international financial and corporate center – played in supporting international growth of the city's professional services, specifically law and accountancy. The study reinforces the conclusions of this book: that while value-added reputation stemmed most of all from local market knowledge and a firm's technical capabilities, international growth was supported by quality relationships with multinational clients strategically based in such international market centers as New York City or Los Angeles in the US, London in the UK, Tokyo in Japan and Frankfurt or Munich in Germany.[4] The case studies presented in Chapters 4 and 6 give direct and compelling evidence that the firms that enjoyed the greatest international growth were headquartered in the world's principal international market centers – alongside many of their major multinational clients who were also investing in foreign property markets.

Real estate advisory services expanded into new service products and foreign markets to capture the clients, the expertise and the market positioning created by the tremendous growth in cross-border investment. The book examines whether the factors that supported the internationalization of real estate services in the four focal countries were associated directly with those factors also influencing the expansion of cross-border real estate investment. These factors included the strength and size of domestic property markets, government regulations, national foreign trade policies, multinational trade by domestic corporations, and the regulation of international financial markets and investment vehicles. Each of these elements was subject to long-term and abrupt economic shifts, which affected the direction and rate of expansion into foreign markets. The ability of individual firms to coordinate innovations across multinational and multifunctional divisions is an equally important factor.

Innovation and expansion

Innovations in services and technical skills, and their diffusion within and between firms, provided the key to an examination of the efficiency with which real estate advisory services expand into foreign markets. While innovations were eventually adopted by real estate advisers worldwide, considerable time-lags occurred between the introduction of innovations and their diffusion to advisory firms in other nations. In this book, "introduction" is defined as the first successful, systematic and profitable application of a new service product that promoted international expansion, rather than an isolated effort to implement an idea that failed to gain market acceptance. "Diffusion" is defined as the liberal circulation or dissemination of information and knowledge between and among firms and countries.

A considerable time-lag between the successful introduction of an innovation and its widespread use among property advisers in other countries would suggest substantial disparities in cross-border investment activity by certain types of investors in these other countries, and perhaps even a weak link in the innovation and diffusion process. Pension fund portfolio management services, for example, followed such a course, as discussed in Chapter 5. Specifically, portfolio services were introduced in the UK in the early 1920s and were freely observable by others, yet did not come into widespread market use in the other countries until the beginning of 1965. The earliest observance in Germany did not occur until this time simply because property investment by insurance companies did not create demand for portfolio management services.

The prime mover of innovation in real estate advisory services appeared to be capital investment flows across borders. Significant changes in inward and outward real estate investment stock and flows, as well as the degree of volatility in the national economy, indicated shifts in the direction of capital markets and the opportunity for innovation. The introduction of major innovations was examined relative to changes in direct real estate investment stock and flows, in annual GDP growth, and in annual property investment yields in the focal countries. Over time and through different investment cycles, innovation became an essential factor in retaining domestic capital and attracting foreign investors.[5] Significant shifts in the stocks of inward and outward direct real estate investment appeared to indicate periods of innovation, such as with public capital and securitized investment services discussed in Chapter 5.

Real estate service firms excelled through local market knowledge and expertise, while gaining a multinational or global reputation and organizational structure. This international recognition broadened a firm's client base and service capabilities, and further equipped its personnel to penetrate widely dispersed local markets. By contrast, the firm profiles and case studies, presented in Chapters 4 and 6 respectively, provide evidence that local and regional firms lacked a national and international reputation and were thus constrained in their ability to expand abroad. Such firms chose to cultivate a regional client base rather than invest in a multiregional and international network.

In all focal countries, regional and national real estate service firms by the 1980s were challenged by competitors to move into international investment markets – foreign regions or foreign clients. Some firms, lacking capital to expand or the managerial resources to grow, affiliated with established foreign firms or joined global cooperative networks. Firms sought to gain competitive advantage by achieving both local market knowledge and multinational access and prominence. The profession concurrently diversified through combination and integration into specialized functions: pension fund management services, accounting services, financial management consulting, legal services, and construction management services. Through diversification, real estate service firms broadened their professional skills (also an important source of innovation) and their client base.

Who should read this book

Real estate advisory service professionals should find *Competition, Growth Strategies and the Globalization of Services* useful in understanding the forces driving their business in the global economy in this century and beyond. For those who want to find the best ways to help their firm expand internationally, this book should be of special interest.

The exploratory discussions, illustrations and entrepreneurial strategies should interest consultants and advisory service professionals such as venture capitalists, pension fund managers, real estate professionals and developers, investment bankers, corporate managers, bankers and attorneys. In addition, academics, students, journalists and anyone interested in studying entrepreneurship, real estate investment and international business should find this book useful in understanding what actually happens and what really works in these fields. This book can also be utilized as a reference tool; reading the entire book from beginning to end is not essential to understanding its main points. For example, you could skip the detailed – and sometimes technical – review of cross-border direct investment in Chapter 2 and still follow the corporate profiles and case studies of specific firms in later chapters.

How the book is organized

An historical analysis of cross-border direct real estate investment is presented in Chapter 2, focusing on trends in inward and outward investment for the US, UK, Germany and Japan.[6] Chapter 3 examines the principal factors that influenced the internationalization of real estate advisory services in the focal countries.

To focus the discussion further, Chapter 4 traces the historical evolution of ten leading firms in each focal country that internationalized at some point during the period between 1960 and 1997. This chapter evaluates service diversification, expansion strategies, management structures and forms of ownership, and also documents the marketplace and/or organizational (strategy and structure) determinants of several "failed" firms, which are defined as enterprises that failed as multinational operations or lost significant capital due to foreign expansion.[7] This collective profile provides the general foundation and analytical framework for the in-depth case studies presented in Chapter 6.

Chapter 5 argues that real estate advisory service firms in the focal countries acquired and deepened their competitive advantage in the international marketplace by continually developing new skills and moving into new markets. This chapter examines major service innovations and market-oriented technical innovations that advanced the internationalization of real estate advisory services throughout the period.

Chapter 6 presents case studies of the international expansion strategies of

8

four leading real estate advisory service firms in each of the four countries: Cushman & Wakefield of the US, Jones Lang Wootton of the UK, Müller International of Germany, and Orix of Japan. By selecting four firms based in four different nations with diverse traditions, cultures, and economic circumstances, this comparative analysis attempted to isolate determinants influencing successful international expansion in real estate advisory services as distinct from idiosyncratic ones. Among the four companies, several distinctions were analyzed: service diversification, response to and promotion of periodic innovations, expansion strategy, ownership structure, and domestic and international organizational structures.

Cushman & Wakefield, founded in 1917, was selected because it diversified its practice throughout domestic and international markets more rapidly than any other US firm, establishing a presence in the European market through a joint initiative with a UK firm. Jones Lang Wootton, founded in 1783, is the most successful UK advisory firm (known as a "chartered surveyor" in the UK) to expand under its own name and ownership throughout the global marketplace. Müller, established in 1958, was the first German firm to move beyond the domestic market, entering alliances with a global real estate services network to broaden its international presence. Orix of Japan is among the first independent non-trading companies involved in international real estate advisory services, expanding from its core business in financial services to acquire a controlling interest in a major US development and investment advisory firm.

Each firm invested substantial capital to diversify its core advisory services in response to the rise of cross-border direct investments in the domestic market and abroad. Moreover, each enterprise developed specific strategies for domestic and global expansion to deepen the firm's penetration of rapidly growing international corporate, development, and investment markets. In summary, the case studies set forth factual evidence that international real estate advisory service firms initially cultivated and achieved a solid reputation in their home nations prior to international expansion. Moreover, service diversification and geographic expansion were not necessarily mutually inclusive strategies. In fact, privately owned service enterprises that were governed by conservative financial management gained competitive advantage through an ability to capitalize service diversification and geographic expansion from retained earnings, as well as infusions of domestic and foreign capital from internal equity partners or shareholders. Simultaneously they formulated an integrated, multidepartmental structure that centralized corporate entrepreneurial control and decentralized localized operational management.

The conclusions presented in Chapter 7 are based on the major findings from the preceding chapters. The strategies for growth listed at the beginning of this chapter, and a forecast for real estate advisory services, are based on these conclusions.

Notes

1 Employment statistics in the real estate sector are used as the economic indicator, or proxy, of domestic property market growth generally.

2 See M.A. Hines, *Marketing Real Estate Internationally* (New York: Quorum Books, 1988), pp. 16–17, 77, 81, 142.

3 S.E. Roulac, "The Globalization of Real Estate Finance", *Real Estate Finance Journal*, vol. 4 no. 2 (1987), p. 39.

4 R. Cohen *et al.*, "The Competitive Advantage of Law and Accountancy in the City of London", The City Research Project (London: London Business School, 1994).

5 A. Baum and A. Schofield, "Property as a Global Asset", Working Papers in European Property (Centre for European Property Research, University of Reading, March 1991), p. 67.

6 Stock data represent the cumulative historical book value of direct investors' equity, including reinvested earnings in and net outstanding loans to their foreign affiliates. However, data on Japan represented the cumulative value of planned projects, not actual stock value. By contrast, flow data represent the total of annual direct investment capital flows of equity, reinvested earnings and intercompany debt.

7 The "universe" of firms that were evaluated was limited only to domestic firms that internationalized at some point between 1960 and 1997. A full recitation of domestic firms in 1960 which subsequently failed in the domestic market was omitted.

2

CROSS-BORDER DIRECT INVESTMENT

Before we look at the internationalization of real estate advisory services, it is important to review trends in cross-border direct investment and international real estate investment in the United States, the United Kingdom, Germany and Japan. The historical review of the growth of real estate advisory services presented in this chapter and the next provides a context for the more detailed discussions in later chapters.

What follows in this chapter is a discussion of the major factors affecting real estate advisory services, including:

- Cross-border direct investment since 1960.
- The liberalization of international capital controls.
- Outward and inward investment trends in each of the focal countries.
- Cycles in cross-border direct investment.

Some of the discussion in Chapter 2 is relatively technical due to the data comparisons for the four countries; if you are not familiar with some of the terminology, you may want to turn to Appendix A where the analytical framework for the book and key terms are explained.

Recent trends in cross-border investment

Cross-border direct investment, c.1850 to 1950

The movement of capital across national borders as a measured phenomenon dates back to the late nineteenth century. Available data on international capital flows indicates that there were three major capital exporters – the UK, France and Germany. The major capital importers were the US, Canada, Australia, Sweden, Italy, South Africa, Argentina and India.[1] Although the data are tenuous and subject to a significant degree of error, scholars have pieced together information that enabled limited estimates of outward direct investment stocks in the late nineteenth and early twentieth centuries. One such estimate indicated the world stock of direct investment abroad totaled

$14 billion in 1914, mostly from the UK ($6.5 billion), US ($2.4 billion), France ($1.7 billion) and Germany ($1.5 billion).[2] Most of this investment was in railways, utilities, land, public works and manufacturing operations. Historical research also indicates that most foreign investment in real estate prior to the 1850s was in land used for crops and cattle ranching, and during the Second Industrial Revolution (c. 1865–1920) in sites for factories. After World War Two, cross-border direct investment in manufacturing and associated service industries began to expand on a larger scale.[3]

Cross-border direct investment, 1950 to 1980

Although cross-border direct investment in land, other natural resources and infrastructure development continued to be important after World War Two, by the late 1950s and 1960s a new phenomenon emerged. The modern multi-national corporation gained in economic power as manufacturing companies expanded into new markets and new products. US multinationals achieved the largest gains during this period, primarily due to their advanced technology, management, marketing and lower cost of capital.[4]

Government restrictions on cross-border direct investment in services,[5] including real estate, were a major factor limiting such investment, particularly in Europe and Japan. In addition to regulatory and cultural barriers in the focal countries, the fragmented nature of real estate markets raised the economic cost of information about overseas markets compared with those costs for domestic markets. Another factor limiting cross-border direct investment in real estate was that financial markets in Western Europe and Japan were more heavily regulated in the 1950s, and financial institutions focused primarily on meeting domestic needs and supporting international trade in goods, not financing foreign investment.[6]

Cross-border direct investment stock data shown in Tables 2.1, 2.2 and 2.3 represent the cumulative historical book value of direct investment, unadjusted for inflation or for changes in market value. These stock data were collected by direct survey of foreign direct investors, and were provided by the focal countries in aggregate country and industry format. Because these stocks were valued at historical cost, they were usually understated, except for years when market values of commercial real estate fell substantially, such as 1974–5. Despite this understatement, compared with either current cost or market value, historical book value data approximated the market value for recent years because the majority of cross-border real estate investment by the focal countries was made in the 1980s. To date, only the US provided current cost and market value estimates of total outward and total inward direct investment. The US did not, however, provide current cost or market value estimates of direct investment in real estate specifically.

Trends in outward and inward real estate investment, 1950–80

Cross-border direct investment in real estate was relatively small well into the 1970s (Table 2.1). The stock of outward direct investment in real estate in 1966 from Germany, Japan and the US collectively totaled $575 million, or only 0.5 percent of the world stock of outward direct investment at that time.[7] This is a low proportion, considering that total outward direct investment from these three countries accounted for over 54 percent of the world stock of outward direct investment at that time. By 1975, parallel real estate data were available for all four focal countries; the UK and Germany were the largest investing countries. Outward real estate investment from both countries had increased to over $2 billion, while from Japan and the US it lagged behind at around $250 million each. By 1980, when Germany, Japan and the US began to provide annual time series data, outward real estate investment from Germany had jumped to over $6 billion, but had increased only minimally for Japan and the US. The UK reported industry-specific outward direct investment data on a triennial basis since 1978; in 1981, outward direct investment in real estate totaled $3.3 billion, representing a modest 17 percent increase since 1975.

Before 1970, none of the focal countries, except Germany, identified inward direct investment in real estate separately. In 1970 only Germany and Japan recorded inward direct investment in real estate: $274 million and $3 million, respectively (Table 2.2). By 1975, the combined stocks of inward direct investment in real estate for all four focal countries rose to $1.6 billion, or about 0.8 percent of the world stock of inward direct investment.[8]

Except for the US, the monetary value of inward real estate investment in the focal countries was relatively small before 1980. In 1980 the US hosted the largest amount of inward direct investment in real estate at $6.1 billion, followed by the UK with $2.1 billion and Germany with $1.7 billion. Most US inward investment in real estate was from Germany, the UK and other European countries. Japan hosted only $23 million, reflecting long-standing government restrictions on foreign direct investment in general.

Liberalization of international capital controls

After World War Two, all of the focal countries except the US placed restrictions on capital outflows in order to relieve domestic shortages of capital and to promote a faster recovery from the disruptions of the war. The US first initiated voluntary controls in the 1960s, and then instituted mandatory controls on capital outflows in response to balance of payments and excess dollar liquidity problems.

During the 1970s, many countries, including the focal countries, began to loosen capital controls on outward direct investment. In part, the major industrial countries reduced their restrictions on international capital markets with

Table 2.1 Stock of outward direct investment in total and in real estate by the focal countries (1950–present, in millions of US dollars)

	Germany[a]		Japan		United Kingdom		United States	
	Total	Real Estate	Total	Real Estate	Total	Real Estate	Total	Real Estate
1950	67	–	–	–	–	–	11,788	38
1956	203	0	–	–	–	–	22,505	81
1957	306	0	–	–	–	–	25,394	–
1958	408	23	–	–	–	–	27,409	–
1959	483	48	–	–	–	–	29,827	–
1960	618	72	348	2	11,798	919[b]	31,865	123
1961	820	125	447	3	12,744	993[b]	34,717	138
1962	1,103	175	546	4	13,690	1,067[b]	37,276	149
1963	1,361	226	671	27	14,636	1,141[b]	40,736	162
1964	1,654	288	790	27	15,583	1,215[b]	44,480	177
1965	1,961	325	949	28	16,469	1,284[b]	49,474	197
1966	2,315	388	1,176	35	17,355	1,353[b]	51,792	209
1967	2,581	400	1,451	35	17,325	1,351[b]	56,560	210
1968	3,041	450	2,008	36	18,241	1,422[b]	61,907	211
1969	3,716	596	2,673	38	19,926	1,554[b]	68,093	213
1970	4,511	813	3,577	44	21,065	1,643[b]	75,480	215
1971	5,689	948	4,435	48	23,304	1,817[b]	82,760	218
1972	7,034	1,218	6,773	103	23,411	1,826[b]	89,878	218
1973	9,200	1,739	10,267	223	35,303[c]	2,753[b]	101,313	220
1974	11,723	2,158	12,663	240	36,061	2,795[b]	110,078	221
1975	12,528	2,136	15,943	251	37,584	2,831[b]	124,050	221
1976	23,315	3,109	19,405	266	39,962	3,117[b]	136,000	224
1977	28,111	3,781	22,211	301	46,444	3,622[b]	145,990	227
1978	37,071	4,704	26,809	399	57,255	7,141[b]	162,727	243
1979	45,181	5,761	31,804	504	69,840	3,723	187,858	235
1980	47,823	6,149	36,497	595	76,823	3,996	215,375	251
1981	49,901	6,029	45,428	778	85,721	3,320	228,348	249
1982	50,971	6,624	53,131	901	84,017	3,280	207,752	550
1983	50,186	6,606	61,276	1,144	83,878	3,274	207,203	558
1984	50,764	6,594	71,431	1,326	86,874	3,870	211,480	445
1985	66,085	8,547	83,649	2,533	101,270	4,557	230,250	384
1986	86,431	11,112	105,969	6,531	121,465	5,465	259,800	348
1987	110,020	13,942	139,333	11,958	158,958	5,811	314,307	1,868
1988	114,465	13,186	186,355	20,599	190,028	6,080	335,893	1,857
1989	133,328	14,555	253,896	34,742	198,650	6,356	372,419	2,025
1990	169,055	17,382	310,808	46,444	226,794	4,560	424,086	1,860
1991	188,401	17,662	352,392	55,343	234,311	5,612	467,844	1,919
1992	197,198	18,844	386,530	60,490	224,447	5,147	502,063	2,435
1993	205,795	19,611	423,863	66,560	250,655	5,039	564,283	1,094
1994	249,581	24,725	465,745	71,836	280,486	4,488	621,044	1,598
1995			518,443	78,016	331,354	4,467	711,621	1,760

14

Sources:
For Germany, total outward direct investment from Deutsche Bundesbank, Statistical Supplements to the *Monthly Report of the Deutsche Bundesbank*, Series 3, Balance of Payments Statistics, March and April issues; Balance of Payments Statistics, *International Capital Links*, May 1996, June 1993, and April issues for earlier years; real estate data for 1957–75 from unpublished estimates by the Balance of Payments Division of the Statistics Department of the Deutsche Bundesbank, and for 1976–90 from the *Monthly Report of the Deutsche Bundesbank*, April issues. For Japan, for 1963–75, Bank of Japan, *Economic Statistics Annual*, 1976; for 1976–90, Japanese Ministry of Finance, *Reported Outward and Inward Direct Investment*, May/June issues. For the United Kingdom, total outward direct investment from levels of assets and liabilities data, Central Statistical Office, *United Kingdom Balance of Payments*, CSO Pink Book, various issues; real estate data from Central Statistical Office, *Census of Overseas Assets*, 1974, 1981, 1984 and 1987. For the United States, for 1950–76, US Department of Commerce, Bureau of Economic Analysis, *Selected Data on U.S. Direct Investment Abroad*, 1950–76, February 1982; for 1977, US Department of Commerce, Bureau of Economic Analysis, *U.S. Direct Investment Abroad*, 1977, April 1981; for 1978–81, US Department of Commerce, Bureau of Economic Analysis, *U.S. Direct Investment Abroad: Balance of Payments and Direct Investment Position Estimates*, 1977–81, November 1986; for 1981–90, US Department of Commerce, Bureau of Economic Analysis, *Survey of Current Business*, August issues.

Notes:
The US Department of Commerce, Bureau of Economic Analysis, performed and confirmed the interpolation of data for the following years the focal countries did publish data: Japan, 1960, total and real estate investment; UK, 1960–73, 1975–9, and 1980–1, total and real estate investment, and for 1982–3, 1986–7 and 1988–9, real estate investment only; US, 1960–76, total and real estate investment.

— Not available.
a   German outward direct investment in real estate before 1976 represents real estate held for personal use; for 1976 forward also represents commercial property. Break in time series in 1975 for all outward direct investment due to revised data collection methodology.
b   Includes insurance.
c   Break in time series in 1973 for both inward and outward UK direct investment due to revised data methodology.

the abolition of the Bretton Woods standard, the advent of the floating exchange rate system beginning in 1973, and the need to facilitate the recycling of dollar surpluses generated from OPEC oil price increases beginning in the early 1970s. Japan liberalized outward investment regulations for Japanese banks in the early 1970s, and later, in 1980, amended the Foreign Exchange Control Law to reduce government restraints on capital outflows. The UK gradually loosened controls on outward investment during the 1970s, culminating in the removal of foreign exchange controls in 1979. Shortly after abolishing its fixed exchange rate system and initiating a floating exchange rate system in the early 1970s, the US officially ended its controls on outward investment in 1974.

This gradual liberalization of general capital controls by each of the focal countries in the 1970s and early 1980s removed major impediments to the international flow of capital, and set the stage for the further expansion of cross-border direct investment, including investment in real estate.

Table 2.2 Stock of inward direct investment in total and in real estate in the focal countries (1950–present, in millions of US dollars)

	Germany[a]		Japan		United Kingdom		United States	
	Total	Real Estate	Total	Real Estate	Total	Real Estate	Total	Real Estate
1950	879	476	–	–	–	–	3,391	101
1951	916	476	–	–	–	–	3,658	109
1952	938	476	–	–	–	–	3,945	118
1953	1,010	476	–	–	–	–	4,251	127
1954	1,076	452	–	–	–	–	4,633	138
1955	1,117	427	–	–	–	–	5,076	152
1956	1,239	405	–	–	–	–	5,459	163
1957	1,412	381	–	–	–	–	5,710	171
1958	1,496	383	–	–	–	–	6,115	183
1959	1,620	360	–	–	–	–	6,604	198
1960	1,794	336	510	0	4,879	48	6,910	207
1961	2,200	325	520	0	5,424	55	7,392	221
1962	2,566	325	550	0	5,968	61	7,612	228
1963	2,868	327	590	0	6,514	65	7,944	238
1964	3,257	302	650	0	7,059	70	8,363	250
1965	3,973	300	680	0	7,812	78	8,797	263
1966	4,410	277	750	0	8,566	85	9,054	271
1967	4,823	275	810	0	8,266	99	9,923	297
1968	5,392	250	840	2	9,251	93	10,815	324
1969	6,219	271	900	2	10,191	102	11,818	354
1970	6,779	274	950	3	11,693	116	13,270	398
1971	8,816	275	1,020	3	14,217	143	13,914	417
1972	9,887	281	1,195	4	14,667	147	14,868	446
1973	13,972	407	1,220	5	17,621	176	20,556	600
1974	16,865	540	1,245	5	24,220	329	25,144	806
1975	15,042	496	1,470	6	24,490	338	27,662	777
1976	33,946	1,033	1,695	6	23,316	373	30,770	799
1977	38,245	1,209	1,920	13	29,955	625	34,595	853
1978	47,619	1,637	2,155	17	36,383	846	42,471	1,161
1979	53,399	1,875	2,679	23	48,953	1,388	54,462	1,820
1980	48,662	1,664	2,979	23	63,014	2,068	83,046	6,120
1981	44,586	1,568	3,411	27	57,263	1,883	108,714	8,964
1982	43,197	1,636	4,418	31	52,150	1,829	124,677	11,520
1983	40,018	1,387	5,571	31	54,009	1,954	137,061	14,636
1984	36,521	1,191	6,064	34	46,376	1,869	164,583	17,761
1985	50,943	1,533	6,844	41	62,561	2,730	184,615	19,402
1986	66,216	2,058	7,604	58	72,752	3,785	220,414	22,512
1987	87,742	2,690	9,551	77	116,256	6,904	263,394	22,025
1988	84,253	2,782	12,794	147	139,294	9,639	314,754	26,867
1989	102,336	3,393	15,654	794	160,282	10,081	368,924	30,386
1990	133,731	4,125	18,432	818	224,834	13,874	396,702	34,552
1991	126,455	4,256	22,771	887	225,795	14,509	419,108	33,577
1992	124,583	4,618	26,855	1,117	185,587	10,815	427,566	32,406
1993	119,749	3,615	29,933	1,213	189,407	11,265	446,666	29,099
1994	142,183	4,362	34,166	1,244	202,430	13,247	502,410	28,452
1995			38,097	1,261	233,077	13,488	560,088	26,518

Sources:
For Germany, total inward direct investment from Deutsche Bundesbank, Statistical Supplements to the *Monthly Report of the Deutsche Bundesbank*, Series 3, Balance of Payments Statistics, March and April issues; Series 3, Balance of Payments Statistics, *International Capital Links*, May 1996, June 1993, and April issues for earlier years; real estate data for 1957–75 from unpublished estimates by the Balance of Payments Division of the Statistics Department of the Deutsche Bundesbank, and for 1976–90 from the *Monthly Report of the Deutsche Bundesbank*, April issues. For Japan, for 1963–75, Bank of Japan, *Economic Statistics Annual*, 1976; for 1976–90, Japanese Ministry of Finance, *Reported Outward and Inward Direct Investment*, May/June issues. For the United Kingdom, levels of assets and liabilities data from Central Statistical Office, *United Kingdom Balance of Payments, CSO Pink Book*, various issues. For the United States, for 1950–79, US Department of Commerce, Bureau of Economic Analysis, *Selected Data on U.S. Direct Investment Abroad, 1950–79*, December 1984; for 1980–6, US Department of Commerce, Bureau of Economic Analysis, *Foreign Direct Investment in the United States; Balance of Payments and Direct Investment Position Estimates, 1980–6*, December 1990; for 1987–90, US Department of Commerce, Bureau of Economic Analysis, *Survey of Current Business*, August issues.

Notes:
The US Department of Commerce, Bureau of Economic Analysis, performed and confirmed the interpolation of data for the following years the focal countries did not publish data: Japan, 1960–75, total and real estate investment; UK, 1960–73, total and real estate investment; US, 1950–72, total and real estate investment.

— Not available.
[a] German inward direct investment in real estate represents real estate held for personal use; for 1976 forward, also represents commercial property. Break in time series in 1975 for all inward direct investment due to revised data collection methodology.

Cross-border direct investment in the 1980s

The 1980s witnessed an unprecedented volume of cross-border direct investment. Divergent monetary and fiscal policies among the major industrial countries, especially among the focal countries, encouraged the flow of portfolio and direct investment capital to the US to help finance the country's large trade and current account deficits. Other macroeconomic factors, including divergent economic growth rates, savings–investment imbalances, and large dollar depreciation, also fostered the rapid growth of cross-border investment. The growing competitiveness of non-US multinationals was another major factor in the rapid growth of foreign direct investment in the United States. Germany, Japan and the UK were three major sources of this increased investment until the late 1980s, when macroeconomic conditions shifted and the flow of foreign investment to the US declined.

Real US economic growth was only about one percent each year during 1988–92.[9] The US balance of payments deficit also began to ease after its peak in 1987 at $160 billion, falling to $92 billion in 1990 and to $9 billion in 1991.[10] Thus, the need for foreign capital subsided and, in response, both foreign direct and portfolio investment flows to the US declined. Intra-European Community (EC) foreign direct investment (both outward and inward) also grew in the latter half of the 1980s in response to faster EC

17

Table 2.3 Real estate as a share of total outward and inward direct investment in the focal countries (1960–present)

	Germany[a]		Japan		United Kingdom		United States	
	Outward (%)	Inward (%)	Outward (%)	Inward (%)	Outward (%)	Inward (%)	Outward (%)	Inward (%)
1960	11.6	18.7	–	–	–	–	–	–
1961	15.2	14.8	0.7	–	–	–	–	–
1962	15.9	12.7	0.7	–	–	–	–	–
1963	16.6	11.4	4.0	–	–	–	–	–
1964	16.7	9.3	3.4	–	–	–	–	–
1965	16.6	7.5	2.9	–	–	–	–	–
1966	16.3	6.3	3.0	–	–	–	0.3	–
1967	15.5	5.7	2.4	–	–	–	–	–
1968	14.8	4.6	1.8	–	–	–	–	–
1969	16.0	4.4	1.4	–	–	–	–	–
1970	15.8	4.0	1.2	*	–	–	–	–
1971	16.7	3.4	1.1	*	–	–	–	–
1972	17.3	2.8	1.5	*	–	–	–	–
1973	18.9	2.9	2.2	*	–	–	–	2.9
1974	18.4	3.2	1.9	*	7.8	1.4	–	3.2
1975	17.0	3.1	1.6	0.3	–	1.4	0.2	2.8
1976	13.3	3.0	1.4	0.4	–	1.6	–	2.6
1977	13.5	3.2	1.4	0.7	–	2.1	0.2	2.5
1978	12.7	3.4	1.5	0.8	12.5	2.3	0.2	2.7
1979	12.7	3.5	1.6	0.9	–	2.8	0.1	3.3
1980	12.9	3.4	1.6	0.8	–	3.3	0.1	7.4
1981	12.1	3.5	1.7	0.8	3.9	3.3	0.1	8.3
1982	13.0	3.8	1.7	0.7	–	3.5	0.3	9.2
1983	13.2	3.5	1.9	0.6	–	3.6	0.3	10.7
1984	13.0	3.3	1.9	0.6	4.5	4.0	0.2	10.8
1985	12.9	3.0	3.0	0.6	–	4.4	0.2	10.5
1986	12.9	3.1	6.2	0.8	–	5.2	0.1	10.2
1987	12.7	3.1	8.6	0.8	3.2	5.9	0.6	8.4
1988	11.5	3.3	11.0	1.2	–	6.9	0.5	8.2
1989	10.9	3.3	13.7	5.1	–	6.3	0.5	8.2
1990	10.3	3.1	14.9	4.4	2.0	6.2	0.4	8.7
1991	9.4	3.4	15.7	3.9	2.4	6.4	0.4	8.0
1992	9.6	3.7	15.6	4.2	2.3	5.8	0.5	7.6
1993	9.5	3.0	15.7	4.1	2.0	5.9	0.2	6.5
1994	9.9	3.1	15.4	3.6	1.6	6.5	0.3	5.7
1995	–	–	15.0	3.3	1.3	5.8	0.2	4.7

Sources: Tables 2.1 and 2.2.

Notes:
Real estate as a percent of total inward and outward direct investment was not calculated for those years in which the data in Tables 2.1 and 2.2 were interpolated.

— Not available.
* Less than one-tenth of one percent.
a German outward direct investment in real estate includes real estate held for personal use in addition to commercial real estate holdings.

economic growth, as well as to increased investment opportunities in anticipation of a more unified market as a result of EC92.[11]

Japanese direct investment abroad surged during the 1980s, especially after 1985, with most of this investment flowing to the US. A number of factors, some specific to Japan, spurred an unprecedented wave of Japanese direct investment abroad. These included:

• A liberal monetary policy in Japan which kept interest rates low and facilitated the recycling of dollar surpluses arising out of the US–Japan trade imbalances;
• Rapid yen appreciation;
• A relatively low cost of capital arising from a soaring Japanese stock market and low interest rates;
• A massive balance-of-payment surplus;
• The unleashing of abundant Japanese savings to world financial markets with the removal of capital controls and a restructuring of Japanese financial regulations and financial markets;
• The relative shortage of, and high prices for, real estate in Japan;
• Improved competitiveness of Japanese multinationals in certain industries arising from superior technology and management skills; and
• An increasingly global outlook in the strategic planning of Japanese companies, including finance, insurance and real estate companies.

The 1985 Plaza Accord on the dollar exchange rate was a major factor supporting yen appreciation during the late 1980s, inflating the net wealth of Japanese investors in dollar terms in a very short period of time. The yen nearly doubled in value against the dollar, appreciating from 239 yen per dollar in 1985 to 128 yen per dollar in 1988. Japanese investors were able to outbid US and other foreign investors for companies and properties for sale in the US.

Trends in outward real estate investment in the 1980s

According to official data, Japanese outward investment continued to dominate the international real estate industry in the first half of the 1990s as it had

19

during the second half of the 1980s. From 1990 through 1995, Japanese outward investment in real estate increased the fastest and by the largest amount of any focal country, and it remained at the highest proportion (15 percent) of any source country's outward direct investment (Table 2.3). Japanese outward investment in real estate grew from $2.5 billion in 1985 to $46.4 billion in 1990 and to $78 billion by 1995. However, Japanese data represent planned rather than completed investment and thus do not reflect any write-downs of actual investment in response to the sharp decline in US and other countries' commercial real estate prices in the 1990s. In fact, write-downs of US-held real estate from historical book values to current values may not yet have occurred among Japanese investors, just as it has not yet fully occurred among the Japanese banks which financed those real estate ventures. European markets, primarily London, Paris and Frankfurt, also attracted Japanese investment in real estate, but to a much lesser extent than the US.

German outward direct investment in real estate also advanced, but at a much slower pace than Japanese direct investment. By 1994, the latest year for which German direct investment data are currently available, the stock of outward investment in real estate totaled about $25 billion, only about one-third as high as Japanese investment in real estate. The majority of property investment through the 1970s flowed to European countries, and a growing portion went to US markets in the 1980s. Outward investment data suggested that German real estate companies concentrated on domestic markets and, in 1989–90, immediate investment opportunities in East Germany;[12] German manufacturing and service companies, by contrast, implemented global strategies.

UK outward investment in real estate increased much less than that of either Germany or Japan, fluctuating between $4 and $5 billion in the late 1980s and in the 1990s. Although the official data showed that UK outward real estate investment grew modestly during the 1980s, data through 1986 might be misleading. For example, US data on inward direct investment in the US real estate industry showed that UK real estate investment in the US alone amounted to $4.3 billion in 1995.[13] It therefore appears that UK outward real estate investment data are understated.

After surging in 1987 to $1.9 billion from only $348 million in 1986, US outward investment in real estate has remained modest at less than one-half of one percent of total US direct investment abroad throughout the late 1980s and up to 1995. Major acquisitions by US companies in the EC, mostly in the UK, were the primary reason for the increases in 1987 and 1992. However, as discussed extensively in Chapter 3, local regulations on foreign real estate investment in Europe and Japan, in contrast to the US, reinforced a less international outlook among US commercial real estate companies and financial institutions and limited the growth of US outward investment in real estate.

Trends in inward real estate investment in the 1980s

The US attracted the largest amount of foreign real estate investment during the 1980s, primarily due to a surge in commercial real estate prices and expectations of future price increases, and to the country's open investment policy. In 1980 the stock of foreign direct investment in US real estate totaled to $6.1 billion, the largest of any focal country. The stock increased steadily during the 1980s, especially after 1987 with the surge in Japanese investment in US real estate, and peaked at about $35 billion by 1990. From 1990 to 1995, the stock declined gradually each year to about $27 billion in 1995, but the US still hosted the largest amount of foreign real estate investment.

The UK had the second largest amount of inward real estate investment stock of any focal country in 1995, amounting to about $13 billion or one-half the size of the US stock. However, relative to the respective size of their economies – the US GDP was about six-and-a-half times as large as the UK's in 1990 – inward investment in UK real estate is quite large. The UK hosted a significant increase in Japanese and other European property investment in the late 1980s, and the overall stock inward direct investment in UK real estate increased from $2.7 billion in 1985 to $14.5 billion in 1991, and then declined to $13.5 billion by 1995.

Despite these surges of inward direct investment in the UK and the US, real estate was not the major focus of cross-border direct investment. In 1995 the US proportion of inward direct investment in real estate was only 5 percent, and in the UK it was only 6 percent (Table 2.3). Cross-border direct investment in manufacturing, trade, petroleum, and in banking, finance and insurance collectively, prevailed in foreign markets.

International real estate investment

Germany: outward real estate investment

Significant increases in Germany's outward direct investment in real estate occurred in the late 1970s and late 1980s, mostly in other European countries, the US and South Africa.[14] The stock of German outward direct investment in real estate increased from $813 million in 1970 to $2.1 billion in 1975, and jumped to $6.1 billion by 1980 (Table 2.1). By 1985, it had grown to $8.5 billion, more than doubled to $17.4 billion in 1990, and rose to $24.7 billion by 1994 (the latest year currently available). Germany's lower cost of capital and appreciating currency favored outward investment. German finance and commercial real estate companies, as well as individual investors, capitalized on lower cost interest rates and deutschemark appreciation in the 1980s, with overseas property values comparing favorably to domestic property values during this time.

In the 1970s, superior technology, as well as the management and marketing skills of German companies in chemicals, electronics and transportation equipment manufacturing, spearheaded an outward surge in direct investment. This success led other German industries – including professional services and real estate – to expand into new markets to service German multinational clients. In the late 1980s, German outward direct investment slowed in the US but expanded in Europe, particularly in the EC and in some countries that joined the EC during this decade (e.g., Spain and Portugal).[15] Two major reasons for this shift in German outward investment were rapid economic growth in Europe following recession in the early 1980s, and anticipation of the more unified markets of EC92, which sparked cross-border mergers and acquisitions. The fall of Communist regimes in Eastern Europe, beginning with Poland in 1989, also opened previously closed markets to Western investors. A relatively small amount of German investment also occurred in East Germany (before unification), Hungary, Poland and Czechoslovakia, including real estate acquisitions.

Germany's outward direct investment in real estate was primarily personal investment in overseas real estate rather than commercial investment. In 1994, out of total German outward investment in real estate of $24.7 billion, $21.2 billion was personal investment in real estate. Personal investment in overseas real estate by German residents was facilitated by large open-end property funds.[16] Other German outward investment was facilitated by real estate advisory service companies, rental and housing agencies, and asset and fund management companies. Also, some foreign investment was channeled through holding companies and pooled international funds, which were classified in the finance industry rather than in real estate; this investment would consequently not be counted in real estate investment stock data. Finally, the relocation to the US of major divisions of German institutional fund management firms, such as Lehndorff, might have lowered reported outward direct investment in German statistics.[17] Taken together, these factors likely resulted in the understatement of the stock of German outward real estate investment.

Germany: inward real estate investment

Inward direct investment in German real estate also surged during the late 1970s and again in the late 1980s. The amounts of inward investment were much smaller than outward direct investment, however.[18] Rapid economic growth in Germany during those two periods attracted more foreign investment, both overall and in real estate. The prospering economy increased profits and reinvested earnings of existing foreign-owned real estate companies. (In addition to new equity investment and intercompany debt, reinvested earnings of foreign-owned companies also increased foreign direct investment stock.) The expansion of the operations of large multinationals located in the EC countries was also a major factor. Increased private investment and government spending associated with the unification of East and West Germany created additional opportunities for foreign investment in German real estate, mostly in the West.

A limited amount of buildable land for commercial structures supported relatively high prices and low investment returns for German property, which, when combined with a strong currency, hindered foreign investment relative to other European countries and the US. Relatively low inflation in Germany also limited the attractiveness of German real estate as an inflation hedge or for price speculation. Thus, despite German tax incentives for offshore companies investing long-term in property, inward investment in German real estate remained low relative to UK and US markets.[19]

Germany's real estate market was further characterized by distinct demographic features. A large proportion of the population live in urban centers – 86 percent versus an average of 78 percent for Europe as a whole, 77 percent for Japan and 74 percent for the US.[20] Fifty percent of the population live on only 7 percent of the land, which has created a high demand for property in cities. Thus, real estate investment in Germany has been concentrated in urban office buildings and high-density commercial and residential developments.

Most property investments have been managed and owned by large German institutions, and, to a lesser extent, by private investment groups and major construction contractors in partnership with investors. Open-end property funds also attracted foreign capital to German real estate.[21] Foreign investors were particularly attracted to Frankfurt and Hamburg, where offshore investments accounted for more than one-third of 1989 acquisitions. Foreign investors also began to invest in Berlin in 1990 and 1991, which prompted such major real estate advisory firms as Müller of Germany and Jones Lang Wootton of the UK to open Berlin offices in 1991.[22] UK investment in Germany historically was through UK-based property companies, such as Hammersons, Slough Estates, MEPC and London & Edinburgh Trust. Japanese investors began to invest in German property markets in the late 1980s, once having established ownership stakes in the UK and the US. This strategy preceded the recession in 1990, at which time only 6 percent of Japanese property investments in Europe were located in Germany.[23]

Japan: outward real estate investment

The economic and demographic factors which supported Germany's outward real estate investment were similar to those in Japan. The country's small land mass, vast mountainous regions, high-density urban development and rising per-capita income supported high real estate prices and created a pent-up demand for real estate. This, together with a loosening of controls on international capital flows, an easy monetary policy, lower interest rates, soaring stock prices and the availability of vast sums of dollars recycled from the US–Japan trade imbalance, boosted Japanese outward real estate investment in the late 1980s to unprecedented levels. Between 1985 and 1990, the Japanese stock of outward real estate investment soared from $2.5 billion to $46.4 billion, and from 1990 to 1995 increased to $78 billion. However, for the reasons noted earlier, these data probably overstate the current value of Japanese outward investment in real estate.

Many Japanese companies and institutional funds were relatively new to foreign real estate investment and tended to concentrate acquisitions in established US urban center and well-known commercial properties, some of which were highly visible, high-quality properties. Mitsubishi Estate purchased an interest in New York City's Rockefeller Plaza, for example, an investment of $1.46 billion in 1989.[24] Japanese investors also acquired major US real estate holdings outside urban areas, particularly shopping centers, golf courses, hotels, and undeveloped land in the states of Hawaii and California.

To broaden their understanding of foreign markets, Japanese investors typically engaged US investment banks and real estate advisory firms, as discussed in Chapters 3 and 6. In Europe, in addition to Paris and Frankfurt, Japanese investors focused on London property between 1985 and 1989, in which they invested approximately $2.8 billion over four years.[25] Among the largest transactions were EIE International's purchase of Britannic House, Moor Lane; 38 Bishopsgate by Kumagai Gumi; the Old Bailey by Mitsui Real Estate; and Bush House, Aldwych, by Kato Kagaku.[26] Through the early 1980s Japanese investors were dominated by construction, development and trading companies (notably Kumagai Gumi, Itoh, Shimizu and Kajima), which typically participated in joint ventures and debt financings, rather than acquiring sole ownership positions.[27] By the late 1980s Japanese life assurance companies became the most active Japanese investors, investing company capital instead of borrowing funds for property investments.

Japanese banks also entered the London market, reportedly to expand international name recognition, to gain direct experience in the global securities business, and to accommodate clients demanding multinational services.[28] Within the 1983–7 period, Japanese banks increased their share of the construction loan market to UK residents from 1 percent of the overall market to 6 percent, a total of $400 million. Japanese bank loans for property acquisitions also grew, from zero to 4 percent of the entire market, a total of $500 million.[29]

The decline of the Japanese stock market beginning in 1990, coupled with a rapid increase in Japanese interest rates and a fall in property values, forced Japanese investors to decrease real estate investments in 1990 and 1991, which severely depleted global capital lending and acquisition sources. This was true particularly in the US, where a high proportion of Japanese investments were focused and where the commercial real estate market had come to depend on rising flows of Japanese capital. During the 1990–1 US recession, industry publications and professional journals reported multiple examples of under-performing Japanese holdings in US markets, investments acquired between 1985 and 1989. Concurrently, however, the UK was also experiencing a recessionary real estate market. Japanese investors subsequently emphasized diversified acquisition strategies, by national markets as well as types of real estate investments.

Japan: inward real estate investment

Similar economic and demographic factors to those that underlay the expansion of Japanese outward real estate investment strictly limited the amount of inward direct investment in Japanese real estate. Exceptionally high real estate prices, low returns, an appreciating currency, and few property sales (in part due to a relatively high capital gains tax of 62.4 percent), acted as major deterrents to foreign investors. In 1995 the stock of inward direct investment in Japanese real estate totaled only $1.3 billion. As points of reference, this volume was the equivalent of only 5 percent of inward direct investment in US real estate, and just 2 percent of Japanese outward direct investment in real estate.

Japanese government restrictions on foreign direct investment in Japan before 1980 suppressed inward real estate investment. The restrictions dated back to the reconstruction period following World War Two and were designed to limit foreign competition while Japanese companies rebuilt factories and re-established domestic markets. Prior to the 1980 amendment to the Foreign Exchange Control Law, direct investors obtained approval from the Japanese Ministry of Finance (MOF) to make inward or outward investments. The amendment, formulated in response to pressure from foreign governments to ease restrictions on foreign direct investment, changed the requirement to notification of the MOF only for a proposed investment, with automatic approval after thirty days if no objection was raised by the MOF. Prior to 1980, the Japanese government was accused of exploiting this law to force foreign investors to accept minority ownership positions with Japanese partners. In March 1991, the Foreign Exchange Control Law was amended again, allowing foreign investors to initiate transactions before notifying the MOF.

Japanese securities laws and the restrictive practices of domestic stock exchanges also discouraged foreign investors from issuing or trading foreign securities on the exchanges. By limiting the amount of stock available for public purchase, interlocking directorates and *keiretsu* arrangements between Japanese companies prevented acquisitions of Japanese companies by foreign investors.

United Kingdom: outward real estate investment

There is a long history of UK outward real estate investment that dates back to at least the seventeenth century. Unfortunately, systematic records began only in the early 1970s. In 1974 the UK sponsored the largest amount of outward direct investment in real estate of any focal country, at $2.8 billion. Although UK statistics did not provide specifics on geographic focus, most foreign property investment reportedly occurred in such developed national markets as Europe and the US, aligning with total UK outward direct investment. The pattern of international expansion undertaken by the UK real estate advisory service firm of Jones Lang Wootton during the 1960s, 1970s and 1980s (which typically aligned with clients' foreign investment targets discussed in Chapter 6), provided selective evidence of the focus of foreign real estate investment by UK investors.

British institutional funds, such as the National Coal Board Pension Fund, remained major investors abroad through the mid-1980s, with substantial real estate investments in the US. British corporations were also active in foreign property markets, including golf course and resort developments in the US. For example, Guinness Enterprise Holdings, Inc., an affiliate of the London-based multinational, purchased an historic hotel and golf course in Vermont in 1991. Also in 1991, the US office of Chesterton International, a UK chartered surveyor, arranged its first golf course community investment with a $5 million participating mortgage. Far-Eastern and European investors, including the Church of England's Deansbank pension investment subsidiary, acquired a 50 percent interest in the same project.[30] UK outward investment in real estate peaked at $5.6 billion in 1991, after which it declined steadily to $4.5 billion in 1995, probably due to the decline in real estate values in the US.

United Kingdom: inward real estate investment

The inward stock of real estate investment in the UK was relatively small until the late 1970s. It increased from $338 million in 1975 to $2.1 billion in 1980. It then stagnated until 1985, when it began to rise over the next five years due to Japanese, Canadian, US and other European investments. It peaked in 1991 at $14.5 billion, before declining to $10.8 billion in 1992 and then rising to $13.5 billion by 1995. Most of the increase in the late 1980s was believed to be directed to UK property companies active in the London office market, based on several reports during this period about Japanese companies buying highly valued properties in central London. It is estimated that, between 1987 and 1990, foreign investors accounted for one-third of all UK property investment, £10 billion.[31]

Foreign investors also made significant indirect (portfolio) property investments in the UK by purchasing significant blocks of domestic public property companies. For example, in 1990 Market Chief, backed by US-based Prudential-Bache and British-based Eagle Star, bought Imry Merchant Developers, US-based JMB purchased Randsworth and acquired 25 percent ownership in Priest Marians, and Canadian-based Olympia & York purchased Stanhope Properties PLC. Indirect investment was also made through bank financings. Between 1984 and 1989, total commercial bank loans to UK property companies increased 600 percent, to £30 billion. Foreign banks accounted for £12 billion in 1989, or 40 percent, up from 20 percent in 1984.[32]

In 1992, UK inward direct real estate investment declined. Japanese companies reduced their UK direct real estate investments along with all foreign property investments, and Canadian and US direct investment also subsided. For example, Canadian and US direct investment in the huge Canary Wharf development project resulted in significant losses and severe refinancing problems for its major sponsor, Olympia & York Developments, Ltd.

United States: outward real estate investment

The US sponsored the smallest stock of outward direct investment in real estate among the focal countries. Until 1987, when US foreign direct investment soared to $1.9 billion, the previous high point was recorded in 1983 at $558 million, which then declined to only $348 million in 1986.[33] US investment in European property markets in the late 1980s stemmed from a rise in perceived market opportunities among US real estate construction and development companies, major institutional investors diversifying abroad, and acquisition of office buildings and industrial facilities by US multinationals. US outward direct investment in real estate jumped to $2.4 billion in 1992 as US investors took part in the ambitious expansion schemes of a major Canadian real estate developer, and dropped sharply to only $1.1 billion in 1993 as the developer went into bankruptcy and the investments were sold or liquidated.

United States: inward real estate investment

Rising outward direct investment by the other focal countries was reflected in a rapid increase in inward direct investment in US real estate. Economic and political stability, a favorable investment climate, a relatively low capital gains tax, and the size of the country's financial and real estate markets, created the world's most attractive and diverse real estate market. Among the four focal countries, and worldwide, the US remained the most active market for real estate investment after the early 1970s. In 1973, when the US Department of Commerce started tracking real estate investment separately from investment in other industries, the inward stock of direct investment in real estate was $600 million. By 1990, the inward stock of direct investment in US real estate peaked at $34.9 billion, and it declined each year thereafter to $26.5 billion in 1995 as the US real estate market tanked. As one gauge of the US market's overall magnitude, this peak level represented less than 1 percent of the value of US land at 1990 prices.[34]

In the late 1970s and early 1980s, Canadian investors led foreign investment in US real estate markets, followed by UK and German firms, respectively, as measured by capital invested. In the mid- to late 1980s, Canadian investment began to slow, while Japanese investment accelerated. German and UK firms remained active in the US into the late 1980s, yet their investments were insignificant by comparison with Japanese capital invested. According to US data, the stock of Japanese inward direct investment rose from $1.5 billion in 1985 to $15.2 billion in 1990. By comparison, the stock of UK direct investment in the US real estate industry declined from $4.8 billion to $3.6 billion, while the stock of German direct investment rose slightly from $1.1 billion to $1.3 billion over the same period.[35] Despite the greater significance of Canadian, UK and German investment in US real estate during the 1970s and early 1980s, highly visible Japanese investments prevailed in the second half of the 1980s. On occasion, this led property rights advocates to seek government intervention, albeit unsuccessfully.

Inward direct investment in US real estate was largely in land, offices, shopping centers, industrial complexes and residential buildings, and also included smaller, specialized projects such as private golf courses. UK investors tended to focus along the Mid-Atlantic coast; Japanese firms around the Pacific coast, Texas and Hawaii.[36]

Cycles of cross-border direct investment

Cross-border direct investment in real estate declined after 1990, marking a shift in rising global property investment in the 1980s.[37] In addition to macroeconomic factors, there were several specific reasons why the real estate market expanded dramatically: real rents increased substantially; major urban markets worldwide experienced low vacancy levels (below 5 percent); and there was an insufficient supply of contemporary, high-quality office space, especially in Europe. Demand for real estate advisory services also expanded in association with the worldwide growth in services industries in the focal countries during this period.

Overbuilding during 1984–90, followed by slow economic growth in the focal countries in 1990–1, however, led to an overabundance of vacant and under-utilized commercial real estate in most major cities in the UK and US. The market value of real estate in all of the focal countries, except perhaps in Germany, subsequently fell, in some instances by as much as 40 percent in one year. For example, in late 1990 Minoru Isutani, a major Japanese developer, bought the Pebble Beach Gulf Links golf course for $841 million. In February 1992, Mr Isutani sold the property for $500 million, a loss of over 40 percent.[38] Such a loss was typical of this period, based on current reports in the press and industry publications.

Many foreign investors also incurred operating losses on their investments. In the US, foreign real estate investors incurred negative income of $1.3 billion in 1990, and $1.6 billion in 1991.[39] In 1990 Canadian direct investors in the US real estate reported total negative cash and capital income of $732 million, German direct investors negative $56 million, British investors negative $131 million, and Japanese direct investors negative $87 million. Other factors which contributed to reduced earnings among real estate entities centered around reduced operating income among commercial properties, decreased real estate values, and reduced demand for new homes and housing construction.[40] The global banking system also significantly decreased new activity in debt and equity issues through 1993 as a means to build reserves and increase profits in order to offset losses on nonperforming loans, especially real estate loans. Lending for investment in real estate diminished to very conservative terms.

Real estate investment cycles

Cross-border direct investment in Europe accelerated after the early 1980s, and further growth can be expected in the 1990s once economic expansion resumes worldwide. Why this relatively positive outlook? The 1980s witnessed the growth of multinational corporations and the globalization of bond and equity portfolios, including real estate. The 1990s have witnessed to date a confirmation of the merits of multinational operations, and global property portfolios have provided economic diversification and the prospect of diminished overall risk.[41] After 1988, Japanese investors focused principally on continental Europe, shifting away from US markets. The central London market, by comparison, continued to sustain the interest of Japanese investors, particularly life insurance companies.

Slower economic growth and the virtual collapse of commercial and residential real estate markets in Japan and the US in 1991 and 1992 fostered expectations among real estate investors that Europe would offer an alternative market, with growth in inward and outward investment aided by deregulation and improved transportation systems within and between countries across the continent.[42] Given the consensus among business analysts and economists that combined national markets offer enhanced investment opportunities, it is no surprise that continental Europe, with its low property-vacancy rates and 360 million customers, generated activity among foreign property investors.[43] UK developers and investors led property investment in continental Europe in the early 1970s, which slowed in the second half of the 1980s. While economists and business analysts widely agree that the high-growth real estate market of the 1980s is past and the internationalization of real estate markets will experience more modest growth over the next decade, there is widespread disagreement as to the long-term consequences for property values and cross-border real estate investment.[44]

In the late 1980s, Waterglade, Heron and Sibec have acquired and participated in German developments. UK institutional investors have participated with UK-based developer Pan European in its portfolio expansion.[45] Hammersons purchased a 277,000-square-foot shopping center in Essen, Germany, for about £60 million (DM 167 million) in January 1990. One year later, the Dutch civil service pension fund Algemeen Burgerlijk Pensioenfonds (ABP) bought a 70 percent stake in the shopping center for an estimated total value of 74.8 million pounds (DM 218 million).[46]

Notes

1 A. Bloomfield, *Patterns of Fluctuation in International Investment Before 1914*, International Finance Section, Department of Economics, Princeton Studies in International Finance, no. 20 (Princeton, NJ: Princeton University Press, 1968), pp. 42–4.

2 J.H. Dunning, "Changes in the Level and Structure of International Production: The Last One Hundred Years", in *The Growth of International Business*, ed. M. Casson (London: George Allen & Unicorn, 1983).

3 Definitions of different types of investment can be found in the Appendix.

4 US Department of Commerce, International Trade Administration, *International Direct Investment: Global Trends and the U.S. Role* (Washington, DC: 1988), pp. 2–3.

5 Government restrictions in the focal countries on cross-border direct investment in services, including real estate, are difficult to document through primary research records. Even the available secondary sources provide only descriptive information, not systematically official records.

6 These regulations included foreign exchange approval requirements, and outright restrictions of domestic residents for offshore finance and banking facilities to prevent international intermediation of funds.

7 US Department of Commerce, International Trade Administration, *International Direct Investment: Global Trends and the U.S. Role* (Washington, DC: 1988), p. 87. The world outward stock of direct investment was $112 billion in 1967.

8 *Ibid.*, p. 91. The world stock of inward direct investment is estimated at $211.1 billion in 1973.

9 US Department of Commerce, Bureau of Economic Analysis, *Survey of Current Business* (Washington, DC: March 1992), p. 25.

10 US Department of Commerce, Bureau of Economic Analysis, *Survey of Current Business* (Washington, DC: June 1991), p. 45 and (March 1992), p. 75.

11 Anticipated market potentials and investment opportunities associated with EC92 may well have exceeded the benefits of combined European markets.

12 Beginning with data for 1991, investment in the former German Democratic Republic (East Germany) is considered as domestic rather than foreign direct investment.

13 US Department of Commerce, Bureau of Economic Analysis, *Survey of Current Business* (Washington, DC: September 1996).

14 M.A. Hines, *Guide to International Real Estate Investment* (New York: Quorum Books, 1988), p. 9.

15 Deutsche Bundesbank, *Monthly Report of the Deutsche Bundesbank*, Statistical Supplement, Series 3 (April 1991), pp. 4, 6.

16 For the other focal countries, personal investment in real estate is either classified as portfolio rather than direct investment, or is not measured at all.

17 When companies transfer their ownership to a foreign country they cease to be foreign direct investors. Since these companies are no longer defined as foreign direct investors, any funds borrowed abroad to finance real estate acquisitions or new developments are also not defined as direct investment. The transfer of Lehndorff operations to the US is described in the case studies in Chapter 6.

18 As shown in Table 2.2, the stock of inward investment in real estate doubled from only $274 million in 1970 to $496 million in 1975, and increased to $1.7 billion in 1980. By 1985, it had declined slightly to $1.5 billion, but it grew to $4.4 billion by 1995.

19 Weatherall, Green & Smith, *German Property Report 1990* (London: May 1990), p. 7.

20 D.J. Kostin, "German Real Estate Market: An Introduction for Non-German Investors", a report prepared for Salomon Brothers (New York: April 1991), p. 23, and personal interview with D.J. Kostin, May 1991.

21 If the ownership level falls below the reporting threshold for German statistics, investment in these funds is defined as portfolio rather than direct investment.

22 See case studies in September 1996.

23 J. Plender, "The Bankers' House of Cards", *Financial Times* (London: 12 November 1991), p. 14.

24 US Department of Commerce, International Trade Administration, *Foreign Direct Investment in the United States, 1989 Transactions* (Washington, DC: June 1991), p. 109.

25 This represented 3.7 percent of total outward direct investment over the same period. "Asian Property Market: Investment in the 1990s", a report issued by Richard Ellis (1990), p. 78.

26 *Ibid.*

27 H. Mitani, "Capital from Japan, Part II: Gaining Access to Japanese Investors", *The Real Estate Finance Journal* vol. 4, no. 4 (1988), p. 19.

28 J.T. Dueser, *International Strategies of Japanese Banks* (London and New York: Macmillan, 1990), p. 115.

29 *Ibid.*, p. 122.

30 "Pension Fund Advisor Funds Golf Resort", *Golf Business & Real Estate News* (8 July 1991), p. 3.

31 P. Hugill, "The International Investor Moves In", *Comment '90* (London: Knight Frank & Rutley, 1990), p. 24.

32 *Ibid.*, p. 24.

33 The US investment data methodology may result in some understatement of US outward real estate investment. See Appendix A.

34 Proportion calculation is based on total value of US land at current cost as reported by Federal Reserve Board of US, *Balance Sheets for the U.S. Economy, 1949–90*, (Washington, DC: September 1991).

35 US Department of Commerce, Bureau of Economic Analysis, *Survey of Current Business*, (Washington, DC: August 1987), p. 90 and (July 1993), p. 65.

36 For example, construction financing for a $100 million resort development in San Antonio, Texas, was provided by the Long-Term Credit Bank of Japan, Ltd. The Japanese bank was joined in its financing by US-based Hyatt Hotels Corporation and two Japanese firms – Shimizu and Kawasaki Steel. *Golf Business & Real Estate News* (15 July 1991), p. 2.

37 D.G. Shulman, "The End of the Global Property Boom", a report for Salomon Brothers (New York: 11 December 1990).

38 "Japanese Purchases of U.S. Real Estate Fall on Hard Times", *The Wall Street Journal* (New York: 21 February 1992), p. A-1.

39 US Department of Commerce, Bureau of Economic Analysis, *Survey of Current Business* (Washington, DC: July 1993).

40 Y. Shima, "Real Estate Industry Update: After the Land Boom", a report by Goldman Sachs (New York: 7 August 1990), p. 1. It is interesting to note that the Goldman Sachs report, in its prediction of a decrease in global land prices, ties the decline in commercial real estate values to a decline in the private housing market, yet there is not always a direct correlation.

41 B. White, chief executive officer of Richard Ellis, a major UK-based international chartered surveyor, untitled speech given at the Melbourne Investment Group breakfast meeting (8 November 1990).

42 F. Dijkstra, "International Property Research: The New Dimension", *Comment '90* (London: Knight Frank & Rutley, 1990), p. 74. However, of the 279 EC directives aimed at harmonizing pan-European services, not one directly mentions property. Arthur Andersen and Nabarro Nathanson, *Building a Stake in Europe: Guidelines for Investors in Real Estate* (Chicago, June 1991), p. 5.

43 B. White, *op. cit.*

44 Y. Shima, *op. cit.*, p. 2.

45 Weatherall Green & Smith, *German Property Report 1990* (London: May 1990), p. 6.

46 D.J. Kostin, "German Real Estate Market: An Introduction for Non-German Investors", report prepared for Salomon Brothers (New York: April 1991), p. 21.

3

THE INTERNATIONALIZATION OF REAL ESTATE ADVISORY SERVICES

In Chapter 2 the stage was set for a closer examination of changes in real estate advisory services, which is the subject of this chapter. The changes such firms encountered as they entered the international marketplace point out the factors that provided competitive advantages for some real estate advisory services, such as:

- The relationship between real estate services and domestic economies and national real estate markets.
- The importance of recruiting skilled professionals.
- The influence of government policy on competition.
- The role of supporting industries.
- The role of multinational corporations in international trade.
- The internationalization of financial markets and investment vehicles.
- The importance of adapting organizational structure to domestic and international business needs.

As this chapter will show, competitive advantage belonged to those firms that first established a strong reputation domestically, recruited skilled personnel, and used a decentralized, multi-division organization in foreign expansion.

Changes in real estate advisory services

Real estate markets throughout the US, UK, Germany and Japan experienced a dramatic restructuring between 1960 and 1997, shifting from a predominantly local orientation to a national and international focus. As documented in Chapter 2, the globalization of the real estate industry during this thirty-year period was driven by the expansion of cross-border direct investment in real estate.[1] Certain professional services – finance, accounting, law, construction, insurance and real estate advisory services – internationalized concurrently with growing cross-border investment activity, supporting foreign investment by following capital and investors across international

33

borders. Market expansion, in turn, enabled these allied services to establish independent channels in global trade.

This chapter reviews the principal factors that supported the internationalization of real estate advisory services in the four countries, focusing particularly on those factors associated with the predominance of certain nations and firms. Through a review of macroeconomic and microeconomic factors, organizational structures and industry structures, the discussion further refines this book's primary thesis – that the internationalization of real estate advisory services was successfully pursued by firms that achieved a solid reputation in their home nations by capitalizing on the domestic economy's maturing capital and real estate markets, then built a diversified, multiregional organization targeted at the cross-border investment activities of multinational clients.

International real estate advisory services cover the full spectrum of the real estate industry: the sale and leasing of property; real estate finance; institutional investment; property and asset management; and project management and construction. Clients who commissioned real estate advisers for outside, "objective" counsel and for specialized expertise about property and financial markets were the source of capital. The client market was unstructured, and included those involved in some facet of real estate as well as those who lacked both the experience and knowledge of buildings and markets. They ranged from individual investors to multinational corporations, from commercial and merchant banks to building societies in the UK and savings and loan associations in the US – insurance and pension funds, universities and local governments, securitized investment and unit trusts, and international developers and construction firms. The advisers, or providers, also encompassed a broad array of specialized disciplines in this unregulated profession. A full-service, diversified firm, such as Jones Lang Wootton of the UK, would offer all disciplines, while a "niche" firm would focus its core business exclusively on a limited number of specializations – brokerage, estate management, appraisal, cost consulting, investment banking, securitization or project management. Other professional service firms, such as accountants, attorneys, mortgage lenders and financial counselors, seeking to expand their services, began to diversify into real estate advisory services in the late 1960s.[2]

Davis and Smales argue that international trade in professional services differs from manufacturing in that knowledge and reputation constitute the imports and exports rather than manufactured products. Labor, moreover, which was culturally specific to each nation, played a central role in successful cross-border services trade.[3] Real estate was ultimately a localized industry that required expert knowledge and understanding of local property and investment markets. A real estate advisory firm, whether a regional, national or international practice, succeeded or failed on its collective local expertise and reputation.

The book's inquiry centers around these questions: How have the dual, and often competing, requirements for responsiveness to local markets and the strategic demands for a multifunctional, multinational structure affected the international expansion by real estate advisory service firms in the focal countries? What benefits were gained, and challenges confronted, by real estate advisory firms from the focal countries expanding into foreign markets? Why did such firms simultaneously diversify into new service products?

International services trade theory

International trade in services only recently became a subject of systematic analyses, and the theoretical literature remains limited compared to that for manufacturing trades.[4] The real estate industry overall, and real estate services in particular, have received only cursory attention by scholars, typically addressed as a subset of generic professional services, and of business and financial services. Yet even this body of literature, as Weiss argued in the "Real Estate History: An Overview and Research Agenda", focused overwhelmingly on residential development and residential finance in domestic markets in the US, UK and Germany, areas which have concerned national public policy since the 1930s.[5] In Japan, real estate investment and real estate advisory services have been evaluated as just one element of the larger corporate history of the *keiretsus* and *zaibatsus*, or large business groups, and this only since 1985. All of these discussions presented either historical studies of the domestic industry and its overseas activities, or "how-to" reference manuals for conducting business in real estate markets abroad.

Weiss provided compelling evidence of the need for further in-depth research and analyses of the flow of capital funds and the complex relationship among various investor groups, builders, owners, national and international regulatory policies, and the professional services that facilitated real estate investment, both at home and abroad. Especially needed, Weiss contended, was systematic analyses of the changing historical role of institutions in the financing of commercial and industrial development.[6] This thesis argued that real estate advisers have played a central role in capitalizing on and directing the international flow of real estate investment funds – and therefore shaping national real estate markets generally – and in influencing particular investor groups in the location and volume of their investment activities.

What factors have sustained the growth of international real estate advisory services? What factors specific to particular national markets and particular firms sustained this incremental growth over the thirty-seven years between 1960 and 1997?

Sampson and Snape added to Wells's thinking in arguing that international trade could also occur without the movement of either the provider or the receiver, simply the transfer of the service – be it oral advice or a written product – thanks to advances in electronic technology over the past three decades.[7] For purposes of prescribing effective national trade policies,

Sampson and Snape claimed, services should be classified by those involving movement of factors of production (the service provider or capital), movement of the receiver (the investor or client), and those requiring no movement by either provider or receiver.[8] Real estate advisory services encompassed all three categories, thus ideally requiring free movement of trade at all levels.[9]

Factor advantages of international real estate advisory services

The international role of real estate services was inextricably linked with domestic economies and national real estate markets after 1960, as reviewed in the next section. Indeed, Dufey argued in his work on Japanese financial services that "there are few uniquely international institutions."[10] Real estate advisory practices depended on long-term growth of the domestic economy and domestic property markets to build established domestic practices and domestic clientele and to survive in the international marketplace.

An important limitation of standard theories of international business as applied to real estate advisory services is their inadequate attention to the role of specialization, technical competence, innovation and the exchange of information within and between firms. Successful differentiation of roles and the management of these functions across broad geographic regions, as Chandler and Casson pointed out, could only be accomplished by people.[11] Casson refined Chandler's theory of the multinational manufacturing enterprise to account for labor's central role in international services trade and the concomitant factor of "innovation through experience".[12] Thus, labor became an essential factor in international trade, as discussed in the "Skilled Labor" section of this chapter.

The third factor focused on the role of government as it influenced the evolution of a nation's competitive environment in a given industry. Because international trade generally, and real estate advisory services particularly, encompassed the transfer of capital, services and personnel across national borders, domestic border regulations and a country's international policy toward foreign service providers and inward and outward direct investment played a major role, as reviewed in "International Policy and Investment Perspective" later in this chapter.[13] Was one nation more protectionist, and another more expansionist? Did domestic regulations raise barriers or open markets to free movement of cross-border transactions? These questions center around such issues as foreign investment, the "right of establishment", and immigration. They can be answered by profiling policies of the focal countries over the 1960–97 period, and, most important, by evaluating the growth of cross-border direct real estate investment over five-year increments and its contribution to each nation's total international direct investment.

A fourth factor was the extent to which supporting industries reinforced the growth of each nation's international real estate advisory service industry.

The emergence of multinational corporations and the internationalization of financial markets and investment vehicles appeared to be most influential, reviewed near the end of the chapter. For all four countries, the rise of heavy industry determined the shape of current urban and economic systems to a large extent. As Hayes and Hubbard documented in their work on global investment banking services and the growth of the Eurobond market, the US, UK, Germany and Japan became generators of surplus investment capital.[14]

Finally, the organizational structure and management of firms competing within the international arena of real estate advisory services represented an important factor. Over the long term, a firm's business philosophy and organizational infrastructure were the defining elements that determined the firm's ability to capitalize on economic growth and defend an international practice in the face of periodic economic decline, to respond to market upturns and downturns, to function across diversified services and multiple cultures as well as various government policies and local markets, to develop innovative service products, to develop the skills to maintain and grow competitive position, and to sustain the loyalty and commitment of experienced people to overcome both internal and external challenges.

The domestic economy and real estate market

The growth and prosperity of international real estate advisory services principally depended on consistent, long-term growth in the domestic economy. By extension, the relative demand for real estate services in home markets determined the competitive strength (or weakness) that each firm experienced in the global market – either providing or limiting opportunities to develop superior capabilities in diversified and innovative services, and to gain exposure to a broad range of clients. The two most reliable measures of economic conditions that affected real estate advisory services were GDP (the size, rate of growth and annual volatility of a nation's economy) and commercial construction investment.

The growth of the economy indicated the relative availability of investment capital, and the size of the economy indicated the relative wealth and diversity of the domestic market. Annual GDP for the US, UK, Germany and Japan increased by 3 percent, 2.5 percent, 3 percent, and 6–7 percent respectively, as each country's domestic financial markets matured concurrently with international financial markets and international trade. In addition, cross-border direct investment in real estate multiplied by substantial multiples of GDP over the thirty-year period, except for the UK between 1970 and 1980. This alone would suggest increased demand for foreign real estate advisory services and the internationalization of property service firms. Moreover, as international financial capital markets matured and investors and multinationals sought to diversify assets and portfolios across global markets, the liberalization of government regulations and changes in tax regulations expanded the competitive environment to include foreign firms and foreign markets increased the demand for real estate advisers.

As shown in Table 3.1, the US economy remained the largest among the four focal countries over the 1960–97 period. GDP growth also rose at a fairly consistent rate during these thirty years, and the volume of commercial construction positioned the US as the premier real estate market in the world, as shown in Table 3.2. The US provided attractive and diverse real estate investment opportunities for both domestic and foreign sources, and US real estate advisers enjoyed wide-ranging opportunities in home markets to service the diverse needs of both US-based and foreign clients. Rather than dedicating financial and professional resources to expand operations in smaller foreign markets, the majority of national firms invested corporate capital in introducing new services and entering new US markets, clearly evident in the ten firms profiled in Chapter 4.

In fact, not until 1989–97, when the domestic economy and capital markets began to contract due to overbuilt property markets and overextended financial institutions, US real estate service firms limited their overseas activities to specific client engagements during the previous decades when US-based multinational clients were increasing international acquisitions. This contrasted with the experience of allied professional service firms, such as banking, accounting, architectural design and law, which internationalized extensively in the 1970s.[15] Perhaps US real estate service firms were hindered by European competitors, which had a virtual lock on continental markets and financing sources, as well as by explicit and tacit Japanese regulatory controls on foreign investment and business development.

The European property market, in contrast to the US, developed along two mutually inclusive tiers: at the local level, in which domestic and foreign clients engaged chartered surveyors for estate management (the heart of the business through the 1960s), and increasingly for knowledge about market conditions, government regulations and potential financial partners; and at the international level, in which domestic clients required advisory services in foreign markets. While the UK economy produced surplus investment funds during the period from 1961 to 1975 and again in the late 1980s, the modest size of British commercial and financial markets and stiff government intervention in the national economy led investors to supplement domestic investment by going abroad – most in the British Commonwealth and Europe.[16]

Moreover, the UK's modest land area – 94,214 square miles – led the government to restrict the amount of new office development throughout Britain in 1964 and again during 1971–76, which limited investment opportunities and prompted cross-border mobility by developers, investors, and real estate advisers.[17] Direct investment in domestic and foreign commercial property had a significant influence on the British economy, accounting for approximately one-third of total investment in the UK economy during the period from 1970 to 1990.[18]

Table 3.1 Gross domestic product[a] in Germany, Japan, United Kingdom and United States (1960–96 in billions of nominal US dollars)

Year	Germany	Japan	United Kingdom	United States
1960	72.6	43.1	72.3	513.4
1961	82.5	53.3	77.0	531.8
1962	90.2	60.6	80.9	571.6
1963	95.9	69.2	85.8	603.1
1964	105.7	81.4	93.3	648.0
1965	115.0	90.7	100.4	702.7
1966	122.1	105.2	107.0	769.8
1967	124.0	123.2	111.3	814.3
1968	133.6	146.6	105.3	889.3
1969	152.1	173.1	112.3	959.5
1970	185.2	204.3	123.8	1,010.7
1971	215.3	231.5	142.0	1,097.2
1972	258.1	303.8	161.0	1,207.0
1973	343.2	412.1	182.0	1,349.6
1974	380.2	457.5	197.6	1,458.6
1975	417.3	498.8	237.1	1,585.9
1976	445.0	561.0	229.9	1,768.4
1977	514.7	690.6	255.8	1,974.1
1978	639.1	970.7	324.5	2,232.7
1979	757.5	1,009.2	419.9	2,488.6
1980	809.8	1,057.5	539.8	2,708.0
1981	679.2	1,168.4	518.4	3,030.6
1982	654.4	1,226.6	488.0	3,149.6
1983	653.5	1,186.1	461.7	3,405.0
1984	615.2	1,264.5	433.2	3,777.2
1985	618.9	1,343.3	461.4	4,038.7
1986	886.6	1,985.6	562.1	4,268.6
1987	1,107.4	2,408.9	689.7	4,539.9
1988	1,193.5	2,898.4	832.3	4,900.4
1989	1,181.3	2,871.8	838.7	5,250.8
1990	1,487.3	2,940.4	980.7	5,522.2
1991	1,566.3	3,362.2	1,018.0	5,677.5
1992	1,723.8	3,750.1	940.1	5,850.1
1993	1,910.2	4,275.5	943.1	6,259.9
1994	2,046.1	4,687.1	1,018.6	6,649.8
1995	2,412.5	5,114.0	1,101.8	6,954.8
1996	2,360.8	4,597.2	1,135.0	7,263.2

Source: International Monetary Fund. For 1992–6 GDP data: National Accounts of OECD countries, Volume 1 (1997).

Note:
[a] Gross domestic product (GDP) is defined as the market value of output of goods and services produced by labor and property located in each focal country. GDP excludes net output produced or consumed in foreign countries and is conceptually equivalent in definition among the focal countries. For Germany, Japan and the United Kingdom, the national currency is converted to US dollars at current exchange rates.

Table 3.2 Total nonresidential fixed investment in Germany, Japan, United
Kingdom and United States (1960–95, structures only,[a] in millions of
nominal US dollars)

Year	Germany	Japan	United Kingdom	United States
1960	5,951	NA	3,260	49,200
1961	7,020	NA	3,806	48,600
1962	7,949	NA	4,184	52,800
1963	8,687	NA	4,203	55,600
1964	10,207	NA	5,001	62,400
1965	10,526	NA	5,402	74,100
1966	10,827	NA	5,693	84,400
1967	9,247	NA	6,194	85,200
1968	9,855	NA	5,934	92,300
1969	11,798	NA	6,277	102,900
1970	16,654	11,722	7,049	106,700
1971	19,561	12,975	8,046	111,700
1972	22,028	16,994	8,916	126,100
1973	27,093	24,277	11,030	150,000
1974	29,164	25,897	13,400	165,600
1975	29,366	27,076	15,597	169,000
1976	29,702	26,960	13,940	187,200
1977	33,081	30,695	13,348	223,200
1978	41,218	41,950	15,705	272,000
1979	51,372	49,042	20,447	323,000
1980	58,156	60,117	27,455	350,300
1981	46,248	64,582	25,290	405,400
1982	42,042	57,106	23,432	409,900
1983	39,200	59,416	20,185	399,400
1984	36,017	61,397	19,571	468,300
1985	34,623	63,595	19,727	502,000
1986	51,015	95,917	24,266	494,800
1987	63,297	113,164	32,571	495,400
1988	67,663	141,990	44,168	530,600
1989	67,617	159,438	51,434	566,200
1990	85,010	174,411	62,206	575,900
1991	89,117	223,035	56,194	547,300
1992	100,768	251,023	51,902	557,900
1993	90,214	284,326	40,045	598,800
1994	91,613	290,725	40,829	667,200
1995				738,500

Sources: For Germany, Japan and the United Kingdom, Organization for Economic Cooperation
and Development (OECD), *National Accounts, Detailed Tables*, volume II, 1996, 1994,
1992, 1990, 1987, 1985, 1984, 1982, 1981, 1980 and 1979 editions. For the United
States, US Department of Commerce, Bureau of Economic Analysis, *Survey of Current
Business*, July 1996 and January/February 1996.

Notes:
[a] Nonresidential fixed investment represents current expenditures on farm and nonfarm buildings and structures, public utilities, and on mining shafts and wells. More detailed
breakdowns of nonresidential fixed investment are not available in a time series for all focal
countries. For Germany, Japan and the United Kingdom, the national currency is converted
to US dollars at average annual exchange rates prevailing in the year recorded and published.

In about 1955, UK investors and advisers began to transport capital and professional resources to markets worldwide where diverse investment opportunities existed. During the late 1950s and early 1960s, developers and investors were principally focused in the London market, retaining quantity surveyors and chartered surveyors for estate and development management.[19] Yet by 1964, when Parliament passed the Brown Ban Act to restrict new building by specifying the amount of new office development in central London and later throughout all of England, several of the UK's leading estate agents, such as Jones Lang Wootton and Weatherall Green & Smith, had already opened overseas offices to assist British clients investing abroad.[20] Investors benefited from the tight property market through inflated asset values in the 1970–2 period, but they were limited in investment opportunities by the restricted amount of developable land. The majority of domestic capital investment occurred through institutional pensions funds, insurance companies, banks, and a growing volume of publicly-issued property bonds.[21] The 1974–5 recession and property crash, as well as the government's rent control edict, further constrained the UK's commercial market.[22] Domestic estate agents thus gained competitive advantage early on by their international perspective and local expertise in foreign markets, as well as through long-standing client relationships with institutional funds, bond funds, and domestic banks.[23]

Germany, by comparison, after 1960, was the second largest advanced industrial economy in the world until 1968 (when Japan surpassed it). Yet the republic was characterized by small, fragmented commercial property markets and highly urbanized development. Eighty-six percent of the German population in 1990 lived in urban areas (similar to Japan), and commercial land remained scarce across the thirty-year period.[24] Throughout the 1960s and early 1970s commercial property in the United Kingdom was viewed as "stones" built for one tenant, rather than as a speculative investment, and major institutional landowners and regional corporations dominated commercial property markets until 1985.[25] Because individual owner-occupiers defined the market's size and structure, independent estate management and quantity surveying was not widely practiced.[26] Overall knowledge of major markets and property cycles was unnecessary and therefore undocumented.[27] The absence of competitive advisory services was exacerbated by the diversity of geographically separate regional economies, markets which were centered around the three largest metropolitan areas of Frankfurt, Dusseldorf and Stuttgart, and the secondary markets of Munich and Hamburg, and Berlin and Leipzig after 1989. German investors remained largely localized in their perspective, and real estate advisory firms that were not affiliated with one of the major bank funds focused on one metropolitan market, such as Frankfurt, with secondary expertise in other metropolitan areas.[28] Unlike the US and UK, no one firm dominated the national market until 1990.

Such a localized industry, together with volatile GDP gains throughout the 1970s and into the early 1980s, hindered the growth and service capabilities of commercial real estate advisory firms. Fragmentation within the industry, and the absence of significant competition for major firms in any of the major markets, was believed to diffuse the economic pressure for a national or an international outlook. While Germany led the other three focal countries in outward direct investment during the 1980–7 period, most German real estate advisory firms lacked an international practice. Instead, only a few firms established operations in major European financial centers, such as London, Paris, Madrid and Rome, where local clients were investing, and usually worked in tandem with one of Germany's large commercial or investment banks. German financial institutions, which sponsored the largest volume of foreign direct investment, maintained the customary practice of retaining local advisers in local markets and typically hired domestic real estate firms in each foreign nation.[29]

Japan's tremendous economic growth over the thirty-year period exceeded gains by the US, UK and Germany, and produced large reserves of excess capital. Yet only a dozen trading conglomerates invested substantial capital reserves to diversify into commercial real estate and establish real estate advisory service divisions. Mitsui, Mitsubishi, Sumitomo and the recently privatized Japan National Railways held title to the country's scarce inventory of developable urban land. Excessive land prices and high capital gains taxes restricted commercial construction and domestic real estate investment throughout the period.[30] Office space in downtown Tokyo, for example, the largest urban market in the country, remained severely undersupplied for two decades, with vacancy rates peaking at 2 percent in 1975 and declining to below 1 percent by 1990.[31]

The major trading companies sponsored the majority of Japan's real estate advisory firms. These were subsidiaries created to serve the leading domestic construction and development firms and to advise sister companies on domestic real estate investments, most of which involved office, hotel and residential development for the corporation and its employees. After 1983, however, when the Ministry of Finance lifted capital export controls and the foreign exchange value of the yen soared, Japanese investors shifted a disproportionate volume of their real estate activities to foreign markets. Japan's largest construction, development and trading companies (such as Kumagai Gumi, Itoh and Kajima) led foreign property investment, followed by the major institutional funds and real estate companies (such as Sumitomo Life, Yasuda Life, Asahi Mutual Life and Mitsui Real Estate). Whether an investment was for the company's own account or in joint venture with a foreign partner, Japanese real estate advisers were brought in to counsel Japanese investors, often coordinating with foreign real estate service firms in the US, continental Europe and the Pan-Asian region.[32]

42

The importance of recruiting skilled professionals

Specialized expertise in local markets laid the foundation for a real estate advisory firm's relative value in the national and international marketplace. Market knowledge and reputation in this business stemmed directly from people – specifically from recruiting and retaining experienced professionals in each local market. This prerequisite for gaining a competitive advantage became more challenging and expensive as a firm expanded into new markets, especially foreign markets, where cultural differences among employees and dispersed operations intensified organizational diseconomies. Because real estate advisory firms gained a reputation through long-term experience in local and national markets, some firms were more successful in minimizing market and geographical disparities and distances than others.[33]

Over the thirty-year period, each of the focal countries cultivated an abundant supply of real estate and financial services professionals who were trained in the business traditions of the country and adaptable to changing market conditions. Historical labor-force and employment data for each of the focal countries indicated that employment in real estate and related services rose relatively slowly but steadily during the 1960s and early 1970s (Table 3.3). Concurrent with the rise of total cross-border direct investment, employment increased at a faster rate in the late 1970s and 1980s, with the largest number of job gains occurring in the US, the UK and Japan. Employment in the commercial real estate sector was believed to be influenced by GDP, relative wages, domestic commercial property investment and total cross-border real estate investment, as it was the willingness and capability of advisory firms to expand overseas and into different markets, and the interests of investors, that came to bear on employment data.

For example, German investors relied on domestic advisers in foreign markets, while US property investors were most likely to reduce their reliance on domestic real estate consultants and use local experts in foreign markets. This book argues that the domestic business culture bore a direct relationship between cross-border property investment and real estate employment. National cultures which tended to be more closed to foreign advisers or property services tended to retain domestic real estate consultants to manage property investments in both domestic and foreign markets. Investors from these countries preferred to retain advisers with whom they enjoyed a cultural affinity and were readily familiar (by reputation or experience). Moreover, multinational corporations with extensive overseas activities often had direct and/or indirect long-standing business associations with a particular home-based real estate advisory firm, and thus were inclined to retain that firm in foreign markets. In cultures historically more open and fluid, such as the US, domestic investors tended to (or were willing to) retain foreign advisory firms when investing abroad.

In the US, real estate employment began growing at a faster pace in the late

1970s, a trend which slowed down throughout the 1980s. Even so, the real estate sector added 358,000 jobs during the period from 1980 to 1990. The UK, with the highest annual growth of 4.4 percent in real estate employment during the 1980s, created 83,000 jobs during this decade. In both the US and UK, "other business services" employment, which included a small (but unquantifiable) number of real estate jobs, nearly doubled between 1980 and 1990, and finance and insurance employment increased by approximately one-third over the same period. Real estate employment in Japan rose by 46,000 jobs between 1980 and 1990, with the majority of job gains occurring concurrently with the boom in Japanese foreign investment and land prices in Japan after 1985. Germany, which reported real estate and business services employment together, added 539,000 jobs during the 1980s, compared to 436,000 new jobs between 1960 and 1970, and 282,000 new jobs during the 1970–80 period.

The rise in cross-border direct real estate investment between 1980 and 1990 is believed to have been an important factor in unprecedented job gains in each of the focal countries. US employment growth was likely supported by the rise of inward investment, while UK job gains were supported by UK investors and real estate advisers expanding in foreign markets. Japan's employment growth was partially supported by domestic real estate service firms expanding abroad, following the extraordinary rise of Japanese investment in the US and UK. Gains in Germany's real estate employment during the 1980–90 period are believed to stem from both the maturation of the domestic market and the increase of outward investment.

The accelerated expansion of real estate service firms into multiple markets, concurrently with a refinement and multiplicity of service products, focused attention on the importance of intrafirm communication and cooperation among people.[34] The experience of internationalizing real estate advisory firms reinforced Casson's argument in *Enterprise and Competitiveness* that "a culture which encourages a high degree of moral commitment among the members of an organization" would reduce internal transaction costs by making personnel more trustworthy and cooperation more fluid.[35] A personalized corporate spirit was essential to maintain standards of quality while diversifying across national borders and multiple cultures.[36] How was such commitment cultivated by both nations and firms? Which nations and firms excelled in professional competence at the local level and cross-border coordination in the international arena?

The UK achieved pre-eminence among the four countries for its high educational standards in real estate services, particularly in the training of professionals and the regulation of professional competence through the Royal Institution of Chartered Surveyors, founded in 1868.[37] UK real estate advisers provided estate and project management services, then land use and country planning services by the late 1960s, having expanded into Europe, Australia, Canada and Africa as early as the 1950s. Such leading firms of chartered

Table 3.3 Long-term employment trends in real estate and related industries in the focal countries (1965, 1970, 1975, 1980, 1985, 1990, 1995, in thousands of employees)

Germany	*1965*	*1970*	*1975*	*1980*	*1985*	*1990*	*1995*[a]
Finance, Insurance, Real Estate and Business Services	945	1,100	1,336	1,540	1,880	2,217	2,534
Finance and Insurance	485	597	703	755	793	893	947
Real Estate and Business Services	460	503	633	785	1,087	1,324	N/A

Japan	*1965*	*1970*	*1975*[b]	*1980*	*1985*	*1990*	*1995*
Finance, Insurance, Real Estate and Business Services[c]	2,844	3,076	4,155	5,004	5,746	6,955	7,909
Finance and Insurance	612	744	965	1,036	1,033	1,085	1,107
Real Estate	37	57	76	71	84	117	141
Business Services[c]	2,195	2,275	3,114	3,897	4,629	5,753	6,661

United Kingdom	*1965*	*1970*	*1975*[d]	*1980*	*1985*	*1990*	*1995*
Finance, Insurance, Real Estate and Business Services	623	893	1,078	1,237	1,989	2,683	3,411
Finance and Insurance	645	544	603	674	784	885	935
Real Estate	NA[e]	110	122	153	193	264	237
Business Services	363	571	648	744	914	1,534	2,239

United States	*1965*	*1970*	*1975*	*1980*	*1985*	*1990*	*1995*
Finance, Insurance, Real Estate and Business Services	4,007	5,087	5,921	7,868	9,958	11,848	13,616
Finance and Insurance	2,452	2,813	3,438	4,247	4,929	5,394	5,476
Real Estate	547	664	756	972	1,165	1,315	1,354
Business Services	1,008	1,410	1,746	2,650	3,865	5,139	6,786

Sources:
For Germany: *Statistisches Bundesamt Wiesbaden*, Facherie 18, Reihe 1.3; OECD, Department of Economics and Statistics, *Labor Force Statistics*; OECD, Statistics Directorate, *National Accounts*, Volume II. For Japan: Ministry of Labor, *Yearbook of Labor Statistics*. For the United Kingdom: Department of Employment, *Employment Gazette*; Department of Employment and Productivity, *British Labor Statistics, Historical Abstract, 1886–1968*. For the United States: US Department of Labor, *Employment, Hours and Earnings, United States, 1909–90*, Volume II, and *Employment*.

Notes:
Employment is classified according to the major activity of each business establishment. Real estate includes the sale and management of commercial and residential real estate; real estate consulting is included in business services; portfolio investment and related management operations would be included in finance. In addition, there may be ancillary real estate investment with associated employment by business establishments classified in non-real estate sectors. Data collection methodologies are not uniform among the focal countries.

[a] Data are for 1993.
[b] Data are for 1969.
[c] Business services include personal services employment.
[d] Data are for 1971. Definition of employment by sector and data collection methodology were changed in 1971. Thus, data for 1971 forward are not comparable with earlier years.
[e] Included indistinguishably in business services; data series changed in 1970 to specify real estate employment.

surveyors as Weatherall, Green & Smith, Jones Lang Wootton and Hillier, Parker, May & Rowden, began to build multinational networks throughout Europe and the British Commonwealth in the late 1950s, integrating an international structure into the operating business long before the rise in cross-border investment activity in the late 1970s and 1980s. Established international networks and expertise in foreign markets contrasted with the regional and national orientations of competitors in the US and Germany. Only when cross-border real estate activity accelerated in the 1970s did firms in these nations begin to establish international offices and bring foreign personnel into the company.

Firm allegiance by senior managers, particularly, played an influential role in international expansion. While UK, US and German real estate advisers identified less with specific firms than with specialized professions – such as brokerage, agency, estate and property management, planning, appraisal, finance, design and construction – most leading real estate advisory firms transferred senior staff abroad to sustain corporate loyalty and internal coordination across widely dispersed regions.[38] UK professionals were most adaptable to foreign practices, likely a result of the country's long history in international expansion. UK firms also demonstrated superior capabilities to US and German counterparts in balancing competing demands for internal corporate commitment and local professional talent in foreign offices.[39] US real estate advisory firms only began to move abroad in the late 1980s, and were less adept at shaping a multinational structure and adapting to foreign practices, even in light of their experience with diverse domestic markets and foreign clients investing in US markets.

Multinational Japanese advisory firms faced their greatest challenges in integrating US and European personnel into Japan's strict corporate culture. Japan's educational system cultivated "society oriented" professionals and an unmatched focus on thorough analysis and innovation. Domestic Japanese businesses excelled in retaining personnel for decades, people who placed the company's interests above their own and who facilitated fluid intrafirm communication across multiple divisions.[40] Yet Japanese firms were less effective in engendering commitment among locally hired professionals in foreign markets. Japanese executives also insisted on retaining centralized control at home, rather than conceding authority to US and European branches or affiliates. In foreign markets, this strategy clashed with long-standing US and European practices of independence and local responsiveness.[41]

During the 1980s, two new phenomena rose to the forefront to weaken company-wide coordination among firms then expanding on an international scale. One was the real estate industry's emphasis on financial expertise, which rewarded individual entrepreneurship, through commission pay structures, at the expense of fee-based teamwork. The second factor was the exponential growth between 1985 and 1990 in personnel employed in real estate and financial services. To varying degrees, internal diseconomies affected Japanese,

US, German and UK firms alike. Overall, UK firms fared better in diversifying into new services and foreign markets, principally because they had
cultivated an infrastructure of professional talent and local expertise in
multiple markets more than twenty years in advance of direct competitors. US
firms, by contrast, were handicapped by the entry of foreign real estate advisory firms capitalizing on the dramatic growth in inward real estate
investment in the US. Foreign firms that established operations in the US
during the 1980s exploited weaker corporate loyalties within US real estate
advisory firms by hiring experienced local professionals away from the best
American firms and business schools.[42]

International policy and investment perspective

National foreign trade policies and domestic investors' orientation to foreign
markets influenced the international expansion of domestic real estate
advisers. Until 1990 professional service firms depended largely on the core
activities of customers, and real estate advisers diversified their operations to
encompass the foreign markets of domestic and foreign clients.

Two measures provided evidence of this phenomenon: the expansion and
contraction of the home nation's inward and outward direct investment, and
the target markets of real estate investors and real estate advisers.[43] Barriers
and incentives to international trade took the form of both implicit business
practices and policies and explicit government regulations. Each effectively
hindered or encouraged the expansion of foreign service firms in certain
domestic markets. Moreover, in such nations as Japan and Germany, where
restrictive investment and financial services laws of the 1960s and 1970s were
liberalized after 1985, domestic demand for services still adhered to long-held
provincial attitudes about foreign real estate advisers. The economic system
could not be easily redirected.

Applied to the flow of services moving in and out of the country, national
trade regulations and international fiscal policies governed direct capital
investment by foreigners in a nation's property assets. Official policies also
defined the nature of professional services for investors in domestic and foreign
markets, and the transfer of personnel to and establishment of satellite operations in foreign nations. For example, preferential treatment of domestic
investors and domestic real estate advisers in Japan strengthened the international competitive standing of domestic firms at the potential (and intended)
expense of foreign firms. Real estate advisory firms, in particular, were able to
broaden corporate reputations and increase fee revenues through unhindered
access to particular geographic regions.[44] To represent foreign investors in
local markets, real estate advisory firms required not only tolerance, but an
open business climate too.

US foreign trade policies and business practices remained the most
liberal among the focal countries throughout the 1960–97 period, reinforcing

international services trade by both foreign and domestic real estate advisers.[45] The 1962 US Trade Expansion Act lowered import–export duties and made America the most open market in the world. This established the tradition of foreign investment. In the early 1970s, the US government further eased administrative and registration guidelines, thereby liberalizing foreign access to the US financial system and the world's largest real estate market as measured by annual output, total inventory and the number of geographic markets.[46] Foreign investment in US real estate was unparalleled worldwide, accounting for 2.8 percent of overall inward investment in US assets in 1975, and growing to 7.4 percent in 1980, 10.5 percent in 1985, and dropping back to 8.6 percent by 1990.[47] Since the mid-1970s, foreign advisers representing foreign investors were unhindered in the openly competitive US environment. US real estate advisers, therefore, "internationalized" principally by targeting foreign investors active in US markets, according to casual observations of industry professionals. Overseas markets, where US real estate advisers were far less knowledgeable and experienced, were distant secondary targets.

S.E. Roulac argued, in "The Globalization of Real Estate Finance", that foreign investors approached the US market "with somewhat more discernment than some of their US competitors". The author contended this practice resulted from the foreign custom of retaining professional advisers for objective counsel in overseas investments.[48] The leading US and German real estate advisers profiled in Chapter 4 gained an unmatched reputation among foreign investors active in domestic markets. Yet their domestic dominance rarely carried over into foreign markets, where US and German real estate service firms struggled to achieve a competitive standing. In fact, only those US accounting and financial services firms that incorporated real estate advisory services into the mainline international business as a complement or a subsidiary – such as the investment bank of Goldman Sachs & Co. or the accounting firm of Arthur Andersen & Co. – succeeded in establishing credible reputations across various foreign markets.

Precisely because US real estate investors, developers and corporations historically imported more foreign capital and services than they exported to major trading partners, US property advisers faced lower risk and higher profitability by targeting foreign investors active in domestic markets rather than enter markets abroad.[49] Even so, during the 1960s, US investors and advisers shifted their primary focus from the UK and other EC countries to Canada. One reason for this was Canada's proximity and the increasing volume of cross-border real estate investment between the two nations. Another reason was that UK real estate advisers virtually monopolized UK and European markets, having decades before set the standards and informal rules by which all advisers operated. The breadth and quality of property education created strict professional standards and business practices among licensed chartered surveyors, which were more limiting to direct investment by foreign competitors and cross-company exchanges in real estate advisory services than official

UK regulations – which actually levied the lowest taxes and VAT fees on foreign entities of all EC nations until the early 1980s.[50]

As early as the 1850s, British civil engineers pioneered the export of advisory services in design, construction, project and portfolio management, and direct investment, mostly in European countries. Founded on a century of experience, by the mid-1950s UK advisers excelled in their access to capital sources in the UK, Spain, France, Belgium and other European nations. In 1965 the Board of Trade established the British Consultants Bureau to promote the interests of UK property and engineering consultants abroad, the only representative body in the UK concerned with advising on overseas property and engineering capital investments.[51]

Yet practical experience in the British Commonwealth was more beneficial than any official promotional initiatives. Through private company initiative, chartered surveyors Jones Lang Wootton and Weatherall Green & Smith, among others, gained knowledge of foreign real estate and learned to transport service innovations to other markets and to overcome onerous local barriers.[52] This became particularly valuable during 1964 and the period between 1971 and 1976, when the government and the Bank of England, respectively, imposed development and financial restrictions on the UK market, prompting such major development companies as MEPC and Slough Estates to expand overseas, primarily to Canada, Australia, Belgium, France and the US.[53] With few exceptions they were guided into new markets by domestic property and financial advisers. Through most of the 1970s, however, UK real estate advisers and investors diminished their activities in foreign markets.[54] The government lifted foreign exchange controls in 1979, prompting UK real estate investors to expand their acquisitions abroad by $2.1 billion in the 1980–5 period, more than double the increase of the previous five-year period.[55] As a result, the major real estate advisory firms expanded their reach into new overseas markets in the early 1980s, such as Washington, DC, Tokyo and Geneva, providing UK advisers with a firmly established clientele and market base for the late 1980s investment boom.

An important advantage enjoyed by UK property advisers was their central geographic position as well as their conventional cultural and moderate political orientation – unmatched by US, Japanese, and even German advisers. The European market was neither uniform in tax and fiscal policies, nor national trade regulations. Yet even before the 1987 Single European Act, which provided a schedule for eliminating non-tariff barriers, UK advisers were particularly well-equipped to enter foreign European markets by virtue of their continental base and heritage.[56] Cross-border mobility and an increasing volume of European property acquisitions by multinational investors in the late 1970s and early 1980s laid the foundation for collaborative opportunities among real estate advisers – such as the European Economic Interest Group created by London-based Goddard & Smith, Paris-based Arthur Lloyd, and Hamburg-based Angermann.[57]

German property advisers were less expansive than their UK counterparts in counseling multinational investors. Beginning in the early 1970s, independent property advisers and the real estate advisory departments of German banks entered foreign markets in London, Paris, New York, Rome and Madrid to serve the outward investment activities of Deutsche Bank, Commerzbank and Dresdner Bank. Only since 1990, when the government lifted regulatory restrictions on foreign investment by German open-end funds, have international property and financial advisers begun to gain prominence with German investors in foreign markets.[58]

If investment in German real estate carried a high level of risk for German nationals, market and regulatory barriers were even higher for foreign investors and developers. Limited commercial land and complicated, multi-tiered public approvals added to the risk of speculative investment by foreign investors, particularly for those represented by foreign real estate advisers. Foreign investors active in one of Germany's metropolitan areas were virtually required to retain a local adviser, even if in collaboration with a foreign real estate service firm.[59] In addition, variable and discriminatory taxes and fees on revenues of foreign advisers and investors created regulatory barriers as formidable as market barriers; the government ostensibly "welcomed" foreign investment but did not encourage it at the expense of domestic entities. The boom in cross-border investment activity and globalization of financial markets after 1985 helped to liberalize German markets and prompted UK and French real estate advisers to enter Germany – Richard Ellis and Healey & Baker in 1988, and August-Thourard in 1990.[60]

Japanese real estate advisers expanded into foreign markets in the 1960s to support the foreign trade initiatives of Japan's large trading companies, their corporate sponsors. Because only corporate-affiliated advisers were privy to the needs of Japanese trading and construction companies, domestic real estate advisers in the US and UK were retained on a limited basis, if at all, to provide only market information (and intelligence) and to assist Japanese corporate real estate advisers, who acquired property to support the nation's financial, manufacturing and tourist trades.[61] Most foreign direct investment was governed by the Foreign Exchange and Foreign Trade Control Law of 1949 and centered around market access to facilitate cross-border trade, particularly with the US. Japanese foreign property investments increased only moderately after 1974, when floating exchange rates strengthened the yen relative to the US dollar and other major world currencies. The Foreign Exchange Control Law of 1980 sharply reduced restraints on capital outflows from Japan, and outward direct investment in total and in real estate rose further.

It took the Bank of Japan to lower the discount rate to 2.5 percent in 1986 – the lowest worldwide – for Japanese financial institutions and corporations to accelerate real estate acquisitions and lending in foreign markets. As the volume of direct property investments grew in proportion to total outward investment, from 3 percent in 1985 to 15 percent by 1990, Japanese investors increasingly retained international real estate advisers to provide objective counsel on speculative commercial investments. Having established extensive financial and trading outposts in the US since the early 1950s, Japanese nationals were most familiar with major US markets, and US real estate investments soared from $1.9 billion in 1985 to $16.5 billion by 1988.[62] Domestic real estate advisory firms with established operations in multiple US markets, such as Cushman & Wakefield and CB Commercial, secured premier acquisition contracts with Japanese investors.[63] Similarly, chartered surveyors with multiple European offices, such as Jones Lang Wootton and Weatherall Green & Smith, secured major Japanese contracts.

Restrictive monetary and lending policies implemented by the Bank and the Ministry of Finance in late 1989 halted Japanese acquisitions and credit worldwide.[64] Several real estate advisory firms in the US and Europe expanded operations and personnel during 1985–8, led by the extraordinary surplus of Japanese investment capital and the heady real estate conditions created by Japan's dominance in foreign markets. Beginning in late 1989 and continuing through 1993, these same firms were forced to contract operations.

While the Ministry of Finance facilitated the global expansion of real estate and financial advisory services after 1985, it continued to hinder foreign trade in Japan. Highly restrictive policies and long-standing business practices dating from the post-World War Two years restrained foreign professional service firms as well as inward real estate investment.[65] Capital liberalization between 1967 and 1971 excluded real estate investment and real estate services, which required screening by government officials and virtual restriction. Even while real estate was one of seventeen industries finally designated by the Japanese government for inclusion in foreign ownership during 1973–6, the business environment's strong aversion to foreign firms remained high.[66]

In addition, the Ministries of Finance and International Trade & Industry maintained onerous requirements for selling services in Japan to domestic trading companies; prohibited foreign services from advising Japan's international banks, pension funds and insurance companies; and selected joint ventures on the basis of obtaining innovative technologies, which effectively eliminated real estate services. Extraordinarily high land prices and a negative investment tax structure were further deterrents.[67] Until 1985, both government regulations and informal government–corporate relationships created a hostile environment for foreign real estate advisers seeking to establish operations in Japan. Even then, the Japanese economy tolerated but did not encourage open competition from foreign services firms.[68]

Each focal country's tax structures and international trade regulations influenced access to particular markets. Such legal structures are believed to have reflected the nation's real receptiveness to inward and outward cross-border trade. By extension, national business practices and market standards were very influential in defining the competitive environment for international real estate advisory services. The US established the foundation for a favorable tax and market system, encouraged a liberal trade and investment climate, and provided the greatest openness to foreign service firms. Japan's and Germany's restrictive domestic regulations, by contrast, reflected tightly linked investor–adviser relationships and closed service networks. The UK established liberal regulatory standards, yet the small and restricted domestic market ultimately limited competition from foreign real estate advisory firms.

International trade and multinational corporations

The unprecedented growth of capital-intensive multinational corporations was the most important impetus behind the globalization of accounting, law and financial services in the post-World War Two era.[69] Real estate advisory services also expanded into international markets during this period, often as subsidiary operations of multinationals, particularly in Japan and later the US. However, because property services remained regionalized in character through the early 1980s, scholarly research in international services trade devoted scant attention to the influence of corporate property investment on the global expansion of real estate services. Even so, investment-grade real estate historically constituted 25 to 40 percent of the total assets of corporations and approximately 20 percent of the assets of financial institutions.[70]

Given this level of investment in commercial property – office buildings, manufacturing plants, warehouses, retail stores, land and hotels – it is interesting that many US and European multinational corporations began to retain international real estate advisers only in the 1980s. Throughout the US and much of Europe, the IBM model of independent subsidiaries based in several nations prevailed, and each foreign operation managed its facilities and real estate requirements separately.[71] Until the last decade, it was more the exception than the rule for a US corporation and many European multinationals to retain an independent real estate adviser when expanding into foreign markets.[72]

Japan's group trading companies pioneered multinational real estate advisory services during the onset of global expansion in the late 1920s.[73] With the rising importance of finance in international trade, the largest group companies – Mitsui, Mitsubishi and Sumitomo – created subsidiary real estate divisions to manage substantial corporate property assets and other direct investments in both domestic and foreign markets. The activities of the groups' multiple subsidiaries supported the real estate divisions, and, simultaneously, the real estate professionals provided market intelligence and project management services in new markets. For example, in the US, Japan's largest trading market, the major trading companies and their group banks – Mitsui Bank, Mitsubishi Bank and Sumitomo Bank – established headquarters in New York City and, on the West Coast, in San Francisco and later Los Angeles. Through the trading companies, Japanese investors gained access to distribution and information networks for the acquisition of US assets.[74]

During the 1960s and early 1970s, Japanese foreign direct investment continued to support trade and focused on raw materials, land, sales networks and banking services, primarily in the US, Hong Kong, Brazil, Singapore and Saudi Arabia. By 1970 and 1972, Sumitomo Realty and Tokyo Land Corporation, respectively, established residential brokerage and land development operations in California, and hotel management and development in Hawaii.[75] In 1972, Mitsui Real Estate Development Co., Japan's leading real estate concern and a pivotal member of the Mitsui group, expanded abroad as adviser, investor and developer. By 1990, it had 201 foreign subsidiaries and affiliates.[76]

Because of Japan's increased economic dependency on foreign trade and export markets, the real estate services firms developed broad-based expertise during the 1970s in research, appraisal, property management, brokerage, finance, accounting and construction management.[77] By the early 1980s, just prior to the surge in Japanese real estate direct investment, real estate subsidiaries of trading companies were intimately familiar with US and European markets, as well as local business practices and the relative value of property.[78] Japanese real estate advisers accelerated their overseas expansions, particularly in US and UK markets, acquiring global–local reputations in the late 1980s by counseling Japanese investors and corporations in landmark acquisitions and joint developments overseas, such as Rockefeller Center in New York City and Paternoster Square in London.[79]

Japanese trading companies also played a vital role in promoting the international reputations of Japanese construction specialists. The largest contractors developed full-service advisory practices, stemming directly from paternalistic relationships within their business groupings – Mitsubishi, Mitsui, Toshiba and Hitachi. These contractors gained financial strength through group banks, the principal financiers of major international projects. They maintained a distinct competitive edge in overseas development projects sponsored by Japanese manufacturing and commercial companies, which tended to sole-source to the group's Japanese construction company manager.[80]

Such Japanese real estate advisory firms as Orix, however, which operated semi-independently from one of the trading groups, tended to expand into foreign markets after 1985 through finance-driven investors and institutions focused on real estate investments, rather than through corporate initiatives and projects. These independent firms, then, lacked the business backing and international foundation of the 1960s and 1970s that group-owned and group-affiliated firms enjoyed. They entered fully mature foreign real estate markets beginning in 1985.

Throughout the 1960–97 period, Japanese advisers deliberately limited business services to foreign US and European clients. Due to the country's restrictive investment policies, Japan's real estate advisers oriented their services only to those non-domestic clients seeking Japanese financial partners. US and European corporations retained a Japanese real estate service company associated with one of the major trading groups, as an introductory vehicle to Japan's domestic economic system or to other affiliates in the group. Such was the case of the Disney Corporation, which was advised by joint venture partner Mitsui Real Estate during 1980–5.

Similar to Japan's limited resources, the UK's modest land area prompted domestic trading and service enterprises to accelerate overseas expansions in the post-World War Two years.[81] UK estate managers first assisted British Commonwealth companies with plant and facility investments worldwide in the late nineteenth century. This activity accelerated during the 1950s as regional differences diminished and a nationalized market emerged. UK chartered surveyors, with unmatched knowledge and experience of Western European markets, advised a broad range of European corporate clients expanding or relocating throughout the EC region.[82]

UK advisers were thus well-positioned to compete favorably for the business of US multinationals entering European markets. The greatest share of US direct investment in real estate during the 1950s was concentrated in the UK, which took second place to Canada in the 1960s. During the 1970s and throughout the 1980s, the UK continued as an important expansion market for US multinationals because of its cultural familiarity, and in spite of its moderate economic size.[83] For example, in 1984 the establishment of US corporations Intel, National Semiconductor and Union Carbide along the M4 motorway between London and Bristol inflated commercial property values and became a major focus of UK property agents and advisers.[84] The prospect of EC market integration in late 1992 heightened European property investment by Japanese and US manufacturers after 1987 – principally electronics, chemicals, machinery and automotive concerns – which concentrated operations in London, Paris and Frankfurt.[85] Market access was the first priority of Japanese companies entering Europe, while US companies placed political stability first and market access second.[86]

UK property advisers enjoyed only moderate success in securing the business of multinational corporations expanding into Germany. Following the passage of the constitutional property rights Basic Law (Grundgesetz) in 1949, which authorized German enterprises and banks to take precedence in property development and property ownership,[87] non-domestic property advisers enjoyed limited opportunities to penetrate German markets. Instead, German advisory firms in each metropolitan area held sway over the majority of German and foreign investors.[88]

Corporate consultancy, or outsourcing to property advisers, was common practice among many European and Japanese corporations by the 1950s. US multinationals, by contrast, while recording a long history of overseas expansions, possessed a short-term outlook on the value of real estate advisory services in domestic and foreign markets. US corporations sponsored the greatest share of international real estate transactions down to the early 1980s, with US foreign direct investment in manufacturing, petroleum production, trade, and mining growing at a faster rate than the US economy between 1955 and 1970. Yet until 1983–4, US businesses typically viewed real estate investment as incidental to the mainline business and approached each market and each asset independently of others in the company's portfolio.[89] McDonald's Corporation, for example, operated in forty-four countries by 1988 and internally managed real estate projects within separate regional offices. The Gillette Company, as well, which opened its first overseas plant in 1904 and had twenty factories abroad by 1970 and thirty by 1990, undertook foreign real estate investments under the auspices of the company's finance personnel or regional managers.[90] Through the early 1980s, these and most other US corporations relied on finance personnel for real estate development and investment, and retained a local property adviser only for large and/or major projects.[91] By extension, US real estate advisory firms lacked an international perspective until the mid-1980s, when foreign clientele brought US advisers into the international marketplace.

Another factor that prompted the internationalization of US real estate advisory firms after 1985 was intensified competition from major investment banks active in international markets. Mellon Bank, Salomon Brothers, Goldman Sachs and Morgan Stanley began to diversify into real estate financial services in the early 1970s to meet the demands of corporate clients. With the emphasis on financial services and financing innovations after the mid-1970s, together with an unprecedented $200 billion rise in the total US stock of outward direct investment between 1985 and 1990, US real estate advisers strengthened their foreign market expertise and their financial services capabilities in concert with the needs of US multinationals.

Internationalization of financial markets and investment vehicles

Real estate advisory service firms accelerated the pace of global expansion and financial services innovations in the early 1980s principally to capitalize on the growth of unregulated international money sources. Prior to this time, debt and equity financial services were largely the domain of domestic banks and life insurance companies, also the primary sources of real estate capital in local markets. The mid-1980s, however, brought new forms of finance, an increasingly dynamic international investment market (particularly in the US) and intense competition from investment banks and the Big Six accounting firms.[92] In this context, real estate service firms competed directly with leading investment and merchant banks active in Eurobonds, international securities, and now real estate services. Firms competed on the basis of access to capital sources and global financial markets, as well as knowledge of property markets.[93]

The creation of the Eurobond market in 1963 prompted innovations in funding vehicles and distribution methods, and drew new business into the international marketplace. Real estate finance, though not a primary sector of the Eurobond market, was certainly integral to most corporate debt and equity issues. During the late 1970s and early 1980s, several leading firms in the focal countries, most of which were investment and merchant banks, established real estate advisory divisions to provide both advisory services and equity capital for real estate transactions. With the tremendous growth of the new-issues market during 1967–87 and the globalization of capital and real estate markets, the number and breadth of real estate financing sources increased in the 1970s and even further in the 1980s.[94]

Real estate advisory firms in the focal countries diversified into innovative financial services and expanded office operations and/or correspondent relationships into the primary financial capitals of New York, London, Tokyo and Frankfurt, in an effort to build a financial services practice linked to international investors and capital markets, and to compete directly with investment and merchant banks in counseling corporate clients on real estate matters. US real estate firms gained the leading position in international finance, stemming from New York's predominance in the Eurobond market during the late 1970s and early 1980s, plus the international strength of the real estate divisions of New York investment banks Morgan Stanley, Credit Suisse First Boston, Lehman Brothers, Goldman Sachs and Salomon Brothers.[95] As foreign real estate loans grew from a $2 billion to an $8 billion market during 1981–9 – a volume 150–200 percent greater than foreign direct investment – the US prevailed as the largest international mortgage market in the world.[96]

By the early 1980s, corporate mergers and acquisitions and leveraged buyouts constituted a growing sector in real estate financial services.[97] Development finance was another major focus of international finance. US advisory firms and investment banks that prevailed in this segment, whether acting as advisers or as equity partners, distinguished themselves from competitors by access to international capital sources and by offering superior financial expertise. For precisely this reason, Japan's Nomura Securities in 1986 acquired a 50 percent interest in Eastdil, the leading US real estate finance firm during the 1970s.[98]

US investment banks sustained their lead through the mid-1980s by shifting significant capital and personnel resources to the London market, then the center of Euromarket activities. This, in turn, intensified competition for US real estate advisory firms, which to date had pursued a domestic-oriented range of services. To remain competitive, such national firms as Cushman & Wakefield and CB Commercial broadened their practices to encompass new forms of international finance and expanded operations into foreign markets, notably London.[99]

UK chartered surveyors also faced new competition from investment banks and the Big Six accounting firms. In the early 1970s, UK merchant banks and

European credit banks established real estate advisory divisions to review short- and medium-term property loans.[100] While insurance companies were the primary sources of long-term debt and equity investment through the early 1980s, such leading merchant banks as Morgan Grenfell, N.M. Rothschild and S.G. Warburg remained an important source of long-term debt for the largest developers and corporate investors, and concentrated financial advisory services on full-service corporate finance, including property.[101] Domestic currency restrictions issued by the Bank of England in 1976 constrained UK real estate credit markets, especially for foreign investments.[102] The banks, guided by their in-house advisers, went in two directions: direct development financings, and/or international loan syndicates such as the Canary Wharf development. A few UK investors in foreign projects secured "back to back" loans with foreign banks, guaranteed by local merchant banks.[103]

UK property advisers gained prominence among financial institutions in the face of the 1973–5 property crash and the Bank of England's 1976 edict.[104] Independent third-party advisers rose in importance and value, as they were called on to prepare independent valuations and financial pro formas for new developments.[105] During the 1980s, clients increased pressure to provide access to international capital sources and to operate as both adviser and principal. The increasing importance of foreign capital in the face of contracting domestic sources heightened the competition with investment banks, merchant banks and accounting firms – which took principal positions in international capital markets.[106] The 1986 Financial Services Act had the effect of expanding the service market for the UK property advisers by regulating the conditions under which such professional firms as lawyers, accountants and chartered surveyors engaged in investment matters and competed with the financial advisory arms of merchant and investment banks. This more restrictive financial services environment enhanced the marketability and stature of quality property advisers.

UK and Germany-based chartered surveyors redefined financial services to encompass transactional representation. German firms such as Müller and Dr. Lubke GmbH Immobilien merged with Commerzbank and Dresdner Bank, respectively; UK firms such as Richard Ellis and Jones Lang Wootton established affiliations with global investment funds and created multi-disciplined financial services divisions that drew on the firms' core brokerage, development consulting and fund management services.[107] Germany's financial institutions enabled domestic real estate advisers to compete on the basis of capital access after 1980, while the real estate affiliates expanded the financial services capabilities of the leading merchant and investment banks. Yet real estate advisory firms did not attempt to compete with German banks as principal agents, nor did they expand operations to the global financial capitals of London, Tokyo and New York to participate in international financial markets.[108] Germany was the world's largest sponsor of foreign property investment for over two decades, 1966–87 (accounting for 12 to 16 percent of the nation's total foreign direct investment).

International financial consultancy constituted one of many divisions of the largest investment and merchant banks. Deutsche Bank, for example, was among the top participants in the Eurobond market since 1963. With the assistance of both in-house and third-party advisers, such as Jones Lang Wootton of the UK, Deutsche Bank aggressively pursued international real estate clients from its earliest years in the late nineteenth century, building up a centralized real estate department in Frankfurt and a foreign network of 300 full-service offices by 1990.[109]

Japanese real estate advisory firms capitalized on the heightened importance of financial services by exploiting their affiliations with domestic financial institutions (typically members of the same group) and followed domestic banking clients overseas. After 1986, Japanese corporations were even more motivated by cumulating stock surpluses to issue convertible Eurobonds and to transfer domestic investments abroad, notably in US real estate.[110]

Japanese real estate advisory firms, in tandem with Japanese banks, extended US and other offshore services to US and European corporations, institutional investors, and property companies.[111] By 1988, the same long-term credit banks which built the largest US presence were also among those that built a significant position in international Euromarket securities and debt sectors – Mitsubishi, Mitsui, Sumitomo, Industrial Bank of Japan and Daiichi Kangyo.[112] Over the 1977–87 period, the growth of foreign direct investment was highly correlated with the growth of commercial and long-term credit banks. For example, as real estate investment rose to 15 percent of total international trade during the 1986–90 period, Japan's largest real estate investor, Mitsubishi, was also the largest Japanese bank in the US during the late 1980s.[113] Moreover, the leading Japanese banking centers in the US were also the leading real estate investment markets – Los Angeles, New York City, Honolulu and San Diego.[114]

The real estate advisory firms affiliated with long-term credit banks were distinguished in US and European real estate markets during the 1985–9 period by their ability to provide financial services and investment capital in both an advisory and an agency capacity, as a source of counsel and capital. These dual roles diminished sharply after December 1989. When the Bank of Japan enforced restrictive monetary standards and Japanese worldwide credit expansion ended, Japanese advisers were no longer sought for their access to real estate funds or for their counsel about real estate investments and financing vehicles.[115]

Industry and organizational structure

The unregulated worldwide industry and minimal differences in real estate service practices across national borders facilitated a liberal flow of market and competitor information after 1960. In this environment, an increasingly internationalized and more capable industry emerged.[116] Japan was the exception; national regulations and business customs hindered foreign competition and the cross-border flow of knowledge and market intelligence.

What did real estate advisory firms expect to gain by engaging in cross-border services trade between the focal countries? What market vehicles did firms rely on to establish a competitive advantage in foreign nations? Measurable differences in national markets, real estate investment yields, and specifically a broad range among major urban centers (London, New York, Los Angeles, Frankfurt, Tokyo, for example) prompted firms with strong domestic reputations to respond to the demands of multinational clients and the rising volume of foreign direct investment.[117] For those firms that established new offices in foreign markets, international expansion was structured to optimize profitability – either by consolidating with domestic firms, by cooperative agreements with potential competitors, and/or by establishing subsidiary operations.[118] Each firm's established reputation in a related market played a key role in internationalization.

J. Kay argued in *Foundations of Corporate Success* that a firm's "reputation was the market's method of dealing with attributes of product quality which customers cannot easily monitor for themselves."[119] Reputation was such a powerful source of competitive advantage, Kay contended, that it directly affected the billing rates and price premiums a firm commanded, as well as market dominance.[120] For real estate advisory services, industry accounts and (public and private) corporate reports provided evidence that real estate advisory firms with solid international reputations began to command rate premiums above national and local firms in the UK and Japan as early as 1960, reflecting the greater emphasis in these markets on cross-border investment and value-added internationalized property services.

For example, internationalized Mitsui Real Estate's hourly billing rates average 10 to 15 percent higher than those of the domestic firm of Tokyu Land in 1960, growing to a premium of 50 to 100 percent by 1975. Similarly, the UK's largest international firm, Jones Long Wootton, commanded rate premiums of 10 percent over the domestic practice of King Sturge & Co. in 1960, rising to almost a 100 percent premium by 1975.[121] It could be argued that international breadth was one among several attributes reflected in such rate premiums. Indeed, industry accounts at the time indicated that the value of personnel, of service capabilities, and of reputation in major markets were as critical to the two internationalized firms' market value as were their cross-border knowledge and international investment services, a value edge each sustained through the early 1980s.

By 1990, US international firms quoted rate premiums relative to domestic competitors. Arthur Andersen's international real estate services group, for example, commanded hourly rates 20 to 25 percent above domestic practices in 1990, such as James Felt Realty of New York City. By contrast, internationalized firms in Germany, the most localized of the focal countries, consistently reported lower billing rates than exclusively domestic firms.[122] The Müller Group, Germany's largest property consultants with offices in both Western and Eastern Europe, reported average hourly fees consistently on a par with or below domestic competitors, suggesting that there was no particular value added for international scope in this most localized and fragmented of national markets. However, the world's largest and, by reputation, leading real estate advisory firm, Jones Lang Wootton, consistently commanded the highest billing rates among all firms analyzed across the 1960–97 period. This would suggest that reputation stemmed from market exposure and market knowledge, and had a direct impact on a firm's real estate service fees.

Firmwide staff growth and billing fees commanded by leading advisory firms in the four countries served as quantifiable measures of reputation. Additional measures could include a firm's historical gross revenue, net revenues per employee, active client roster, and revenue by client and service division. These latter measures, however, remained largely confidential and unattainable for a collective analysis of the forty firms in the real estate services profession. The work of Davis and Smales (1989) also highlighted how "the crucial feature of expert services" was "very difficult for buyers to monitor", thus making "reputation an important factor in attracting customers to service firms". [123] Again, the core issue of measuring reputation was addressed but not resolved. Indeed, reputation was such a crucial feature of valuing the merits of professional services generally and real estate advisory services particularly that further, full-scale research would be warranted.

This study has determined that, since the 1960s, property advisory firms competed on the basis of access to markets, capital and clients; reputation stemmed from securing these domestic and international sources to the maximum and earliest extent; and internationalization of the profession was driven by the globalization of financial markets and multinational investors. In the nature of the business of property investment and advisory services, competitive advantage implied that real and perceived conflicts of interest were balanced against a firm's knowledge and representation of other major investor clients. For example, Kraft General Foods selected Cushman & Wakefield real estate advisers to manage the multinational's real estate functions because of the firm's national and international network of professionals and its in-depth knowledge of other corporate competitors' business and property portfolios (which were also clients). In a business that placed equal value on information and technical capability, potential conflicts of interest between clients were cautiously avoided and deliberately overlooked by investors in the interest of access to expertise and markets.[124]

While Ricardo's price theory of international trade in goods is largely inapplicable to an analysis of international real estate services trade, the essence of Ricardo's free trade argument remained valid: capital investment in domestic trade tended to be diverted to other markets where profits and yields were expected to be higher.[125] Unrestricted trade yielded the greatest economic efficiencies and benefits to both export and import markets. As in real estate investment, Japanese firms exported real estate advisory services to the US and Europe in the hope of increasing returns on investments in personnel and service innovations. UK chartered surveyors were also principally export-oriented, focusing foreign services trade in the country's primary real estate investment markets – other EC nations, the US, and the British Commonwealth. Conversely, where such "invisible" imports were restricted or wholly prohibited – as in Germany and Japan – market participants incurred higher costs from limited competition, limited access to professional expertise and market knowledge, and delays in technological transfer and service innovations.[126] Such formal and informal restraints on real estate services trade hindered long-term national gains, as Hindley and Smith argued for international services trade generally.[127] Indeed, international investors in the US stood to gain the most from the country's most liberal import policy for services and real estate expertise; information and innovations flowed freely across borders and through the national market.

By the mid-1980s, real estate services firms based in free-trade national markets were able to exploit the benefits of intensified international competition and an increased dependency on cross-border transfer of information – access to innovations, clients and capital – at the expense of advisory firms headquartered in more restricted markets. An indigenous trait among real estate advisory firms was that, when information and expertise were harbored, colleagues and competitors closed off channels of mutually-beneficial communication. Two extremes exemplified this practice: UK chartered surveyors responded promptly to market shifts, service innovations and national inward–outward investment cycles; Japanese advisers, in contrast, innovated and expanded in response to macro trade forces (such as capital credit markets), rather than to shifting real estate markets and advancing service innovations.

Real estate advisory subsidiaries in larger, diversified financial and professional services organizations – UK merchant banks, German investment banks and US accounting firms – also appeared to be less responsive to property market shifts and industry innovations. By contrast, independent real estate advisory firms, such as those presented in the case studies in Chapter 6, tended to be most pliable to market shifts and more innovative than their competitors in banking, accounting and product trade.[128] The optimum organizational structure accommodated the pressures of both an integrated global strategy and local responsiveness: a centralized multiregional and multinational network of offices and subsidiaries; an autonomous but cooperative multidisciplined departmental system; an international perspective toward markets and clients; and an adequate capital reserve to fund incremental expansion and new businesses.[129] UK real estate advisory firms were most successful in developing a complex structure that integrated a multimarket, global presence with locally autonomous offices and diversified service divisions. Over several decades beginning in the early years of this century, such firms as Jones Lang Wootton and Weatherall, Green & Smith retained central control over expansion into multiple national markets by enabling the most profitable local offices to subsidize the firmwide strategy of expanding services beyond a provincial business environment and broadening the scope of international trade.[130]

At the other end of the spectrum were global, multi-firm networks. One notable UK chartered surveyor, Ronald Collier, who practiced in the UK and Australia, established in the 1960s the earliest known multinational, multi-firm network – throughout the British Commonwealth in Malaysia, Singapore, Hong Kong and Canada.[131] By the late 1980s, Colliers, headquartered in Boston, Massachusetts, had built a network of thirty-four firms in twelve countries. Over time, however, eroding commitments by member firms weakened the reputation and market acceptance of Colliers and other multinational networks.[132] Most networks were founded in the 1970s and early 1980s and prided themselves on meritocratic organizational structures and no nation-state allegiances – though the majority originated in the UK and US. Only one multinational network, the International Commercial Property Association (ICPA) of Europe, which was founded and managed since 1972 by UK-based Hillier Parker, retained centralized control through a hierarchical organizational structure and succeeded in balancing competing demands for multiregional vs. local expertise.[133]

In the 1990s a new major player in global real estate services emerged: New America Network. It is the largest consortium of commercial real estate brokerages in the world, with more than 150 member firms serving over 210 offices throughout the US, Canada, Europe, Latin and South America. Total sales and leases consummated within the Network were worth approximately $16 billion in 1996. New America Network is headquartered in Hightstown, New Jersey, and has approximately 3,000 real estate agents. It provides brokerage services, corporate services, financial services, property and facilities management, strategic information services and advisory services. The Network also offers specialized services to niche markets such as restaurants and entertainment, hospitality, housing for senior citizens, land, biotech and telecommunications. In 1996, New America Network formed an alliance with PHH Corporation, a residential real estate service in Mexico, to provide a variety of real estate services throughout Mexico.

US firms, by comparison, tended toward decentralized management of services and regional markets, and simply lacked the international experience to institute a unified global network. Regional expansion in US markets after 1960 was principally driven by local–national clients and the potential profitability of adapting existing services to local conditions. Even as late as 1990, when faced with the formidable presence of international competitors, many established US firms – as well as the US subsidiaries of international accounting and insurance organizations – lacked the leadership and centralized control to coordinate multinational operations and capitalize on the global reputation of diversified services organization.[134]

Competitive advantages

What determined competitive advantage for real estate advisory services in the international marketplace? Different national markets cultivated different skills in response to real estate cycles, inward and outward investment flows and investor demands. Variations in real estate markets and capital investment flows defined the historic evolution and relative strength of firms in each nation. US and UK advisory services were built on brokerage, agency, investment sales, corporate real estate, and pension fund management. Japanese firms focused on financial services, and German advisers oriented their practices to agency services, and institutional and bank investments.

Throughout the period from 1960 to 1990, even in the face of an internationalizing marketplace, domestic firms held a prima facie advantage over foreign competitors in domestic markets.[135] While the US encouraged a free flow of information and professional expertise, and US and foreign firms alike were afforded equal access to investors – in contrast to more limited market environments in the UK, Germany and Japan, where domestic advisers enjoyed a clear advantage over foreign advisory firms – US firms still enjoyed unmatched expertise in widely dispersed local markets.

The size and stability of inward and outward investment flows also influenced the long-term competitive standing and reputation of real estate advisory firms. UK firms gained dominance early on in the 1950s and 1960s because of the nation's long history in outward investment. US firms and foreign firms active in the US marketplace acquired international prominence across the 1980s due to the sustained growth of foreign real estate investment – from the UK, Japan, Germany, Netherlands and Canada. Japanese and German property advisers lacked consistent exposure to international investor demand throughout the period between 1960 and 1997, and therefore lacked a solid investment climate for sustained innovation.

Notes

1 Also see S.E. Roulac, "The Globalization of Real Estate Finance", *The Real Estate Finance Journal*, vol. 4 no. 2 (1987), p. 39.

2 M.A. Hines, *Marketing Real Estate Internationally* (New York: Quorum Books, 1988), pp. 16–17, 77, 81, 142.
3 E. Davis and C. Smales, "The Internationalization of Professional Services", Working Paper Series no. 66, Centre for Business Strategy, London Business School (April 1989).
4 Comparative statistical models that analyze dependent factors of international trade in services have only recently been developed, notably by Louis Wells and Mark Casson. The author has drawn from this work in analyzing factor advantages in international real estate advisory services.
5 M.A. Weiss, "Real Estate History: An Overview and Research Agenda", *Business History Review,* vol. 63 no. 2 (Summer 1989), pp. 241–82.
6 *Ibid.,* p. 257.
7 G.P. Sampson and R.H. Snape, "Identifying the Issues in Trade in Services", *The World Economy* vol. 8 no. 2 (June 1985), pp. 172–3.
8 *Ibid.,* p. 173.
9 As reviewed in Chapter 2, and discussed further in this chapter, such liberal, completely open trade has not historically existed in the US, UK, Germany and Japan.
10 G. Dufey, "The Role of Japanese Financial Institutions Abroad", in *Japanese Financial Growth,* eds C.A.E. Goodhart and G. Sutija (London: Macmillan Academic and Professional Press, 1990), pp. 132–66.
11 A.D. Chandler, Jr., *Scale and Scope: The Dynamics of Industrial Capitalism* (Cambridge, MA: The Belknap Press of Harvard University Press, 1990); M. Casson, ed., *The Growth of International Business* (London: George Allen & Unwin, 1983); and M. Casson, *Enterprise and Competitiveness* (Oxford: Clarendon Press, 1990).
12 *Ibid.,* p. 5.
13 See Appendix B for a detailed discussion of government regulations, taxation policies and fee requirements affecting real estate direct investment and professional services in each of the focal countries.
14 S.L. Hayes III and P.M. Hubbard, *Investment Banking: A Tale of Three Cities* (Boston: Harvard Business School Press, 1990), p. 319.
15 *Ibid.,* p. 323, for discussion of US investment bankers and international experience. For the accounting profession, see C.P. DeMond, *Price, Waterhouse & Co. in America* (New York: Arno Press, 1980); and for international architectural services, see A.O. Dean, "European Forecast" and N.R. Greer, "Americans Abroad: Some Coming Attractions"; "Foreign Exchange", *Architecture* (September 1990), pp. 101–5; M. Casson, *Enterprise & Competitiveness,* pp. 2–3.
16 C.G. Powell, *An Economic History of the British Building Industry, 1815–1979* (London: Methuen, 1982), pp. 152–3.
17 *The Economist* (5 November 1966), p. 610; (11 November 1967), p. 639; (18 March 1972), p. 8; (10 June 1978), pp. 3–11.
18 S. Currie and A. Scott, "The Place of Commercial Property in the U.K. Economy", paper presented to The London Business School (January 1991), p. 1.
19 "Development, the Economy and the Chartered Quantity Surveyor", *Chartered Surveyor* (5 November 1965), pp. 243–6; and (May 1966), pp. 595–7; A.T. Brett-Jones, "The Future Role of the Quantity Surveyor", *Chartered Surveyor* (July 1969), pp. 13–15; A. Bailey, "Property People", *The Estates Gazette,* vol. 219 (31 July 1971), pp. 597–601.
20 E.L. Erdman, *People & Property* (London: B.T. Batsford Ltd., 1982), p. 181; O. Marriott, *The Property Boom* (London: Abingdon Publishing, 1967, reprint 1989), pp. 120, 138–9, 150–60; and *The Economist* (11 November 1967), p. 639.

21 *The Economist* (18 March 1972), p. 8; (1 July 1972), p. 22.

22 P. Scott, "MEPC PLC", *International Directory of Company Histories* IV, edited by A. Hast (London: St. James Press, 1991), pp. 710–11.

23 *The Economist* (10 June 1978), pp. 3–11; (2 August 1980), p. 67; S. Cowan, *The Guide to European Property Investment* vol. 1, (London: Waterlow Publishers, 1989), pp. 3–7.

24 D.J. Kostin, "German Real Estate Market: An Introduction for Non-German Investors", (New York: Salomon Brothers, April 1991), p. 3.

25 *The Economist* (25 November 1972), p. 124; (13 July 1985), p. 480.

26 R. Marshall, "The QS in Europe", *Building* (24 September 1976), p. 61.

27 R. Gop, "The League Table of Estate Agents: The Leaders Stay Ahead of the Field", *Immobilien Manager* (February 1992), pp. 17, 18.

28 Germany's largest banks, such as Deutsche Bank, Commerzbank and Dresdner, created real estate advisory service divisions in the 1970s in response to the foreign investment activities of major banking clients. Because of their diversified European operations and leading involvement in the international Eurobond market in London, these banks were well-positioned in major local markets abroad in the 1970s and 1980s to advise on foreign direct real estate investment. See Deutsche Bank, "Deutsche Bank – A Brief History", press release, Frankfurt am Main (December 1989); and J.A. Gosling and A.J. Thornley, "The Role of the European Property Professional: France, Spain, The United Kingdom and Germany", Working Papers in European Property, Centre for European Property Research, University of Reading (March 1991).

29 J. van den Bos, "JLW Signs Up to Manage Germany Buying Spree", *Chartered Surveyor Weekly* (31 January 1991), p. 7.

30 *The Economist* (13 July 1985), p. 480.

31 L.S. Bacow, "The Tokyo Land Market: An Essay", Working Paper Series No. 26, Center for Real Estate Development, Massachusetts Institute of Technology (October 1990), pp. 5–8.

32 A. Froggat and T. Oliver, "Japanese Investment in European Property", *World Property* (May 1990), pp. 25–7; S. Hayes and P.M. Hubbard, *Investment Banking* (1990), p. 278; M.A. Hines, *Guide to International Real Estate Investment* (1988), p. 89.

33 J. Kay, in *Foundations of Corporate Success* (Oxford: Oxford University Press, 1993), pp. 89–90, argued that the reputation of products is revealed by one of three processes: (1) research; (2) immediately on consumption; and (3) through long-term experience.

34 S.L. Hayes III and P.M. Hubbard, *Investment Banking* (1990), p. 320; M. Casson, *Enterprise and Competitiveness* (1990), p. 13.

35 *Ibid.*, pp. 87–8. In a history of UK chartered surveyors Drivers Jonas, H. Barty-King argued that a firm must maintain a personalized corporate spirit throughout growth and diversification, in *Scratch a Surveyor* (London: William Heinemann Ltd., 1975), p. 253.

36 S.B. Sagari argued that skilled labor was also a comparative national advantage for international financial services, in contrast to large endowments of arable land and surplus capital, which have a negative impact on international trade; her findings are statistically documented in "The Financial Services Industry: An International Perspective", (PhD dissertation, Graduate School of Business Administration, New York University, 1986).

37 *The Economist* (10 August 1968), pp. 12–13; J.A. Gosling and A.J. Thornley, "The Role of the European Property Professional: France, Spain, The United

Kingdom and Germany", Working Papers in European Property, Centre for European Property Research, University of Reading (March 1991).

38 Professional allegiance originated in the US and UK in the late nineteenth century with specialized training and technical schools, then was sustained through licensing requirements and professional organizations. J. Bennett, R. Flanagan and G. Norman, "Capital & Counties Report: Japanese Construction Industry", Centre for Strategic Studies in Construction, University of Reading (May 1987). R. Volhard, D. Weber and W. Usinger, eds, *Real Property In Germany: Legal and Tax Impacts of Development and Investment* (Frankfurt: Fritz Knapp Verlag, 1975, 1991), pp. v, 23. S.L. Barter, ed., *Real Estate Finance* (London: Butterworth, 1988), pp. 30–2.

39 Throughout the 1960s, many leading chartered surveyor firms and senior professionals accepted equity positions in foreign projects, while also providing "objective" counsel to clients. Challenged by RICS and the Estate Agents Council on the basis of conflicts of interest, this practice had diminished considerably by the mid 1970s. *The Economist* (10 August 1968), pp. 12–13; R. Sobel, *Trammell Crow, Master Builder: The Story of America's Largest Real Estate Empire* (New York: John Wiley & Sons, 1989), p. 109.

40 G. Dufey, "The Role of Japanese Financial Institutions Abroad", in *Japanese Financial Growth,* eds C.A.E. Goodhart and G. Sutija (London: Macmillan Academic and Professional Press, 1990), pp. 151–2.

41 J. Bennett, R. Flanagan and G. Norman, "Capital & Counties Report: Japanese Construction Industry", Centre for Strategic Studies in Construction, University of Reading (May 1987). pp. 11–15; and S. Hayes and P.M. Hubbard, *Investment Banking* (1990), p. 290.

42 Interviews and primary observations by author with CB Commercial; Cushman & Wakefield; Goldman Sachs & Co.; Arthur Andersen & Co.; Harvard Business School; Wharton Business School, University of Pennsylvania.

43 The source of data on the target markets of investors included interviews by the author with real estate investors as well as direct surveys of the ten largest real estate advisory firms in each of the focal countries, detailed in Chapter 4.

44 Domestically focused service firms have had the most difficulty in managing cross-border regulations and cultures, "and thus have had most way to go [sic] in developing internationally", according to E. Davis, G. Hanlon and J. Kay in "Internationalization in Accounting and Other Professional Services", Working Paper Series No. 78, Centre for Business Strategy, London Business School (April 1990), p. 3. See Appendix B, "A Brief History of Restrictions on International Investment by the Focal Countries".

45 The caveat to this statement, discussed in the preceding section, is that foreign real estate advisory firms active in the US partially diminished the competitive advantage of US firms in their home market by hiring skilled real estate professionals away from many domestic firms.

46 M. Wilkins, "Japanese Multinationals in the United States: Continuity and Change, 1879–1990", *Business History Review* 64 (Winter 1990), p. 608.

47 Chapter 2, Table 2.2.

48 S.E. Roulac, "The 'Globalization' of Real Estate Finance", *The Real Estate Finance Journal,* vol. 4 no. 2 (Spring 1987).

49 Real estate constituted less than 1 percent of all outward direct investment throughout the 1960–97 period. In addition, 85 percent of US entities that did participate in overseas investment focused their activities in one foreign country, most in the culturally compatible European Economic Community. M. Wilkins, *The Maturing Multinational Enterprise: American Business Abroad from 1914 to 1970*

(Cambridge: Harvard University Press, 1974), pp. 341, 350; L.S. Bacow, "Foreign Investment, Vertical Integration, and the Structure of the U.S. Real Estate Industry", Working Paper No. 25, Massachusetts Institute of Technology Center for Real Estate Development (Cambridge, MA,: January 1990); also P.A. Geroski and S. Toker, "Picking Profitable Markets", Working Paper Series No. 59, Centre for Business Strategy, (London Business School, November 1988).

50 S. Cowan, *The Guide to European Property Investment* I (London: Waterlow Publishers, 1989), pp. 7–12, 7–16; Arthur Andersen & Co. and Nabarro Nathanson, *Building a Stake in Europe – Guidelines for Investors in Real Estate* (Chicago: June 1991), p. 140.

51 *Ibid.*, pp. 198–9.

52 E. Davis and C. Smales argued that international expansion by service firms, and gaining competitive advantage, involved the importation of "creative services" into new markets in "The Internationalization of Professional Services", Working Paper Series No. 66, London Business School (April 1989), p. 10.

53 P. Scott, "Slough Estates PLC", *International Directory of Company Histories* IV, edited by A. Hast (London: St. James Press, 1991), p. 722; P. Scott, "MEPC PLC", *International Directory of Company Histories* IV (London: St. James Press, 1991), pp. 711–12; *The Economist* (3 April 1976), pp. 117–18; (11 September 1976), pp. 99–100; Leslie Hannah, Barclays Bank, ms. (January 1994), pp. 277–87.

54 P. Scott, "MEPC PLC", *International Directory of Company Histories* IV (London: St. James Press, 1991), p. 711.

55 Chapter 2, Table 2.1.

56 M. Hsia, "Corporate Location in Europe: The Implications of a Single Market", Working Papers in European Property, Centre for European Property Research, University of Reading (March 1991), pp. 1–2, 13.

57 *Chartered Surveyor Weekly* (12 March 1992), p. 6.

58 Jones Lang Wootton, *JLWorld*, privately published corporate brochure (May 1991), p. 19; and "News Briefs", *National Real Estate Investors* (July 1991), p. 16.

59 For example, UK property developer MEPC, assisted by Jones Lang Wootton, spent six years seeking development permission for a Munich site it controlled. It finally sold the property to the largest Munich real estate developer, and planning permission was promptly granted. D.J. Kostin, "German Real Estate Market: An Introduction for Non-German Investors", (New York: Salomon Brothers, April 1991), p. 19; R. Volhard, D. Weber and W. Usinger, eds., *Real Property In Germany: Legal and Tax Impacts of Development and Investment* (Frankfurt: Fritz Knapp Verlag, 1975, 1991), pp. vii, 36, 114–16.

60 *Ibid.*, pp. 82–121; R. Gop, "Player + Profile", *Immobilien Manager* (February 1992), p. 11; S. Cowan, *The Guide to European Property Investment* I (London: Waterlow Publishers, 1989), pp. 8–9; Arthur Andersen & Co. and Nabarro Nathanson, *Building a Stake in Europe* (1991), pp. 51–2, 56.

61 On Japanese foreign direct investment in Europe, notably the UK, see R. Strange, *Japanese Manufacturing Investment in Europe: Its Impact on the UK Economy* (London and New York: Routledge, 1993) and M. Mason and D. Encarnation, eds, *Does Ownership Matter? Japanese Multinationals in Europe* (Oxford: Clarendon Press, 1994); M. Wilkins, "Japanese Multinationals in the US: Continuity and Change" *Business History Review* 64 (Winter 1990), pp. 601–8, 617.

62 Direct investment in foreign corporations that owned property assets were included in the total asset value of the particular industry in national stock statistics; real estate was not identified separately. In the US, real estate invest-

ments included manufacturing plants for SONY and hotels in Hawaii for affluent Japanese tourists.

63 Kenneth Leventhal & Co., "Japanese Capital Flows: Availability and Constraints", unpublished report, Los Angeles, 1992; Kenneth Leventhal & Co., "1991 Japanese Investment in United States Real Estate", unpublished report, Los Angeles, 1992.

64 In addition, in 1988 the Bank of International Settlements in Basle, Switzerland, introduced minimum capital standards for international banks to strengthen the stability of international banking system, requiring that capital must equal at least 8 percent of risk-adjusted assets. This action, plus restrictive monetary policy, the declining Japanese stock market, the banking industry's low profit margins, and declining land prices in the principal Japanese markets, reduced the flow of Japanese investment capital. *Ibid.*, pp. 1–2.

65 H. Yoshihara and S. Khan, *Strategy and Performance of Foreign Companies in Japan* (Westport, CT: Quorum Books, 1994); M. Mason, *American Multinationals and Japan: The Political Economy of Japanese Capital Controls, 1899–1980* (Cambridge, MA: Council on East Asian Studies, Harvard University, 1992).

66 M.Y. Yoshino, "Japan as Host to the International Corporation", *The International Corporation* (Cambridge, MA and London: The MIT Press, 1970), pp. 350, 368–9; M.Y. Yoshino, "Japan as Host to the International Corporation", *The Japanese Economy in International Perspective*, ed. I. Frank (Baltimore, MD and London: The Johns Hopkins University Press, 1975), pp. 276–89.

67 J.C. Baker and T. Kondo, "Joint Ventures in Japan and How to Obtain Managerial Control", *MSU Business Topics*, vol. 19, no. 1 (Winter 1971), p. 49; R.M. March, "Foreign Firms in Japan", *California Management Review*, vol. 22 no. 3 (Spring 1980), pp. 42–6; W.E. Brock, "A Simple Plan for Negotiating on Trade in Services", *The World Economy*, vol. 5 no. 3, p. 235; M.A. Hines, *Investing in Japanese Real Estate* (New York: Quorum Books, 1987), pp. 8, 121.

68 S.L. Hayes III and P.M. Hubbard, *Investment Banking: A Tale of Three Cities* (Boston: Harvard Business School Press, 1990), pp. 158–74, 278.

69 A.D. Chandler, Jr., documented in *Scale and Scope: The Dynamics of Industrial Capitalism* (1990), pp. 140–1, that such capital-intensive industries as oil, rubber, paper, glass, aluminum and other metal manufacturers enjoyed significant economies of scale and cost advantages by diversifying over widely dispersed geographic regions. E. Davis and C. Smales further argued that the demands of multinational corporations were the principal force behind the globalization of service industries in "The Internationalization of Professional Services", Working Paper Series No. 66, London Business School (April 1989).

70 S. Currie and A. Scott, "The Place of Commercial Property in the U.K. Economy", (London, January 1991), p. 1.

71 A. Baum and A. Schofield, "Property as a Global Asset", Center for European Property Research, University of Reading (May 1987), p. 63.

72 Western European corporations had a longer history than US firms in retaining real estate specialists for leasing and building facilities. The tradition was first established in the post-World War Two years, when national and multinational businesses were involved in real estate development and financing. See M.A. Hines, *Marketing Real Estate Internationally* (1988), pp. 14–15.

73 Japanese trading companies became well-established in several foreign nations by the post-World War One era, then opened branch banks to arrange financing for Japanese trade. See M. Wilkins, "Japanese Multinationals in the United States: Continuity and Change, 1879–1990." *Business History Review* 64 (Winter

1990), pp. 586–90; and M.A. Hines, *Guide to International Real Estate Investment* (New York: Quorum Books, 1988), p. 89.

74 M. Wilkins, *ibid.*, pp. 586–96; M.A. Hines, *ibid.*, p. 11.

75 Tokyu Land Corporation was established in 1953 as a subsidiary of Tokyo Electric Express Railway Company to manage the urban development, gravel transportation and recreational property businesses of its parent. In T.H. Tucker, "Tokyu Land Corporation", *International Directory of Company Histories* IV, ed. by A. Hast (London: St. James Press, 1991), p. 728. During its first decade, Sumitomo Realty, established in 1949, primarily served the real estate management and investment needs of the Sumitomo group. L.M. Kalanik, "Sumitomo Realty & Development Co., Ltd.", *International Directory of Company Histories* IV, ed. by A. Hast (London: St. James Press, 1991), p. 726.

76 J. Harpham, "Mitsui Real Estate Development Co., Ltd.", *International Directory of Company Histories* IV, ed. by A. Hast (London: St. James Press, 1991), p. 715.

77 M.A. Hines, *Investing in Japanese Real Estate* (New York: Quorum Books, 1987), pp. 97–100, 155–9, 242–3, 253.

78 The largest international real estate services firms in Japan included Mitsui Real Estate, Mitsubishi Real Estate, Sumitomo Realty and Development, Nippon Steel Real Estate Corporations and Seibu Railway Company. M. Wilkins, "Japanese Multinationals in the United States: Continuity and Change, 1879–1990." *Business History Review* 64 (Winter 1990), pp. 607–13; M.A. Hines, *Investing in Japanese Real Estate* (New York: Quorum Books, 1987), pp. 242–3.

79 L.M. Kalanik, "Mitsubishi Estate Company", *International Directory of Company Histories*, IV (London: St. James Press, 1991), pp. 713–14; J.T. Dueser, *International Strategies of Japanese Banks: The European Perspective* (London: Macmillan Academic and Professional Ltd., 1990), pp. 51, 62–6, 116. Also, *Nikkei Annual Corporation Reports (Kaisha nenkan)* (Tokyo: Nihon Keizai Shinbunsha, 1960, 1970, 1980, 1990), which publishes financial statistics and annual stock and flow financial data, and a synopsis of investment activity in Japan by foreign companies; and *Gaikoku Shihon no Tainichi Toshi: Gaikukuhen* (Tokyo: Kaizai Chosa Kyoka, 1969, 1970, 1980, 1990), which publishes an annual synopsis of each foreign firm investing and doing business in Japan.

80 J. Bennett, R. Flanagan and G. Norman, "Capital & Counties Report", (1987) pp. 19, 26, 36–7, 73.

81 Thirty percent of the UK's gross domestic product in 1989 was generated by exports of goods and services; cited in S. Cowan, *The Guide to European Property Investment* I (1989), p. 7–11. Also see A.D. Chandler, *Scale and Scope*, p. 250.

82 Corporations involved in trade or service emphasized rail and air transport as well as the cost and suitability of office/plant space when evaluating sites for European relocations. C.G. Powell, *An Economic History of the British Building Industry, 1815–1979* (London: Methuen, 1982), pp. 179–83; M. Hsia, "Corporate Location in Europe: The Implications of a Single Market", Working Papers in European Property, Centre for European Property Research, University of Reading (March 1991), pp. 27, 46–7; also see J.H. Dunning and G. Norman, "The Theory of the Multinational Enterprise: An Application to Multinational Office Location", *Environment and Planning*, vol. 15 (1983), pp. 675–92.

83 M. Wilkins, *The Maturing Multinational Enterprise: American Business Abroad from 1914 to 1970*, Cambridge, MA: Harvard University Press, 1974, pp. 341–2.

84 *The Economist* (3 November 1984), p. 334.

85 During the 1986–90 period, 185 Japanese companies opened plants and offices in European nations, including the UK, Germany, France and Spain; 230 US

plants opened over the same period in the UK, France, Ireland, Netherlands and Germany. R. Buck, "New Japanese and US Investments in Europe", *Site Selection Europe* (Nov./Dec. 1990), p. 14 and (March 1992), pp. 12–13.

86 Louis Harris and Associates, Inc., "The Cushman & Wakefield/Healey & Baker European Business Real Estate Monitor: American and European Businesses Rate Europe", unpublished survey (July–August 1990).

87 J.A. Gosling and A.J. Thornley, "The Role of the European Property Professional: France, Spain, The United Kingdom and Germany", Working Papers in European Property, Centre for European Property Research, University of Reading (March 1991), pp. 41–4, 73.

88 R. Gop, "Player + Profile", *Immobilien Manager* (February 1992), p. 11.

89 M. Wilkins, *The Maturing Multinational Enterprise* (1974), pp. 329, 375; M.A. Hines, *Guide to International Real Estate Investment*, p. 12.

90 Xerox Corporation was among the few largest US multinationals to manage its property as an investment portfolio, forming a separate real estate subsidiary akin to the Japanese model. By the time Xerox Real Estate Company was organized in 1975, the parent had been established in foreign markets for two decades and received 40 percent of corporate revenues from overseas operations, having established its first joint venture abroad in 1956 in the UK. M.A. Hines, *Guide to International Real Estate Investment*, p. 12.

91 S. Goldenberg, *Hands Across the Ocean: Managing Joint Ventures* (Boston: Harvard Business School Press, 1988), pp. 3–4, 74.

92 S.L. Barter, ed., *Real Estate Finance* (London: Butterworth, 1988), pp. 31–2.

93 Author's interviews with industry executives and casual observations from multiple professional articles.

94 The US new-issues market grew 25 percent annually, 1967–87, cited in S.L. Hayes III and P.M. Hubbard, *Investment Banking: A Tale of Three Cities* (Boston: Harvard Business School Press, 1990), pp. 51–3, 63. The globalization of real estate finance particularly emphasized mortgage-related securities rather than equity investments. See discussion in S.E. Roulac, "The 'Globalization' of Real Estate Finance", *The Real Estate Finance Journal*, vol. 4 no. 2 (1987), p. 40.

95 See annual listings of lead managers in Eurobonds, 1963–87, in S.L. Hayes III and P.M. Hubbard, *Investment Banking: A Tale of Three Cities* (Boston: Harvard Business School Press, 1990), pp. 37–9, 44, 51, 55, 59, 350–1.

96 M.A. Louargand, "Foreign Bank Participation in United States Mortgage Markets", Working Paper No. 24, Center for Real Estate Development, Massachusetts Institute of Technology (December 1989).

97 *Ibid.*, pp. 62, 132.

98 S.L. Hayes III and P.M. Hubbard, *Investment Banking: A Tale of Three Cities* (Boston: Harvard Business School Press, 1990), p. 278.

99 See Chapter 4, Table 4.1.

100 *The Economist* (18 March 1972), p. 8.

101 Clearing banks and merchant banks occasionally provided longer-term finance during the period 1969–75. After the 1973–5 property crash and until the early 1980s, many secondary clearing banks were unwilling to provide construction loans; the merchant banks continued to lend to developers with a healthy capital base. *The Economist* (April 3, 1976), pp. 117–18; S.L. Hayes III and P.M. Hubbard, *Investment Banking: A Tale of Three Cities* (Boston: Harvard Business School Press, 1990), p. 211; Royal Institution of Chartered Surveyors, *Finance in Property* (London: Royal Institution of Chartered Surveyors, October 1977), p. 24.

102 *The Economist* (11 September 1976), pp. 99–100.

103 R.J. Wolfe, "Debt Finance", in *Real Estate Finance*, ed. S.L. Barter (London: Butterworth, 1988), pp. 83, 96; and E.L. Erdman, *People & Property* (London: B.T. Batsford Ltd., 1982), pp. 181–2.

104 The 1975–6 period was a significant turning point for the UK property market and UK property advisors. However, the 1976 edict was ineffective after October 1979, when the dollar premium was abolished, together with previous barriers between wholesale capital markets and international capital markets in London and domestic credit markets. Since 1980, the Bank has had no effective authority over sterling investments and credit markets.

105 H. Barty-King, *Scratch a Surveyor* (London: William Heinemann, 1975), p. 255.

106 S. Currie and A. Scott, "The Place of Commercial Property in the UK Economy", (paper presented to the London Business School, January 1991), pp. 15–19.

107 S.L. Barter, ed. *Real Estate Finance* (London: Butterworth, 1988), pp. 4, 30–4.

108 R. Volhard, D. Weber, and W. Usinger, eds, *Real Property in Germany* (1975, 1991), pp. vii, 81, 119–21.

109 Deutsche Bank, "Deutsche Bank – A Brief History", press release, Frankfurt am Main (December 1989).

110 R.S. Dohner, "Japanese Financial Deregulation and the Growth of Japanese International Bank Activity", USJP Occasional Paper 89–05, The Center for International Affairs and the Reischauere Institute of Japanese Studies (Cambridge: Harvard University Press, 1989); J.T. Dueser, *International Strategies of Japanese Banks: The European Perspective* (London: Macmillan Academic and Professional Ltd., 1990), p. 58; Kenneth Leventhal & Co., "Japanese Capital Flows: Availability and Constraints", unpublished report, 1992, pp. 11–12.

111 M. Wilkins, "Japanese Multinationals in the United States: Continuity and Change, 1879–1990." *Business History Review* 64 (Winter 1990), p. 620.

112 *Ibid.*; S.L. Hayes III and P.M. Hubbard, *Investment Banking: A Tale of Three Cities* (Boston: Harvard Business School Press, 1990), pp. 170, 183.

113 Loans collateralized by property accounted for over half of the loan growth of Japanese city banks during 1987–8. See discussion in Kenneth Leventhal & Co., "Japanese Capital Flows: Availability and Constraints", unpublished report (1992), p. 4. M.A. Louargand, "Foreign Bank Participation in United States Mortgage Markets", Working Paper No. 24, Center for Real Estate Development, Massachusetts Institute of Technology (December 1989), pp. 30–1.

114 Kenneth Leventhal & Co., "1991 Japanese Investment in United States Real Estate", unpublished report, Los Angeles (1992).

115 See discussion of rise and fall of the international credit flows of Japanese real estate banks, 1986–91, in Kenneth Leventhal & Co., "Japanese Capital Flows: Availability and Constraints", unpublished report, Los Angeles (1992).

116 G.B. Richardson argued that a fluid industry structure enabled information to flow freely, thus allowing entrepreneurs to make adjustments in investments based on market intelligence about competitors, in *Information and Investment: A Study in the Working of the Competitive Economy* (Oxford: Clarendon Press, 1990), pp. xxii, 51–2. Internationalization by the "Big 8" accounting firms after 1920 was facilitated by similar professional standards among nations, in E. Davis and C. Smales, "The Internationalization of Professional Services", Working Paper Series No. 66, London Business School (April 1989), p. 7.

117 See Appendix. Documentation of real estate yields and volatility in US and UK, 1983–8, in Salomon Brothers, "Real Estate versus Financial Assets – An Updated Comparison of Returns in the United States and the United Kingdom", unpublished report (16 February 1989).

118 G.B. Richardson discussed the competitive benefits of different organizational structures in *Information and Investment: A Study in the Working of the Competitive Economy* (Oxford: Clarendon Press, 1990), pp. 227–33.

119 J. Kay, *Foundations of Corporate Success* (Oxford: Oxford University Press, 1993), p. 87.

120 *Ibid.*, pp. 88–9.

121 Company reports and direct surveys: King Sturge, senior partner of Office Consulting; Jones Lang Wootton information was affirmed by a partner and third party clients; Tokyu Land, affirmed by senior vice president; Mitsui Real Estate information confirmed by executive vice president, New York City.

122 Company reports and direct surveys: James Felt Realty information confirmed by senior partner, New York City. Senior partner of Arthur Andersen (formerly Gladstone Associates) provided information; Dr Seebauer was founded in 1985, but was a local consulting firm in 1975. Information was confirmed by senior partner (Financial Office); Müller information was confirmed by senior partner (in early years, Müller was providing very little consulting).

123 E. Davis and C. Smales, "The Internationalization of Professional Services", Working Paper Series No. 66, Centre for Business Strategy, London Business School (April 1989), p. 4.

124 C. Harlan, "Firms Use Outside Real-Estate Managers", *Wall Street Journal* (4 June 1992), p. B1.

125 M. Morishima provided a critical assessment of David Ricardo's theory in *Ricardo's Economics: A General Equilibrium Theory of Distribution and Growth* (Cambridge, MA: Cambridge University Press, 1989), pp. 5, 126–34. The discussion in this chapter also revealed the limitations of the Heckscher–Ohlin–Samuelson model in determining the prime movers of trade flows; international trade in real estate advisory services depended on additional factors of production beyond just capital and labor endowments in the different national markets.

126 The latter consequence emerged in 1989–90, when limited market perspective and finance-driven investments in the US and Europe resulted in disproportionately high losses for Japanese investors. For a history of "invisible" UK imports and exports, see D. Liston and N. Reeves, *The Invisible Economy: A Profile of Britain's Invisible Exports* (London: Pitman Publishing, 1988).

127 B. Hindley and A. Smith contended that "a country gains from importing services or allowing immigration of labor or receiving foreign direct investment if the terms on which these transactions take place are more favorable than the terms available on domestic transactions." In "Comparative Advantage and Trade in Services", *The World Economy*, vol. 7 no. 4 (December 1984), p. 375.

128 S.L. Hayes III and P.M. Hubbard found the same tendency in international investment banking services, discussed in *Investment Banking: A Tale of Three Cities* (Boston: Harvard Business School Press, 1990), p. 321.

129 Comparative advantage is gained by integrating an international strategy with local market responsiveness, discussed in C.K. Prahalad and Yves L. Doz, *The Multinational Mission: Balancing Local Demands and Global Vision* (New York and London: The Free Press, 1987), pp. 37–47. E.T. Penrose argued that a firm's growth is restrained by managerial diseconomies and increasing costs in *The Theory of the Growth of the Firm* (White Plains, NY: M.E. Sharpe, 1959, reprinted 1991).

130 C.G. Powell, *An Economic History of the British Building Industry, 1815–1979* (London: Methuen, 1982), p. 154; Healey & Baker's European expansion strategy is chronicled in J. Ozanne, "Teaming Up to Trade on the Continent",

Estate Times European Supplement, 2 March 1990, p. 8; K. Holmes and R. Butler, "1992: Joint Ventures in the EC", *Single Market Monitor*, vol. 2 no. 7 (April 1990), p. 56. Richard Ellis, which opposed joint ventures in foreign markets, embarked on a rapid, and flawed, expansion strategy in the late 1980s, depleting reserves and ultimately resulting in the worldwide firm's demise; see A. Reinbach, "Ellis Principals Do Buy-Out", *Pensions & Investment Age* (12 June 1989), p. 37.

131 J. Gladstone and N. Nohria, compilers, *Colliers International Property Consultants Case Study*, (Cambridge, MA: Harvard Business School Press, 1990).

132 *Ibid.*, p. 3. Another international network which has a strong US presence is Oncor, formerly The Office Network, chronicled by S. Brown, "Real Estate Networks", *National Real Estate Investor* (July 1989), p. 94. Also see P. Kavanaugh, "Levy, Younce, Roth Ease US Firms' Entree Into Europe", *Commercial Property News* (16 April 1991), p. 14.

133 J. Ozanne, "Teaming Up to Trade on the Continent", *Estate Times European Supplement* (2 March 1990), p. 7; B.W. Selvin, "Networks Help Firms Branch Out", *Real Estate* (17 July 1990); Hillier Parker Ltd., *The Hillier Parker Magazine*, published corporate brochure (1989), p. 12–13; W. Taylor, "The Logic of Global Business: An Interview with ABB's [Asea Brown Bovery] Percy Barnevik", *Harvard Business Review* (March–April 1991), p. 92.

134 C.P. DeMond, *Price, Waterhouse & Co. in America* (New York: Arno Press, 1980), pp. 307–8, 332–7. E. Davis, G. Hanlon and J. Kay argued that a service firm's reputation is the key factor in internationalization, rather than production economies, in "Internationalization in Accounting and Other Professional Services", Working Papers Series No. 78, Centre for Business Strategy, London Business School (April 1990), pp. 9–10.

135 For international real estate advisory services, the author endorses the argument set forth by G.P. Sampson and R.H. Snape that "the broader the front across which the liberalization of trade operates, the more likely that the allocation of resources will be improved", in "Identifying the Issues in Trade in Services", *The World Economy*, vol. 8 no. 2 (June 1985), p. 178.

4

HISTORICAL PROFILE OF REAL ESTATE ADVISORY SERVICE FIRMS

Evaluating successful firms

This chapter presents a historical profile of leading real estate advisory service firms in each focal country. An evaluation of the internationalization of forty prominent firms provides a comparative reference for the detailed analysis of the growth and internationalization of four major real estate advisory service firms in Chapter 6. The case study approach departed from pure narrative analysis, in that business history can be documented through the chronology of particular firms and major events in the profession, an approach which Chandler pioneered in the early 1960s.[1]

Why would such a collective profile be necessary in conjunction with the preceding historical survey of the growth of real estate advisory services and the following detailed case-study biographies? The real estate services sector, as with most professional services, was not previously documented by economic analysts and historians, and the quantitative evidence for this point largely depended on national economic and cross-border direct investment statistics.[2] In fact, all the property service firms profiled in this chapter moved into new services or foreign markets without the benefit of national and international benchmark performance data on markets, firms and products. Such an uninformed perspective contrasted with the experience of most other major industries. Only real estate firms which moved into foreign markets or into international services were included in this analysis. This evaluation, together with the comprehensive analysis of the four case study firms, gathers otherwise unobtainable data essential to an understanding of the history of real estate advisory services in four countries.

An important finding of this survey was that thirty-seven of the forty firms, or 92.5 percent of those surveyed, increased in size (measured by the number of personnel employed) over the period, and thirty-four of the forty firms, or 85 percent, expanded their operating business into foreign countries. These findings suggest that a high incidence of multidivisional growth into dispersed and foreign markets defined the evolution of firms within this professional services sector over the period. A key question, then, is what were

74

the conditions prompting change (or growth), and what methods did firms use to implement change most effectively and efficiently?

These profiles will begin to illustrate how a firm's organizational structure hindered or helped growth, geographic expansion and service diversification, and the degree to which changes in organizational structure were intimately related to the way in which the enterprise did, and was able to, expand. This discussion will be further expanded in the case studies in Chapter 6. If, as argued by Coase, Chandler and Williamson, the primary goal of administrative structure is to economize a firm's transaction costs, internally and externally, then the profiles would likely reveal which form of coordinated super-structure was most effective in administering an international enterprise in the real estate services sector.[3]

The intent of the present evaluation is to isolate the essential factors influencing international growth in property services by evaluating uniform facts about forty firms relative to broader historical developments impacting professional services, property markets, cross-border real estate investment and real estate advisory service firms.[4] It also provides the framework for further refining the discussion presented in Chapters 2 and 3, and for establishing the context of the discussion on innovations in Chapter 5 and the case studies in Chapter 6.

The profile of each firm was based on direct surveys, published corporate reports and unpublished company documents, and interviews with senior personnel, present and past. The firms were selected based on three criteria: staff size in 1990, with each firm ranking among the largest in each national market; the existence of an international practice (with or without establishment of personnel or an affiliate in a foreign country); and the recommendations of recognized professional authorities in each focal country.[5]

Growing markets, changing client demands, and service innovation

Foreign expansion and service diversification took shape differently and at various times in each focal country, as well as among the different firms. As illustrated in Tables 4.1 and 4.2, foreign expansion among Japanese firms occurred between the mid-1920s and mid-1950s, and typically within a decade of the firm's founding. Yet, for these firms, which were vertically integrated within multinational group companies, international expansion did not necessarily require a foreign presence. Five of the ten firms did not establish a foreign office and instead served a Japanese clientele of international investors from a domestic base. Because Japanese multinationals (in alliance with the Ministry of Finance) virtually dominated the country's economy, as the discussion in Chapter 3 made clear, Japanese advisers sought to reach a larger pool of clients by investing resources to expand in domestic markets.[6]

Nine of the ten UK firms, by contrast, internationalized to a greater number of foreign markets than did firms in any other focal country. UK advisers established offices abroad several decades after the firms' founding between 1958 and 1968, concurrent with a significant rise in outward direct real estate investment by UK sponsors. During the 1960–97 period, foreign expansion exceeded domestic growth, with UK firms entering twelve new foreign nations and growing by forty offices worldwide over the thirty-year period, on average.

German property advisers began to internationalize in the late 1970s and early 1980s. Two recently established firms, Apollo (1988) and Eureal (1990), only entered foreign markets in the 1990s, and two of the firms surveyed, Comfort and Brockhoff & Partner, did not establish offices outside Germany until the mid-1990s. German advisers approached international expansion in a provincial manner, just as they approached regionalization in domestic markets. On average, they opened five new offices and entered two foreign markets. Rather than investing their capital resources in opening an office abroad, most (except Müller) affiliated with a foreign firm, or firms, or joined a global network association.

US firms, the last among the focal countries to expand abroad, internationalized between 1975 and 1990 in response to increased multinational activity by domestic clients and the liberalization of globalized financial markets.[7] Relative to UK firms, however, US advisers invested more corporate capital and personnel resources in geographic diversification in domestic markets, where foreign investors were most active, than in foreign markets. On average, US real estate advisers increased the number of offices by thirty-four, yet entered only four to five foreign nations over the 1960–97 period.

Davis *et al.*'s hallmark studies on internationalizing professional services argued that the key asset of an internationalizing service firm was reputation, at home and abroad. This was because customers typically bought and priced services (or products) based on a firm's reputation in a specific market or a specific practice area.[8] In cross-border real estate investment, when clients and/or investment capital entered foreign markets to build, acquire and finance real estate assets, investors sought to retain property advisers with strong credentials and known expertise in a particular market or a particular technical service. This study found that reputation was clearly among the key factors, but the research concluded that local market knowledge was precedent to a firm establishing market reputation and pricing value with clients.

Perceived and real "value creation" was crucial to each firm's growth and profitability. Because of this, shifts in client needs and patterns of where and how clients invested during certain periods directly influenced the strategies of these forty real estate advisory firms, both in terms of the services offered and the geographic location/concentration of established personnel.

The business expansion experienced by the forty firms during the period, complemented by rising cross-border direct investment, clearly appeared to provide an important national factor advantage in the growth and interna-

Table 4.1 Summary profile of ten leading real estate advisory service firms in each of the focal countries

		Year Established	Foreign Expansion	Staff Size in 1997[b]
United States Firms				
1	Cushman & Wakefield/ Healey & Baker	1917	1990	1,750
2	CB Commercial/DTZ Debenham Thorpe	1969	1980	3,960
3	Grubb & Ellis	1958	1984	3,100
4	Arthur Andersen	1963	1990	260
5	LaSalle Partners/Savills	1966	1978	2,100
6	Colliers International	1967	1967	4,400
7	Landauer Associates	1946	1979	95
8	Morgan Stanley Realty/ Dean Witter	1935	1975	1,820
9	Eastdil Realty	1967	1975[a]	43
10	Goldman Sachs & Co./ Whitehall	1974	1979	235
United Kingdom Firms				
1	Jones Lang Wootton	1783	1958	3,735
2	Knight Frank	1896	1963	2,780
3	Healey & Baker/ Cushman & Wakefield	1820	1963	1,750
4	Hillier Parker	1896	1963	6,000[b]
5	Richard Ellis	1773	1963	1,200
6	DTZ Debenham Thorpe	1853	1972	1,700[c]
7	Weatherall Green & Smith/Staubach	1860	1963	630
8	Savills/LaSalle	1855	1982	700
9	Chesterton	1805	1985	2,000
10	Erdman Lewis/Colliers	1934	1959	400
German Firms				
1	Müller International	1958	1977	190
2	Aengevelt Immobilien/ ICPA	1910	1975	85
3	DTZ Zadelhoff Deutschland	1979	1983	1,100
4	Angermann Internationale/Goddard Loyd	1953	1982	25
5	Volckers, King & Co./ King Sturge - UK	1853	1980	NA[d]

Table 4.1 Summary profile of ten leading real estate advisory service firms in each of the focal countries (continued)

		Year Established	Foreign Expansion	Staff size in 1997[b]
6	Brockhoff & Partner/ Colliers	1986	1997[f]	27[e]
7	Deuteron Holding/ Lambert Smith Hampton	1976	1978	47
8	Eureal Gesellschaft	1990	1992	8
9	Comfort Gesellschaft/ Müller	1978	–	22
10	Apollo Gesellschaft/ Colliers	1988	1991	20
Japanese Firms				
1	Mitsui Real Estate/ Mitsui Fudosan	1941	1946	1,296
2	Mitsubishi Real Estate	1937	1937	2,043
3	Sumitomo Realty and Development	1949	1956	715
4	Heiwa Real Estate	1947	–	110
5	Tokyo Tatemono	1896	1926	407
6	Osaka Real Estate	1923	-	127
7	Tokyu Land	1939	1946	819
8	Hankyu Realty	1947	–	331
9	Daiwa Danchi	1948	–	898
10	Towa Real Estate Development/Fujita	1957	–	776

Source: Direct surveys of companies, conducted 1993–March 1994; public corporate reports; private company reports and memoranda.

Notes:
a   International division established, but personnel not transferred or employed
b   With network, associations and alliances
c   With several associations
d   Bankruptcy
e   Without Colliers membership
f   With Colliers

tional expansion of real estate advisory services. It can be concluded that the availability of skilled labor also constituted a primary factor in the growth of real estate services. Even though national markets temporarily competed on the basis of low-cost investment capital during the finance-driven 1980s (which was true of financial services generally), for real estate advisory services an educated workforce appeared to be a more important long-term factor advantage.[9] In fact, while low-cost capital was a definite advantage for

Table 4.2 Size of firms before (1960) and after (1997) internationalization of real estate advisory services

		Number of Offices		
		1960	*1997*	*Change*
United States Firms				
1	Cushman & Wakefield	2	65	+63
2	CB Commercial	30[a]	200	+170
3	Grubb & Ellis	5	86	+81
4	Arthur Andersen	1[b]	23	+22
5	LaSalle Partners	3[c]	36	+33
6	Colliers International	13[c]	190	+177
7	Landauer Associates	1	28	+27
8	Morgan Stanley Realty	4	7	+3
9	Eastdil Realty	1[c]	3	+2
10	Goldman Sachs & Co.	5[d]	24	+19
United Kingdom Firms				
1	Jones Lang Wootton	4	72	+68
2	Knight, Frank & Rutley	2	71	+69
3	Healey & Baker	1	16	+15
4	Hillier Parker	1	56	+55
5	Richard Ellis	1	39	+38
6	DTZ Debenham Thorpe	1[e]	26	+25
7	Weatherall Green & Smith/Staubach	1	19	+18
8	Savills/LaSalle	9	28	+19
9	Chesterton	3	28	+25
10	Erdman Lewis/Colliers	2	38	+36
German Firms				
1	Müller International	1	12	+11
2	Aengevelt Immobilien/Hillier Parker	1	2	+1
3	DT2 Zadelhoff	1[f]	7	+6
4	Angermann Internationale/Goddard Loyd	1	7	+6

Table 4.2 Size of firms before (1960) and after (1997) internationalization of real
estate advisory services (continued)

		Number of Offices		
		1960	1997	Change
5	Volckers, King & Co./ King Sturge[g]	1	18	+17
6	Brockhoff & Partner	-	1	0
7	Deuteron Holding/Lambert Smith Hampton	1[h]	3	+2
8	Eureal Gesellschaft	-	1	0
9	Comfort Gesellschaft/Müller	1[i]	7	+6
10	Apollo Gesellschaft/Colliers	-	1	0
Japanese Firms				
1	Mitsui Real Estate/Fudosan	1	27	+26
2	Mitsubishi Real Estate	5	9	+4
3	Sumitomo Realty and Development	6	9	+3
4	Heiwa Real Estate	2	4	+2
5	Tokyo Tatemono	3	7	+4
6	Osaka Real Estate	2	2	0
7	Tokyu Land	1	3	+2
8	Hankyu Realty	4	8	+4
9	Daiwa Danchi	3	9	+6
10	Towa Real Estate Development/Fujita	5	8	+3

Notes:
[a]1969 figures; [b]1963 figures; [c]1967figures; [d]1974 figures; [e]Renamed DTZ Debenham Thorpe
in 1990; [f]Established in 1979; [g]1996 bankruptcy; [h]1976 figures; [i]1978 figures

Japanese firms during the late 1980s, across the entire period of this study
Japanese firms gained competitive strength due to their investment in financial expertise and skilled professionals.

This was particularly evident among UK firms: the British system was
unmatched in its consistent commitment to both superior property education
and the internal advancement of chartered surveyors. The ten US firms, as
well, consistently invested corporate capital in recruiting and retaining well-
educated professionals. All the senior managers believed that a trained,
credentialed staff provided a sound foundation for technical innovations and
adaptability to market changes, and had longer-term value in national and
international competition than low-cost investment capital.

In addition, structural changes in financial and economic markets over the period brought new types of clients and new service demands into international real estate investment. Tables 4.3 and 4.4 illustrate the degree to which shifting client demands and competitive pressures prompted real estate advisory firms in all focal countries to introduce innovative services and diversify into new practice areas. Most firms pursued diversification to broaden their reach across overlapping markets, different client types and periodic weaknesses in specific market sectors (such as development, leasing, finance, or corporate expansions/relocations).[10] Real estate advisory firms diversified into new services through different means: by recruiting or increasing staff in multiple functions, by developing innovative services and technical capabilities, through merger and acquisition with potential competitors, and through affiliation with an established business (and also a potential competitor).[11]

Each country's property advisers emphasized their expertise in different services during different times, typically in response to the prevailing demands of domestic clients, which, on average, remained the dominant source of revenues in all countries throughout the period. For example, US advisers focused on feasibility studies and development services for insurance companies and retail/residential developers in the 1960s, emphasizing in the 1970s appraisal and portfolio management for pension and mutual funds and insurance companies, then corporate real estate and financial services for major corporations, mixed-use commercial developers, and large-scale investors and investment funds in the 1980s.[12] UK advisers, who faced fierce competition from in-house corporate property managers as well as accountants, attorneys, planners, management consultants and environmental experts, focused their practices on such basic services as acquisitions and dispositions, rent reviews and ratings, valuation, investment services, portfolio management, development services, and research by the late 1980s.[13] Internationalized German advisers sustained their focus on portfolio management and advisory services for pension funds and other institutional investors throughout the period, and in the late 1980s supplemented weakening client demand for leasing and development services with asset management services for newly privatized agencies and investors in former Eastern Bloc regions.[14]

The degree to which cross-border real estate investment influenced this process can only be inferred from the rate of growth of foreign (versus domestic) personnel and fee revenues, for each firm individually and for each country overall. Few firms, however, could operate on a large enough scale to support a fully integrated operation in every market, finding, as Williamson argued, that it was more efficient to affiliate, contract or merge with a third party for certain services in certain regions, at home and abroad.[15]

As the profession evolved during the 1960s and early 1970s, real estate advisers in all countries could be categorized by one of two operating philosophies: those that were entirely independent of their clients' investment activities, and those that were linked in a participating (partnership) position.[16] Among the forty firms, UK and German advisers tended to be

Table 4.3 Client profile of fee revenues by category for real estate advisory service firms[a] (1960–97)

	Manufacturing and Trade Corps (%)	Pension and Insurance Funds (%)	Financial Institutions (%)	Development and Construction Companies (%)	Government and Other Professional Service Firms (%)
United States					
1960	30		20		
1970	30	10	15	30	15
1980	30	15	15	30	10
1997	30	20	15	20	15
United Kingdom					
1960	15	20	15	30	20
1970	15	20	15	35	15
1980	25	15	15	35	10
1997	40	10	15	25	10
Germany					
1960	40	10	40	5	5
1970	40	15	30	5	10
1980	30	15	30	10	15
1997	25	15	25	10	25
Japan					
1965	23	7	50	20	0
1975	33	7	18	33	9
1980	38	9	16	34	3
1997	36	9	21	25	9

Sources: Public corporate reports and private company documents; direct surveys of forty firms, 1993–7.

Note:
[a] Average of 10 leading firms in each focal country.

Table 4.4 Service diversification of real estate advisory firms (1960–97)

	Brokerage/ Agency	Property Manage- ment	Development Consulting	Appraisal Portfolio Valuation	Market Research	Asset Manage- ment	Corporate Services	Financial/ Investment Banking
United States								
1960	x	x					x	
1970	x	x	x	x			x	
1980	x	x	x	x	x		x	x
1990	x	x	x	x	x	x	x	x
1997	x	x	x	x	x	x	x	x
United Kingdom								
1960	x	x	x	x				
1970	x	x	x	x				
1980	x	x	x	x		x	x	
1990	x	x	x	x	x	x	x	x
1997	x	x	x	x	x	x	x	x
Germany								
1960	x	x		x				
1970	x	x		x		x		x
1980	x	x		x	x	x	x	x
1990	x	x	x	x	x	x	x	x
1997	x	x	x	x	x	x	x	x
Japan								
1960	x	x						x
1970	x	x	x					x
1980	x	x	x				x	x
1990	x	x	x	x	x	x	x	x
1997	x	x	x	x	x	x	x	x

Sources: Public corporate reports and private company documents; direct surveys of forty firms, 1993–7.

most independent from clients, and presumably the most objective, with only one of the ten in each country (Edward Erdman and Apollo, respectively) having an equity interest in either development companies or building projects. In the US, the investment and merchant banks of Goldman Sachs, Eastdil (originally Eastman Dillon), Morgan Stanley, Landauer, LaSalle Partners and Coldwell Banker (mortgage banking) often acted as both an adviser and an entrepreneurial agent in client investments. Japanese advisers without exception were integrally tied with an industrial or trading group company: Mitsubishi was a pivotal member of the Mitsubishi group; Sumitomo originated as the real estate administrator to the Sumitomo family; Osaka was closely related to the Sumitomo Group; Tokyu Land was a subsidiary of the major electric railway Tokyo Comp Excels; Hankyu was a subsidiary of an industrial group; and Towa Real Estate was affiliated with the major general contractor Fujita Corporation.

The role of the real estate advisory firm, either as an independent or a participating agent, appeared to have only a marginal effect on its international expansion. US investment and merchant banks capitalized on established European and Asian financial services and securities operations to expand real estate advisory services in foreign markets. Japanese advisers capitalized on the established reputations and business networks of the group company to subsidize foreign expansion. However, UK advisers, who experienced the greatest international growth over the period, rarely advanced in foreign markets by way of an equity or participatory relationship with a client or a client's operations.

Patterns of geographic expansion and international growth

An analysis of the forty companies indicated that personnel and office growth tended to stem more from geographic expansion than from service diversification (Table 4.5). Geographical dispersion responded to increasing levels of domestic and foreign real estate investment, growing commercial property markets domestically and abroad, and the investment activities of existing and prospective clients. Sheer staff size and gross revenue levels proved to be less significant to the reputation and organizational structure of the market's top leaders than did geographic breadth and service diversification. For example, the difficulties with international expansion encountered by CB Commercial of the US (the nation's largest real estate advisory firm in 1990) and Richard Ellis of the UK (the nation's fifth largest chartered surveyor firm in 1990) will be discussed later in this chapter; the relative success of the case-study firms in Chapter 6 highlight the significance of geographic and service diversity.

During the 1960s and until 1977, UK investors sponsored the greatest amount of direct outward real estate investment. This cross-border activity would suggest the existence of a lucrative platform to support overseas expansion of UK advisers. Indeed, eight of the ten UK property advisers entered foreign markets through "organic" expansion (Table 4.6). Such vertical integration was matched only by a minority of firms in the other focal countries, which chose instead to affiliate or merge with potential competitors in foreign markets. Perhaps because a global perspective was part of the national culture, UK firms were most adaptable to foreign customs and they drew on well-established capabilities to exploit economies of scale. In addition, UK firms initially moved across continental Europe and into British Commonwealth regions when they first internationalized, thus ameliorating the most challenging aspect of foreign expansion by entering markets with familiar customs.[17] The complexity and cost of managing several offices across different regions and cultures became the highest barrier for internationalizing real estate advisory service firms.[18]

The UK's DTZ Debenham Thorpe aggressively responded to the rising management and acquisition costs of international expansion by incorporating the partnership of Debenham Tewson & Chinnocks and taking it public on the London Stock Exchange in 1987. The company chose to float a public offering at the market's and economy's peak, deleveraging to acquire new capital for domestic and international expansions and acquisitions across the 1988–92 period.[19] The prospectus provided only moderately more enlightenment about the company, its clients, professional staff, and service revenue than private research obtained, rather than laying out a detailed and systematic chronology since 1922 of the company's history and domestic office openings and subsequent international expansion – France (1972), Australia (1973), Turkey (1975), the Netherlands (1977) and the US (1980).[20] Documented in company reports were the functions of the umbrella holding company, which centrally managed the international operations of DTZ Debenham Chinnocks, including 23.5 percent ownership in DTZ BV European operations (the balance owned by partners in Belgium, France, Germany and the Netherlands) and financial interests in private real estate service companies in Spain, Greece, Turkey, Russia, Hungary and the Ukraine. Partial equity ownership in different operating business maximized DTZ's international expansion in multiple markets and with multiple partners, made possible by an infusion of public capital for operations and future expansion.

Among US, German and Japanese firms, nonequity affiliations as well as equity mergers and acquisitions were adopted in roughly an equal number of international expansions. When a firm independently entered a foreign market, it gained direct market knowledge and a singular reputation among clients. Equity and nonequity combinations, by comparison, typically achieved two objectives: a limited degree of market coverage and an expansion of the firm's scope of services or expertise. When choosing the location and the form of geographic expansion, each firm assessed the cost and risk relative to the potential gain, recognizing, as Coase and Chandler argued, that local rela-

Table 4.5 Domestic and foreign personnel in ten leading real estate advisory service firms in the focal countries (1960–97)

		1960			1970			1980			1997		
		Domestic	Foreign	Total	Domestic	Foreign	Total	Domestic	Foreign	Total	Domestic	Foreign	Total
United States Firms													
1	Cushman & Wakefield	75	0	75	175	0	175	410	0	410	650	1100	1750
2	CB Commercial	*	*	*	600	0	600	4500	2	4502	3800	160	3960
3	Grubb & Ellis	1050	0	1050	2200	0	2200	3450	0	3450	2200	900	3100[e]
4	Arthur Anderson	5	0	5	50	0	50	75	5	80	145	115	260[e]
5	LaSalle Partners	*	*	*	40	10	50	240	200	440	1250[b]	850	2100
6	Colliers International/Affiliations	*	*	*	28	0	28	34	4	38	2900	1500	4400
7	Landauer Assoiates	10	0	10	110	0	110	150	0	150	90	5	95
8	Morgan Stanley Realty	*	*	*	200	0	200	1200	50	1250	1700	120	1820
9	Goldman Sachs & Co./Whitehallstar	*	*	*	3	0	3	45	5	50	175	60	235
10	Eastdil Realty	*	*	*	5	0	5	75	0	75	40	3[d]	43
United Kingdom Firms													
1	Jones Lang Wooton	60	20	80	170	60	230	700	300	1000	800	2935	3735
2	Knight Frank	65	0	65	130	25	155	300	150	450	980	1800	2780
3	Healey & Baker	300	0	300	300	100	400	350	150	500	575	1175	1750
4	Hillier Park	60	0	60	200	50	250	450	180	630	670	5330	6000
5	Richard Ellis	60	0	60	170	50	220	350	150	500	500	700	1200
6	DTZ Debenham Thorpe	40	0	40	200	20	220	525	75	600	1300	400	1700
7	Weatherall Green & Smith	55	0	55	180	40	220	275	85	360	380	250	630
8	Savills/LaSalle	200	0	200	300	0	300	350	5	355	500	200	700
9	Chesterton	120	0	120	160	0	160	180	0	180	1200	800	2000
10	Erdman Lewis	50	5	55	65	15	80	160	60	220	330	70	400[f]

German Firms

1 Müller International	6	0	25	25	75	5	80	185	5	190[g]
2 Aengevelt Immobilien	30	0	36	38	64	3	67	80	5	85
3 Zadelhoff Deutschland/DTZ	*	*	*	*	10	0	10	180	920	1100
4 Angermann Internationale/Goddard Loyd	6	0	30	30	52	0	52	20	5	25
5 Volckers, King & Co.	7	0	10	10	20	0	20	N/A	N/A	N/A
6 Brockhoff & Partner	*	*	*	*	10	0	10[c]	27	0	27[f]
7 Deuteron Holding	*	*	*	6	6	7	13	35	12	47
8 Eureal Gesellschaft	*	*	*	*	*	*	*	8	0[b]	8
9 Comfort Gesselschaft	*	*	*	3	3	0	3	22	0	22[h]
10 Apollo Gesellschaft	*	*	*	5	5	0	5[a,i]	20	0	20

Japanese Firms

1 Mitsui Real Estate/Fudosan	487	0	690	690	808	10	818	1284	12	1296
2 Mitsubishi Real Estate	1630	0	1759	1759	1852	0	1852	1709	334	2043
3 Sumitomo Realty and Development	959	0	776	776	518	0	518	397	318	715
4 Heiwa Real Estate	75	0	79	79	97	0	97	110	0	110
5 Tokyo Tatemono	104	0	230	230	258	0	258	350	57	407
6 Osaka Real Estate	107	0	180	180	153	0	153	127	0	127
7 Tokyu Land	1050	0	1027	1050	1356	0	1356	795	24	819
8 Hankyu Realty	194	0	216	194	240	0	240	331	0	331
9 Daiwa Danchi	170	0	226	170	312	0	312	873	25	898
10 Towa Real Estate/Fujita	240	0	307	240	412	0	412	776	0	776

Notes:

* Indicates the firm or the firm's real estate practice/personnel not formally established

a Established in 1988; 1988 figures

b Affiliated with Savills and, therefore, LaSalle/Galbreath

c Established in 1987; 1987 figures

d Nomura Securities merged with Eastdil Realty in 1987

e 1993 figures; in 1990 the real estate advisory service firm of GA/Partners (est. 1961–3) was acquired by Arthur Andersen

f In UK without Colliers, Brochoff during 1997 in Colliers Affiliation/employees are not included

g Oncor affiliation was terminated

h Affiliate of Müller

i Colliers affiliate and terminated relationship in 1997

tionships and local market knowledge were ultimately most effective and economical.[21] Because real estate investment remained highly sensitized to local markets, local effectiveness was a critical element in each firm's decisions about how to organize international expansion.

For example, Japanese firms acquired ownership interests in US firms in the 1980s to gain access to pools of investors (or sources of supply) and to participate directly in higher yielding property assets – Nomura Securities acquired 50 percent of Eastdil, Dai-Ichi bought 40 percent of LaSalle Partners, Sumitomo acquired 12.5 percent of Goldman Sachs, Orix acquired 70 percent of Rubloff, Mitsubishi acquired 51 percent of The Rockefeller Group (which had acquired Cushman & Wakefield in 1975), and Tobishima bought 18 percent of William Zeckendorf.[22] The US partners anticipated reciprocity in Japanese markets and among Japanese investors, yet rarely received such benefits. Indeed, in markets where the "right of establishment" proved onerous or too expensive relative to expected fee revenues – such as in Japan for all foreign real estate service firms, and Germany for US and Japanese firms – foreign property advisers chose to operate through an affiliate or limited partner rather than invest corporate capital in a satellite office. However, those property service firms which made an upfront investment of corporate capital (public or private) to expand abroad – either through diversification or by a merger/acquisition with a foreign partner – typically received a greater proportion of fee revenues from foreign sources than did firms that internationalized through a nonequity affiliation or a global network (Table 4.6).

Higher investment costs tended to accrue higher long-term benefits. This would suggest that, at a minimum, an equity investment in geographic expansion was typically required – either to diversify the firm or to merge with another – to build an international practice that exceeded at least 15 percent of the firm's gross revenue. Yet even some equity-based mergers or diversifications failed to achieve this level of return, such as Germany's Aengevelt and Volckers, King (presently in receivership), and Japan's Mitsubishi, Tokyo Tatemono, Osaka and Tokyu Land, perhaps stemming from certain diseconomies that one or more partner brought to a merger.[23]

The most important finding from Table 4.7 is that, while cross-border real estate investment and real estate advisory services increasingly moved toward an international business throughout the period, by 1990 only five of the firms surveyed received more than one-half of their fee revenues from foreign sources. UK firms, the most internationalized of the firms studied, produced an average 1990 revenue mix of 56 percent domestic sources and 44 percent foreign. Thus, while sizable gains were achieved in establishing international reputations and diversifying into widely dispersed foreign markets, the dominant value and core business of most leading real estate advisory firms remained centered in domestic markets.

Table 4.6 Average annual staff growth of real estate advisory service firms in the focal countries (1960–97)

		Staff Size		Annual Growth	Foreign Expansion Structure
		1960	1997		
United States Firms					
1	Cushman & Wakefield	75	1,750	56	A, M
2	CB Commercial	2,200[a]	3,960	59	D, A
3	Grubb & Ellis	1,050	3,100	68	A
4	Arthur Andersen	5	260	9	M, D
5	LaSalle Partners	200[b]	2,100	63	D
6	Colliers International	50[c]	4,400	145	A
7	Landauer Associates	10	95	32	M
8	Morgan Stanley Realty	25	1,820	60	M
9	Eastdil Realty	5[c]	43	1	M
10	Goldman Sachs & Co.	3[d]	235	8	M
United Kingdom Firms					
1	Jones Lang Wootton	80	3,735	122	D, M
2	Knight, Frank & Rutley	65	2,780	91	D, M, A
3	Healey & Baker	300	1,750	48	A, D
4	Hillier Parker	60	6,000	198	D, M, A
5	Richard Ellis	60	1,200	38	D, A
6	Debenham Tewson & Chinnocks	40	1,700	55	M
7	Weatherall Green & Smith	55	630	19	D, A
8	Savills	200	700	17	D
9	Chesterton	120	2,000	62	D, M
10	Edward Erdman	55	400	12	M
German Firms					
1	Müller International	25	190	6	D, A
2	Aengevelt Immobilien	30	85	2	A, D
3	Zadelhoff Deutschland	10[e]	1,100	36	A, M
4	Angermann Internationale	6	25	63	D

Table 4.6 Average annual staff growth of real estate advisory service firms in the focal countries (1960–97) (continued)

5	Volckers, King & Co.	7	NA	NA	M
6	Brockhoff & Partner	-	27	6[f]	
7	Deuteron Holding	13[g]	47	1	
8	Eureal Gesellschaft	-	8	-	
9	Comfort Gesellschaft	3[h]	22	1	
10	Apollo Gesellschaft	-	20	1[i]	

Japanese Firms

1	Mitsui Real Estate	487	1,303	27
2	Mitsubishi Real Estate	1,630	1,832	7
3	Sumitomo Realty and Development	959	715	(8)
4	Heiwa Real Estate	75	93	1
5	Tokyo Tatemono	204	356	5
6	Osaka Real Estate	207	127	(3)
7	Tokyu Land	1,050	1,004	(2)
8	Hankyu Realty	194	313	4
9	Daiwa Danchi	170	617	15
10	Towa Real Estate Development	240	556	11

Sources: Direct surveys of each firm, 1993–4; public corporate reports; private company documents.

Notes:
— Indicates the firm or the firm's real estate practice/personnel not formally established
D   Internal Expansion
A   Alliance or Affiliation
M   Merger or Acquisition
[a]   1969 figures
[b]   1966 figures
[c]   1967 figures
[d]   1974 figures
[e]   1979 figures
[f]   Established in 1987
[g]   Established in 1978; 1980 figures
[h]   Established in 1978
[i]   Established in 1988

Table 4.7 Domestic vs foreign sources of fee revenue in ten leading real estate advisory service firms in each of the focal countries (1960–97)

		1960		1970		1980		1997	
		Domestic (%)	Foreign (%)	Domestic (%)	Foreign (%)	Domestic (%)	Foreign (%)	Domestic (%)	Foreign (%)
United States Firms									
1	Cushman & Wakefield/Healey & Baker	100	0	100	0	90	10	37	63
2	CB Commercial/DTZ Debenham Thorpe	–	–	100	0	95	5	85	15
3	Grubb & Ellis	100	0	100	0	95	5	95	5
4	Arthur Andersen	100	0	100	0	95	5	80[a]	20[a]
5	Lasalle Partners	–	–	95	5	90	10	80	20
6	Colliers International	–	–	90	10	55	45	55	45
7	Landauer Associates	95	5	90	10	90	10	85	15
8	Morgan Stanley Realty/Dean Witter	–	–	95	5	90	10	80	20
9	Eastdil Realty	–	–	75	25	25	75	25	75
10	Goldman Sachs & Co./Whitehall	–	–	100	0	85	15	60	40
Average		99	1	95	5	81	19	73	27
United Kingdom Firms									
1	Jones Lang Wootton	90	10	75	25	70	30	21	89
2	Knight Frank	100	0	90	10	67	33	30	70
3	Healey & Baker/Cushman & Wakefield	100	0	95	5	90	10	80	20
4	Hillier Parker	100	0	85	15	75	25	50	50
5	Richard Ellis	100	0	95	5	65	35	33	67
6	DTZ Debenham Thorpe	100	0	95	5	90	10	75	25
7	Weatherall Green & Smith/Staubach	100	0	85	15	75	25	70	30
8	Savills/Lasalle	100	0	95	5	90	10	80	20
9	Chesterton	98	2	95	5	92	8	83	17
10	Edward Erdman/Colliers	95	5	85	15	75	25	25	75
Average		98	2	90	10	79	21	56	44

Table 4.7 Domestic vs foreign sources of fee revenue in ten leading real estate advisory service firms in each of the focal countries (1960–97) (continued)

German Firms

1	Müller International	100	0	90	10	85	15	85	15
2	Aengevelt Immobilien/ICPA	100	0	97	3	96	4	94	6
3	Zadelhoff Deutschland/DTZ	–	–	–	–	90	10	70	30
4	Angermann Internationale/Goddard Lloyd	100		90	10	80	20	65	35
5	Volckers, King & Co./King Sturge–UK	100	0	100	0	95	5	92	8
6	Brockhoff & Partner/Colliers	–	–	–	–	90[b]	10[b]	85	15
7	Deuteron Holding/Lambert Smith Hampton	–	–	–	–	90	10	75	25
8	Eureal Gesellschaft	–	–	–	–	–	–	90	10
9	Comfort Gesellschaft/Müller	–	–	–	–	100	0	79	21
10	Apollo Gesellschaft/Colliers	–	–	–	–	90	10	90	10
	Average	100	0	94	6	91	9	83	17

Japanese Firms

1	Mitsui Real Estate/Mitsui Fudosan	100	0	92	8	80	20	75	25
2	Mitsubishi Real Estate	100	0	95	5	92	8	93	7
3	Sumitomo Realty and Development	99	1	93	7	85	15	90	10
4	Heiwa Real Estate	100	0	98	2	97	3	95	5
5	Tokyo Tatemono	100	0	100	0	98	2	96	4
6	Osaka Real Estate	100	0	97	3	98	2	98	2
7	Tokyu Land	100	0	100	0	97	3	98	2
8	Hankyu Realty	100	0	95	5	97	3	98	2
9	Daiwa Danchi	100	0	100	0	96	4	96	4
10	Towa Real Estate Development/Fujita	100	0	98	2	98	2	94	6
	Average	100	0	97	3	94	6	95	5

Sources: Direct surveys of each firm, 1993–7; public corporate reports; private company reports and documents.

Notes:
— Indicates the firm or the firm's real estate practice/personnel not formally established
a Weighted average of 1990–3 period
b 1987 figures, when firm was established

Organizational structure and management of growth

The collective profiles illustrate the extent to which a firm's organizational structure hindered or helped growth, geographic expansion and service diversification. Each firm's early (1960s) or previous organizational structure tended to influence the manner and pace in which the firm grew. For example, Japanese advisory firms remained highly centralized and integrated within the publicly-held, family/group company. Geographic diversification followed the expansion patterns of other company divisions, and all divisions and subsidiaries were ultimately administered by the central headquarters office in Japan and major shareholders. Thus, Japanese advisers indicated a propensity to pursue service diversification and geographic diversification only to respond to the immediate needs of clients. The firms' organizational structures were only nominally (if at all) altered by international expansion. When real estate markets worldwide contracted in the post-1989 period, Japanese firms had the least structural flexibility to respond to changing markets and client needs, affirming Chandler's basic argument that "growth without structural adjustment can lead only to economic inefficiency".[24]

European and US firms which sought only access to and information from major foreign markets, rather than an established presence or a globalized network, tended to prefer to affiliate with a reputable firm, to capitalize on a foreign partner's reputation and practice. The intent, or strategy, ideally dictated the most efficient structure. For example, Cushman & Wakefield of the US and Healey & Baker of the UK entered into a nonequity affiliation to acquire access and knowledge about their respective domestic markets. Globalized networks made up of several firms represented a broader version of two-way affiliations and were favored among European and US real estate advisers in the mid-1970s. Networks enabled a federation of local firms to pool resources in the international marketplace without a substantial equity investment.[25]

Property advisers who chose to internationalize by entering a foreign market independently or by merging with a foreign firm faced the greatest challenges in shaping a fluid structure among multiple service divisions and geographic regions. The ideal result was a complex administrative structure with a coordinated managerial hierarchy that facilitated management and growth of various departments across widely dispersed regions.[26] The firms that effectively created a semi-decentralized, multidivisional structure

93

remained among the most successful international real estate advisory firms –
LaSalle Partners and Arthur Andersen of the US, Jones Lang Wootton, Knight
Frank & Rutley, Hillier Parker, Savills, and Weatherall Green & Smith of the
UK, and Müller of Germany. Why were they successful in local and foreign
markets? Because the organization, generally, encouraged initiative and innovation at the divisional and local levels. Also, because each firm was privately
and directly owned by partners/principals and/or employees, corporate
managers enjoyed a greater degree of control and freedom to implement long-
term structural changes than did, for example, public companies answerable
to shareholders.[27]

One important challenge that property service firms faced in managing
growth and geographic expansion was balancing the nuances of real estate
markets and investments, which were highly localized and highly
entrepreneurial, with administrative needs to have uniform coordination
across domestic and foreign markets.[28] Perhaps one reason that German firms
limited their foreign expansion to only a few major financial capitals was due
to the atomistic structure of the domestic industry, which produced organizational inefficiencies by its very nature: fifteen of the country's largest
population regions constituted only 38 percent of the national market in
1990.[29] UK firms, by comparison, were forced in the 1960s to consolidate
into multidisciplinary firms to respond to growing demands by domestic
clients, who were increasingly critical of the multiplicity of professionals they
had to employ and coordinate. Mergers and acquisitions thus became prevalent among British property advisers in the mid- to late 1960s.[30]

The causes of failure: markets and management

Firms that failed to internationalize effectively typically experienced one of
two problems: an inability to remain knowledgeable about local markets and
cultivate client relationships at the local level, and/or an inability of senior
managers to create an efficient yet flexible administrative structure that
acknowledged the complexity of a growing enterprise across diverse regions
and multiple service functions. Two notable failures of the 1980s, Richard
Ellis of the UK and CB Commercial of the US, are discussed below. A third
firm, Gladstone Associates (later Arthur Andersen's Real Estate Services
Group in the US) was a domestic firm that failed in internationalization, until
it was acquired by Arthur Andersen S.A., which subsequently globalized the
real estate service group. A fourth failure in the international marketplace was
Orix of Japan, reviewed in Chapter 6.

Richard Ellis

Richard Ellis, which was founded in 1773 and first moved abroad in 1963,
faced a major management crisis during the 1983–9 period. The firm's inter-

national structure remained highly centralized in the London office and among the sixteen London-based partners. The US operation, which began in 1976 with two professionals, had grown to 280 employees in five offices in New York, Chicago, Atlanta, Los Angeles and San Francisco by 1989, and principally served a client base of corporate and institutional pension funds, 60 percent domestic and 40 percent foreign (Dutch, Japanese and British). In 1983, several US managers and partial owners resigned due to a disagreement with the UK owners over the relative lack of authority of the US partners generally, and the New York headquarters specifically. The London partners maintained that control should be centralized and coordinated in London (first) and New York (second), rather than decentralized through the regional offices. The resigning US board members and owners argued that, to cultivate a strong regional network for marketing real estate services, the firm should distribute ownership among local and regional partners, not centralize authority.

In 1989 the conflict between London and the US operation climaxed when the London partners decided that all offices worldwide would provide a full menu of property services to international clients, de-emphasizing the US group's business in fiduciary investment management for foreign and domestic institutions. London failed in this decision to consult or acknowledge the US partners, who consequently implemented a 49 percent buyout of the New York-based company. The London partners acquired the remaining 51 percent. The former US principals created The Yarmouth Group, retaining eleven tax-exempt clients and $5 billion of managed property assets.[31] In that same year – 1989 – Richard Ellis returned with the merger of REI Ltd and the Lexington Co., based in Chicago. The new firm, Richard Ellis Inc., opened headquarters in Chicago and offices in New York, Washington and Minneapolis.

During the 1990s Richard Ellis merged with Hepper Robinson, and in 1996 the firm established a joint venture with General Electric Capital. The new company was called Pangaea Real Estate Capital Services, and its goal was to promote and manage new property funds throughout the Asia/Pacific region. By that time, Richard Ellis International Property Consultants employed 700 partners and staff in the UK and 1200 directors and staff outside the UK.

CB Commercial

CB Commercial's failed international expansion illustrated the critical importance of in-depth local market knowledge and an entrepreneurial perspective in managing the organization. In 1968 Sears Roebuck & Co., the publicly held retail conglomerate, acquired Coldwell Banker, a residential brokerage and mortgage banking house predominantly located in the Far West and Southwestern regions of the United States.[32] The next year Sears established the commercial division of Coldwell Banker, which became CB Commercial in 1980. Sears incorporated Coldwell Banker into the diversified organizational structure, centralizing management in Chicago corporate headquarters and altering the incentive-based compensation (or reward) structure to align with other retail divisions. Both of these actions limited cross-communication between regional offices and different service divisions among the real estate advisory professionals, and worked as a disincentive against entrepreneurial innovation.

Then, in 1979–80, Sears transferred two real estate service professionals to the London satellite office to establish a European base for Coldwell Banker. Both lacked experience and direct knowledge of UK and continental markets, as well as of international investment practices. By 1988, just as cross-border real estate investment was peaking, the London real estate advisory group ceased operations and the larger US firm was experiencing negative revenue growth as well as internal staff turmoil. Sears, moreover, lacked the ability and initiative (and perhaps the understanding) to dedicate management and financial capital to restructuring Coldwell Banker, forced as it was to dedicate corporate resources to a weakening retail business, especially after 1989. In 1990 The Carlyle Group, a US-based multinational investment holding company and merchant banker, acquired the real estate services firm and continued to invest surplus capital and professional resources in rebuilding the company's management structure, compensation structure and revenue base.[33] Carlyle changed the firm's name to CB Commercial.

During the early 1990s, CB Commercial struggled to reduce its debt. CB began the 1990s with a number of consecutive quarterly losses. In 1991 the firm announced a long-range plan to restructure $240 million in debt. The restructuring deferred dividend payments due to CB's preferred shareholders, all based in Japan: Sumitomo Real Estate Sales L.A. Inc. (CB's chief lender), Kajima USA Inc., and General Lease Co. Ltd. Debt was still a problem for the firm in 1996, when $232 million in long-term debt was reported. In November 1996, CB announced an initial public offering of $80 million to reduce debt and provide capital for its expansion plans.

During this period, CB continued its efforts to expand in the global marketplace; by 1995 the firm had alliances in twenty-three countries. In 1992 CB entered an international alliance with Debenham Tewson & Chinnocks and its partners in DTZ, a joint venture of leading European firms, to provide a full range of commercial property services; in 1995, C.Y. Leung and Co. Ltd, a prominent Hong Kong firm, joined the alliance, contributing expertise about the Chinese marketplace and thereby simplifying and expediting transactions involving China. In 1995, CB formed alliances with three firms in South America: L.J. Ramos Brokers Inmobilaros in Argentina, Commercial Properties in Brazil, and P & G Larrain in Chile.

CB also continued to make acquisitions. In 1995 Westmark Realty Advisors LLC, an investment management and advisory service, was acquired, creating a $4 billion portfolio of managed property. CB provides its investment management and advisory services primarily to large institutions and pension funds, through Westmark, which employs over 100 professionals and operates from CB's headquarters in Los Angeles. In the same year CB purchased Langdon Rieder Corp., a tenant advisory service, thereby diversifying its clients' services. In 1996 the firm bought L.J. Melody & Co., a mortgage banking company located in Houston, Texas, significantly improving its position in the mortgage market. In addition, CB signed a letter of intent to combine operations with Koll Real Estate Services, a national leader in commercial property and corporate facilities management.

In addition, CB continued to diversify its services. In 1992 CB announced a joint venture with Kennedy-Wilson Inc., a leading real estate auction and marketing firm in the US. In 1994 CB made arrangements with Merrill Lynch to provide commercial real estate financing. The CBC Land Group was created in 1995 to provide real estate information to homebuilders. In 1997 CB and Nomura announced a joint program to provide conventional refinancing for properties subsidized under the US Housing Opportunity Program Extension Act of 1996.

By 1996 CB had more than 4,000 employees in 216 offices in thirty countries. The company provided a full range of services to commercial real estate tenants, owners and investors, including brokerage (facilitating sales and leases), investment properties (acquisitions and sales on behalf of investors), corporate services, property management, real estate market research, mortgage banking, investment management and advisory services, as well as valuation and appraisal services.

Arthur Andersen

Perhaps those domestic firms that built successful real estate advisory practices in international markets in the late 1980s (rather than earlier in the 1960s and 1970s) were those which were acquired by or merged with large, multi-service international holding companies – such as Coldwell Banker and The Carlyle Group. Another was GA/Partners of the US and Arthur Andersen & Co. S.A. GA/Partners, founded in 1961 as Gladstone Associates, a sole proprietorship in Washington, DC, developed a highly successful and technically specialized domestic practice during the 1970s and early 1980s. Clients included Fortune 50 corporations in leading US industries, major national developers, financial institutions and Federal government agencies. In the mid-1970s, the firm had opened three small satellite offices in Los Angeles, Boston and Miami, which were consolidated back into the central headquarters office in 1979 in a move to centralize management and ownership in Washington. In 1981 the firm's founder, Robert Gladstone, sold the practice to six active partners who created an egalitarian partnership of equal shares and responsibilities.

As in the 1960s and 1970s, GA/Partners continued to be respected by clients and in major and secondary domestic markets as a leader in real estate consulting in the US with in-depth market knowledge, relationships with premier clients, premium professional fees, a highly educated professional staff, and an ability to innovate to respond to changing service and technical needs. And while the firm had a token few international assignments each year – in Canada, Singapore, Mexico, British Columbia – the partners lacked the capacity to establish profitable, ongoing relationships with foreign investors in US markets or to retain work abroad. GA/Partners was firmly entrenched in domestic markets and respected for its domestic reputation and practice.

Enter Arthur Andersen in 1985, one of the six largest, globalized, full-service accounting firms. Seeking to expand into real estate services in the US and subsequently abroad, Arthur Andersen viewed a merger and acquisition of GA/Partners as a foothold into an underdeveloped and complementary practice area for the accounting firm. For GA/Partners the acquisition meant loss of autonomy, control and ownership by the six partners, yet offered the ability to expand the practice nationally and internationally by capitalizing on Arthur Andersen's domestic clientele and global office network. The acquisition was completed in early 1986. By late 1990, the real estate services group of GA/Partners–Arthur Andersen had grown more than two-fold in professionals; foreign personnel and fees had increased ten-fold. In addition, access to international investors active in US markets expanded by an indeterminate, exponential amount – global financial institutions, foreign pension and insurance funds, and high-net-worth individual investors. Prior to Arthur Andersen's acquisition, the partners and the fifty to seventy-five professionals at GA/Partners lacked the financial and personal resources to gain and sustain in-depth knowledge of local foreign markets and clients.

Arthur Andersen's global office network and existing clientele worldwide expanded the firm's international capacity and was the essential vehicle to facilitate an ongoing profitable business and international reputation.[34] For example, in 1994 Arthur Andersen formed a strategic alliance with Chadwick & Co. to provide fairness opinions, used in assessing the financial fairness of transactions involving the consolidation of real estate assets, such as REITs. In addition, as part of an ongoing expansion of services, in 1995 the firm created a new position to direct real estate operations in Pacific Rim cities.

By 1995 the Arthur Andersen Real Estate Services Group (RESG) had become one of the largest international real estate advisory services, with over 6,000 clients and 1,500 personnel. RESG had successfully diversified into a wide range of services in addition to real estate consulting, including accounting, audit, tax, information systems, hospitality and appraisal services. In 1996 the firm launched Real Estate OneSource to help clients adapt to the new technology required for electronic commerce. The initiative involved moving the firm's real estate advisors to regional offices; previously they were all located in Washington, DC.

The causes of success

This collective profile of forty firms provides a reliable account of the representative universe of firms in the four countries between 1960 and 1980, portraying firms that internationalized quite successfully, firms that developed a modest foreign practice, and firms that failed in internationalization. Leading firms, both domestic and international, consistently invested corporate capital in recruiting and retaining well-educated professionals. The quality of a firm's professional staff directly affected reputation, and reputation was key to a firm establishing its value with clients. Perceived and real "value creation" was crucial to each firm's growth and profitability. Because of this, shifts in client needs – patterns of where and how clients invested during certain periods – directly influenced the strategies of these forty real estate advisory firms, both in terms of the services offered and the geographic concentration of a firm's personnel.

Service diversification was prompted by client demand and by competitive pressures from other real estate advisory firms and other allied professional service firms, such as the major investment banking houses and accounting firms. Only by diversifying into new service areas and new markets could firms broaden their range of exposure among different types of clients, and thus broaden sources of potential revenues. In addition, innovations were motivated by the prospect of attracting and retaining clients and by maintaining and growing profitability margins.

Diversification and expansion tended to occur concurrently with the growth of the domestic economy and with rising cross-border investment in real estate. As such, firms in each focal country undertook foreign expansion during different periods. Increasingly more complex organizations characterized real estate advisory firms, stemming from the maturation of real estate markets worldwide, the increase in more sophisticated techniques and types of services, and the growth in the number of multiregional operations. The challenge for each firm was how to manage standards of quality, efficiency and effective service delivery across these multiple layers. Firms that centralized authority and decentralized decision-making and innovation to regional markets and functional divisions tended to be most responsive to shifts in markets, client demands and economic circumstances. Moreover, privately-owned and privately-operated firms had the greatest capital and reputation at risk, yet also enjoyed the greatest flexibility to grow, contract and/or expand offices incrementally relative to shifting property and investment markets.

Notes

1 A.D. Chandler Jr., *Strategy and Structure: Chapters in the History of American Industrial Enterprise*, Cambridge, MA: MIT Press, 1962.
2 In the US and the UK, the real estate sector and foreign investment have been largely unregulated and unevenly documented; in Germany, through 1990,

property and financial market data was unpublished and restricted; in Japan, even though real estate service firms were publicly-traded enterprises, the real estate division's activities and profitability indicators were not itemized in published reports. Moreover, the Ministry of Finance maintained tight controls on government data, effectively closing off access to detailed statistics on property, investment and the real estate sector.

3 A.D. Chandler, Jr., *The Visible Hand: The Managerial Revolution in American Business*, Cambridge, MA: Belknap Press of Harvard University Press, 1977, p. 6.

4 It should be noted that the author did not include Orix, the Japanese firm examined in the Chapter 6 case studies, among the ten Japanese real estate services firms analyzed in this chapter. The ten firms that are evaluated all originated as subsidiaries of group trading companies, while Orix was created out of an equipment leasing company. The firms are, therefore, believed to be uniformly comparable for the purposes of collective analysis.

5 In the United States, the author consulted with the Association of Real Estate Counselors and the research division of the National Realtors Association, as well as the International Federation of Real Estate Consultants for all countries. For Japan, the author consulted with the Real Estate Companies Association in Japan, ALL Japan Real Estate Association, the Association of Real Estate Agents, Shuwa Investments Corporation, The Nomura Group of Japan, Nippon Life, C. ITOH Real Estate, the International Chamber of Commerce in Tokyo, and the *Japan Company Handbook*, for the largest publicly-listed real estate service companies, which all Japanese real estate advisory firms are. For Germany, the author consulted with the editor of the annual *Immobilien Manager's* Player + Profile survey of real estate consultants, the Association of German Chambers of Industry and Commerce (DIHT), Ring Deutscher Makler (RDM), the research division of Gesellschaft für Informationsverarbeitung mbH, Deutsche Immobilien Anlagegesellschaft mbH (Deutsche Bank), and Commerz Grundbositz Investmentgesollschaft mbH (Commerzbank). For the UK, the author consulted Ernst & Young (chartered accountants), the Royal Institute of Chartered Surveyors research division, and the annual edition of *The Chartered Surveyors Survey*, 1979–93.

6 Refer to Chapter 3.

7 M.A. Hines, "Global Real Estate Services," *The Appraisal Journal* (April 1992), pp. 206–13.

8 E. Davis, G. Hanlon and J. Kay, "Internationalization in Accounting and Other Professional Services," Working Paper No. 78, Centre for Business Strategy (London Business School, 1990), p. 3; and E. Davis and C. Smales, "The Internationalization of Professional Services," Working Paper No. 66, Centre for Business Strategy (London Business School, 1989).

9 S.B. Sagari, "The Financial Services Industry: An International Perspective," (PhD dissertation, New York University, 1986), pp. 67–8.

10 See H. Barty-King, *Scratch a Surveyor* (London: William Heinemann Ltd., 1975), pp. 250–2.

11 Innovation will be evaluated in detail in Chapter 5; organizational structures are reviewed in Chapter 4 and again in Chapter 6.

12 *The Wall Street Journal* (19 January 1970), pp. 1, 19; (6 March 1970), p. 3; (30 July 1970), p. 10; (20 March 1980), p. 1; (8 October 1984), p. 37; (15 October 1980), p. 31; (3 April 1990), p. 46; (13 September 1990), pp. C1, C9. R. Derven, "Goldman Sachs Credits Innovative Financing for Success in a Changing Mortgage Market", *National Real Estate Investor* (June 1986), p. 131.

13 *Chartered Surveyors Survey* (London: Tann vom Hove, 1987–91); A. Bailey, "Putting the Professional Under One Roof", *Director* (April 1988), pp. 37–8; *The Wall Street Journal*, (25 January 1990), p. C6.

14 Dr Seebauer, "From East and West to unified Germany: Real Estate Market and Real Estate Financing Market", (July 1991); "The French Are Coming – International Investors in Germany", *European Real Estate Insider*, vol. 2 no. 3 (Fall 1992), pp. 3–5, 12; R. Gop, "Player + Profile: New Game Rules", *Immobilien Manager*, no. 6 (December 1993), pp. 9–20. Interview with author, Caspar Frhr. von Weichs, Dr Seebauer & Partner, GmbH, Munich (15 December 1993 and 26 January 1994).

15 O.E. Williamson, *Markets and Hierarchies: Analysis and Antitrust Implications*, New York and London: Free Press, 1975, pp. 56, 82ff; also see L.S. Bacow, "Foreign Investment, Vertical Integration, and the Structure of the U.S. Real Estate Industry", Working Paper No. 25, Massachusetts Institute of Technology Center for Real Estate Development (January 1990), pp. 16–17.

16 *The Economist* (18 March 1972), p. 8. A real estate advisory firm could have a participating or partnership stake in a client's project without an investment of equity by the professional service firm; instead, incentive fees and percentage-based commission pay structures were common in the UK, Germany and the US.

17 *The Economist* (20 January 1973), pp. 90–2; R. Marshall, "The QS in Europe", *Building* (24 September 1976), pp. 60–1.

18 R.H. Coase, "The Nature of the Firm", in *The Firm, the Market, and the Law*, edited by R.H. Coase (Chicago: University of Chicago Press, 1988), pp. 333–4, 338.

19 This statement is implied rather than explicitly stated in the data and information contained in public offering documents and reports.

20 DTZ Debenham Thorpe, "Background to DTZ Debenham Thorpe", "DTZ Debenham Thorpe – A Brief history (1984–1994)", "DTZ Debenham Thorpe – International Statement", public company reports and prospectus documents (1987–94). The flotation was valued at £41.6 million; by 1990 it was valued at £39.2 million.

21 A.D. Chandler, Jr., *Scale and Scope: The Dynamics of Industrial Capitalism*, Cambridge, MA: Belknap Press of Harvard University Press, 1990, pp. 38–9; R.H. Coase, "The Nature of the Firm", in *The Firm, the Market, and the Law*, edited by R.H. Coase (Chicago: University of Chicago Press, 1988), pp. 55–8; L.S. Bacow, "Foreign Investment, Vertical Integration, and the Structure of the U.S. Real Estate Industry", Working Paper No. 25, Massachusetts Institute of Technology Center for Real Estate Development (January 1990), p. 7.

22 *The Wall Street Journal* (9 February 1990), p. B11C; (13 September 1990), p. C1; L.S. Bacow, "Foreign Investment, Vertical Integration, and the Structure of the U.S. Real Estate Industry", Working Paper No. 25, Massachusetts Institute of Technology Center for Real Estate Development (January 1990).

23 As G.J. Stigler explained, in *The Organization of Industry*, Chicago: University of Chicago Press, 1968, p. 99, sufficiently large diseconomies of scale deplete a merger of profits and ultimate success, including commitment of financial resources, personnel, efficient management and coordination.

24 A.D. Chandler, Jr., *Scale and Scope: The Dynamics of Industrial Capitalism*, Cambridge, MA: Belknap Press of Harvard University Press, 1990, p. 16.

25 Networks established corporate guidelines among member firms, which outlined territorial boundaries and exclusive market coverage. Each firm retained local autonomy, and paid membership fees to the network corporation or partnership. In a few cases, network affiliation fostered a merger of two firms, such as the UK–France merger of Erdman Thouard.

26 A.D. Chandler, Jr., *Strategy and Structure: Chapters in the History of American Industrial Enterprise*, Cambridge: MIT Press, 1962, p. 33; *ibid.*, pp. 31, 41; O.E. Williamson, *Markets and Hierarchies: Analysis and Antitrust Implications*, New York and London: Free Press, 1975, pp. xi, 52–6.

27 Alfred P. Sloan, Jr., General Motors chairman in the 1920s, effectively introduced the "decentralized" multidivisional corporate structure, believing that divisional independence focused "line" staff on operations and freed central managers to deal with planning. See A.D. Chandler, Jr., *Scale and Scope: The Dynamics of Industrial Capitalism*, Cambridge, MA: Belknap Press of Harvard University Press, 1990, pp. 133, 284.

28 L.S. Bacow argued that vertical integration as applied to the real estate industry and foreign expansion was inappropriate, in "Foreign Investment, Vertical Integration, and the Structure of the U.S. Real Estate Industry", Working Paper No. 25, Massachusetts Institute of Technology Center for Real Estate Development (January 1990), p. 8.

29 J.L. Blysh, "Baukostenplanung [Quantity Surveying in Germany]", *The Quantity Surveyor* (July/August 1972), pp. 3–5; Statistisches Bundesamt, Dr Seebauer & Partner (1991).

30 I.A. Leslie, "Service to the Industry", and J.B. Sermon, "In the Contracting Camp", *Building* (2 May 1969), p. 91; J. Nisbet, "The Future Private Practice", *Chartered Surveyor* (July 1969), pp. 33–6.

31 K. Blanton, "Dispute Over Control Leads to Richard Ellis Departures", *Pensions & Investment Age* (17 October 1983), pp. 2, 44; "Richard Ellis and County Bank Join Forces", *Accountancy* (July 1986), p. 34; A. Reinbach, "Ellis Principals Do Buy-Out", *Pensions & Investment Age* (12 June 1989), pp. 37, 39; "Richard Ellis Inc. Sold to Executives in All-Cash Deal", *National Real Estate Investor* (July 1989), pp. 28–30.

32 Sears's diversification into some financial services, such as residential mortgage and retail credit cards, was successful because they were more closely allied with the mainline retail market, while commercial property services were oriented to a very different client market.

33 "Head Start", *Forbes* (1 October 1970), p. 46; Coldwell Banker annual reports (1970–9); Coldwell Banker and CB Commercial annual reports (1980–93).

34 The sacrifice to GA/Partners in the Arthur Andersen acquisition was the phased-out use of the Gladstone name and loss of the identity-based reputation. Within a decade of the acquisition, the Gladstone and GA/Partners identities were virtually unrecognized by most, except long-time professionals and clients in the US.

5

INNOVATIONS IN INTERNATIONAL REAL ESTATE ADVISORY SERVICES

Chapter 5 examines the major service innovations and market-oriented technical innovations that advanced the internationalization of real estate advisory services. In addition, the conditions that enabled firms to achieve competitive advantage are analyzed by looking at economic cycles, organizational structures, market-entry strategies and the competitive environment in the industry. The focus then narrows to important turning points in markets, innovations and technical skills; in particular, attention is given to developments in the following areas:

* International pension and insurance fund management
* International corporate real estate services
* International financial and investment banking services
* Public capital and securitized investment services.

The chapter reviews the primary sources of innovation and the economic cycles from which they were derived. The most successful real estate advisory service firms acquired competitive advantages in the international marketplace by continually developing new skills and moving into new markets. Local specialists were the primary sources of innovation, and local market knowledge was the basis for developing new skills.

New skills and new markets

Real estate advisory service firms in the focal countries acquired competitive advantage in the international marketplace by continually developing new skills and entering new markets. Innovations in services and market-oriented techniques, together, advanced the internationalization of real estate advisory services throughout the thirty-seven-year period. While such international trade theorists as Wells, Casson, and Sampson and Snape defined trade in services as the cross-border transfer of just service factors, real estate services trade involved the mobility of both service *factors* (investors and professional advisers) and/or local service *products* (real estate investment and investment

103

advisory services). To promote internationalization, real estate advisory firms innovated by moving into new products (services) and new functions (foreign markets and foreign investor clients).[1]

Indicators of innovation in real estate advisory services

What macroeconomic conditions, if any, enabled firms and nations to achieve competitive advantage in innovative products to sustain internationalization? The prime mover of innovation in international real estate advisory services appeared to be total capital flows across borders. Significant changes in inward and outward real estate investment stock and flows, as well as the degree of volatility in the national economy,[2] indicated shifts in the direction of capital markets and opportunities for innovation. In addition, other conditions of innovation in international real estate advisory services included the national industry's structure and competitive environment, and the organizational structure of leading national firms. The following sections review the introduction of major service innovations and technical innovations, discussed relative to changes and/or events in direct real estate investment stock and flows to annual GDP growth, and to annual property investment yields in the focal countries.

Economic cycles and innovation

Changing economic environments necessitated new approaches to real estate acquisitions, dispositions, financings, management and development. During recessionary cycles, corporations, investors and real estate developers demanded new mechanisms to strengthen or salvage yields on property investments. Rising stocks of real estate investment also tended to prompt service and technical innovations, to reinforce international investment activity in property, and to improve investment yields relative to real estate costs.[3] Investors became uncertain in unusually strong or weak market environments and tended to intensify demand for more and new types of real estate investment. Exceptionally active cross-border markets, such as the UK in the 1960s (outward investment), Germany in the 1970s (outward investment), and the US and Japan in the 1980s (inward and outward investment, respectively), stimulated a higher degree of innovation.[4]

Significant shift in GDP growth or decline was a second indicator of turbulence in the national economy, and usually, in down cycles, created new forces in the real estate marketplace that transformed standard practices to daunting challenges.[5] The dynamics of the market thus attracted prominent investors and qualified professionals, and enlarged the national market's opportunities for investors, professional skills and ongoing innovation.[6]

Innovation became an essential factor in attracting and retaining domestic and global investors throughout periodic, up-and-down investment cycles.[7]

For example, when foreign investment capital increased globally after 1978, US investment banks introduced innovative debt and equity instruments to finance real estate investment worldwide, thereby attracting an abundance of real estate capital to diverse and profitable US markets.[8]

Based on a review of primary and secondary historical and contemporary sources, equity investors appeared to be the most prevalent entrants into international markets at the bottom of a cycle. Economic growth generated excess capital, which gave way to higher leveraged investment vehicles and strategies. Innovations that emerged from such rapid local economic realignments moved efficiently into national and international markets, especially during the advanced globalization of the late 1970s and 1980s.

Industry structure and competitive environment

Taking a locally developed service product or technical product into the international marketplace required an open industry structure that enabled innovations introduced in one particular sector or local market to flow by competitive supply-and-demand forces throughout the national system. In essence, the broadly defined and relatively flexible structure of this industry and its profession encouraged innovation and diversification.

Real estate advisory firms, unlike other professional services such as law or medicine, defied classification into distinct groups. As the real estate industry and property professions matured nationally and internationalized, real estate advisers in the focal countries called on different professional services to complement and expand existing practices. Many sectoral firms – including pension funds, insurance companies, commercial and merchant banks, investment banks, developers and contractors, equity funds, and investment trusts – diversified vertically to integrate some form of property consulting into the mainline business. Firms that gained competitive advantage nationally and globally would extend services and technical skills through existing expertise, rather than create or acquire wholly new products; furthermore, they possessed the administrative, financial, tactical and political capabilities to export innovations to new foreign markets and investors.[9]

Restraints and barriers on trade in international markets most of all limited the effective and efficient transfer of skills, services technologies and specialization to foreign markets.[10] Persistent protectionism through strict immigration and labor laws in Japan and local ownership rules in Europe and Japan hindered the progress of internationalizing real estate service firms as well as other professional services.[11] Since the 1950s, for example, most European nations have required foreign investors to secure offshore funding, rather than to rely only on domestic sources for real estate acquisitions. Provincial investment practices encouraged both domestic and foreign real estate advisers to expand operations across multiple countries in Europe to diversify risk and gain an adequate return on investment. In this environment, domestic UK and German firms enjoyed a competitive advantage over US and Japanese real estate advisory firms. Even German real estate service firms, being highly localized in their operations, were at risk in challenging international competitors on a purely local approach.[12] As discussed in Chapter 3, inegalitarian market access in the UK, Germany, and Japan in particular, hindered the cross-border transfer of innovative services among foreign competitors.[13] Instead, most innovations throughout the 1960–97 period depended largely on fluid communications among professionals and firms in each country.

Organizational structure and innovation

The international marketplace represented the ultimate arena of service and technical innovations originally conceived in local and national markets. How did locally developed innovations emerge into international markets? More importantly, how did such locally cultivated techniques and services assist internationalization?

In the best circumstances, several of a firm's geographic and functional divisions contributed to developing innovative responses to local market opportunities, then transported these new skills into foreign markets and/or with foreign clients. Firms that achieved a competitive advantage among foreign clients developed an effective network to bring locally cultivated services into the international marketplace. The research for this book suggests that the strongest competitors were companies sensitive to market, technical and analytical trends and were able to exploit new services globally in a prompt and efficient manner (Table 5.1). The development and distribution of local-to-global innovations demanded that senior managers centralize standards of quality and decentralize authority to divisions and regions to permit flexible communication channels. Japanese real estate service firms were the exception in this regard. They typically pursued centralized research and development, and they advised clients in different markets during the 1985–8 period on the basis of fairly uniform, though innovative, financing criteria and techniques. This lack of market-based responsiveness resulted in huge losses from 1989 to the mid-1990s in US, UK and German markets, among others, and by Japanese and foreign clients.

Any one firm's foundation for service innovation rested on its breadth of experience in diversified markets and with a diverse range of clients.[14] Not dissimilar to product manufacturers, real estate services firms moved into overseas markets to gain access to new market knowledge and to sustain the competitive position gained in home markets, usually with existing customers. Firms that incrementally diversified or expanded operations in the early 1960s or before – Jones Lang Wootton, Richard Ellis, Cushman & Wakefield, Mitsubishi – tended to be structurally organized to disperse more efficiently into multiple domestic and foreign markets in the 1970s and 1980s and to incorporate new functions into the core business.[15] In this way, Jones Lang Wootton of the UK was the exemplary model, as reviewed in Chapter 6.

The results of the case studies of forty firms in Chapter 4 indicate that the motivation for entering a new business or a new market, either through integration, consolidation or cooperation, was to exploit access to existing and distinctive resources – skills, experience, markets, clients – which were more expensive for competitors to acquire.[16] As US and UK investment and merchant banks became involved in real estate advisory services in the late 1970s and early 1980s, they applied expertise in securities, mergers and acquisitions and international investment management, to real estate advisory services. For example, the US, UK, Germany and Japan dominated global financial markets during the 1980s, accounting for up to 80 percent of all Euromarket issues. Such wide-ranging influence enabled a distinct coterie of leading investment banks to be easily accepted by clients and competitors in affiliated functions, and to introduce innovative financial structures to property investment.[17]

Since 1960 the competitive marketplace demanded new combinations of services through vertical integration or well-conceived coordination between specialized disciplines.[18] Innovations typically emerged when firms had perceived intensified competition from new entrants or lower profitability from existing businesses. Investment in people and advanced skills and technologies were the essential ingredients of innovation in real estate advisory services.

While vertical integration of functions enhanced innovation through cross-cultivation of information about investor needs, markets and technological approaches and solutions, the evidence was mixed as to whether returns from innovation in a vertically integrated enterprise were higher than in a so-called "niche" service firm.[19] The niche firms evaluated in Chapter 4, such as Goldman Sachs and Morgan Stanley, did not necessarily incur higher transaction costs when real estate services were vertically integrated into the mainline business. Conversely, when a real estate advisory firm and an investment bank – or another sectoral enterprise – joined in a cooperative engagement, the cost of innovation was typically higher (by bringing two firms together), but the results, or profits, to the firms and the investor client were also greater. Because of their ability to act as both adviser and principal, US, UK and German investment banks were more profitable in real estate financial services in the late 1980s than most of the full-service real estate advisory firms in these countries.[20]

The ultimate issue was sustaining profitability growth. Competing theories argued by Williamson and by Porter and Millar addressed the benefits of diversification versus specialization: diversified firms enjoyed greater opportunities to deepen market penetration and to increase market share by broadening competitive scope, contended Williamson; specialized firms enjoyed lower cost margins and therefore higher profitability margins by targeting particular market segments, argued Porter and Millar.[21] Because local market knowledge lay at the heart of real estate advisory services, most real estate service firms tended to diversify into allied functions (rather than specialize in one or a few distinct services) to create a foundation for nurturing innovative capabilities and complementing existing services.[22]

The following sections of this chapter discuss specific turning points in national and international markets, and innovations in services and technical skills that emerged during particular economic environments. As reviewed in the section titled "International pension and insurance fund management", UK chartered surveyors developed new portfolio management skills in the mid-1920s and led the industry in counseling insurance and pension funds investing in foreign markets. Beginning in the late 1930s, Japanese advisers were the first to engage in corporate real estate services as a means to acquire access to foreign resources and strengthen financial gains in overseas markets, discussed in the section on "International corporate real estate services". International investment banks diversified into real estate advisory services in the early 1960s to protect existing relationships with corporate and institutional clients by integrating property finance into personal and corporate services; this prompted property advisers to incorporate financial or real estate investment banking services into the business. In the global real estate recession of the late 1980s, securitized real estate portfolio services were introduced by US firms to attract equity investors worldwide and thereby increase fund management fee revenues, as discussed in "International financial and investment banking services" later in this chapter.

International pension and insurance fund management

Institutional funds were invested in foreign real estate to diversify investment portfolios, rather than as a means of seeking higher investment yields than were available in domestic markets.[23] Because national regulations prohibited the creation of international co-mingled funds, except in the UK, international funds retained real estate advisers in the host country for advice on acquisitions and asset management. Investment and merchant banks, securities firms, international accounting firms and independent investment advisers competed directly with real estate advisory service firms for institutional fund management business.[24]

Pension and insurance funds became the single largest source of funds for domestic real estate investment in the UK in the 1930s, then in Germany and the US in the mid-1960s and mid-1970s respectively, and finally in Japan in 1985–6. UK real estate advisers introduced portfolio management services around 1924 and led the industry in counseling insurance and pension portfolio funds investing in foreign markets. Insurance company property investment emerged in the early 1920s, rising precipitously in the inter-war years to become the principal source of domestic real estate equity in the

Table 5.1 Innovations in real estate advisory services in the United States, United Kingdom, Germany and Japan

Innovation	Country and Date of Innovation	International Diffusion	Time Lag	Widespread Market Use
Pension & Insurance Fund Portfolio Management Services[a]	UK, 1924	1965	41	Germany, 1965 US, 1975 Japan, 1985
Corporate Real Estate Services[b]	Japan, 1937	NA	NA	UK, c. 1965 US, c. 1978–79 Germany, c. 1981
Financial and Investment Banking Services[c]	Germany, 1963	1981	18	US, 1981 UK, 1981 Japan, 1985
Public Capital and Securitized Investment Services[d]	UK, 1953	1960	7	US, 1960 Germany, 1970 Japan, 1959

Sources:
S.E. Roulac, "The Globalization of Real Estate Finance", *The Real Estate Finance Journal* 4, no. 2, Spring 1987, p. 40; S. Tolliday, ed., "Business History of Real Estate", *Business History Review*, Summer 1989; L.S. Bacow, "The Internationalization of the U.S. Real Estate Industry", Working Paper No. 16, MIT, Center for Real Estate Development, Nov. 1988; A. Baum and A. Schofield, "Property as a Global Asset", Working Papers in European Property, Centre for European Property, University of Reading, March 1991; Peter Scott's PhD dissertation; D. Neidich and T.M. Steinberg, "Corporate Real Estate: Source of New Equity", *Harvard Business Review* 4, July–August 1984, pp. 76–83; S.L. Hayes and P.M. Hubbard, *Investment Banking* (1990); privately published industry and company reports (see Bibliography); Author interview with several leading property professionals and property economic analysts during the conduct of project research and twenty-year professional career.

Notes:
[a] "Pension and Insurance Fund Portfolio Management Services" include systematic analysis and strategic planning and management of real estate investments (assets, mortgages and equity interests) held by institutional pension and insurance funds; these services may be outsourced or retained internally, often depending on the proportionate size of the institution's real estate portfolio relative to total investment assets.
[b] "Corporate Real Estate Services" include advisory services undertaken on behalf of a non-real estate private corporate entity to maximize the value of owned/leased assets and minimize financial exposure relative to the mainline business; these services can include tenant representation, project management, sale/leaseback arrangement, and takeover defense strategy (to utilize the residual value of real estate assets to bolster overall corporate value).
[c] "Financial and Investment Banking Services" include real estate advisory services that involve investment banking techniques and vehicles that were originally designed to expand the universe of corporate investment capital, such as equity financing, participating mortgages, commercial paper, mezzanine financing and SWAPs.
[d] "Public Capital and Securitized Investment Services" include real estate investment services that utilize public capital markets and securitized investment vehicles, such as Real Estate Investment Trusts, Property Unit Trusts, Eurodollar bond financing, and publicly-traded corporate equity shares.

1950s and 1960s.[25] Investments in land property and ground rents constituted 20 percent of total insurance investments in 1964. When in 1965 the capital gains tax prompted institutional investors to hold property for their own account (rather than through developers and be taxed on profits),[26] insurance companies with their property advisers introduced property bond funds in 1966 to invest directly in real estate. Pension funds then invested 25 percent of portfolios in property-linked life policies or property bonds.[27]

By 1958, institutional portfolios had begun to invest in foreign real estate. Foreign purchases accelerated after the 1964 Brown Ban and the high inflationary period of the early 1970s.[28] Major insurance companies, for example, funded the foreign expansion of The Hammerson Property Investment & Development Corp. during the late 1950s and 1960s in Australia, New Zealand and the US – as advised by Jones Lang Wootton.[29] MEPC, too, expanded into continental Europe, Australia, Honolulu, Munich and Frankfurt from 1961 to 1973, backed by Equitable, London Life and National Provident Institution.[30] And the Imperial Tobacco pension fund formed a joint development company with City Centre Properties in 1961 to pursue domestic and US projects.[31] The first offshore bond fund, the Tyndall Property Fund of 1970, was structured by UK estate managers Allsop & Co.[32]

Because domestic and foreign real estate investments accounted for a disproportionate share of the growth of insurance and pension fund investments, portfolio advisory services played an important role in the evolution of chartered surveyors property services throughout the thirty-year period. Insurance funds increased property investments from 8.6 percent of total assets in 1958 to 9 percent in 1960, 16 percent in 1976, and 18.3 percent by 1980. Commercial and residential property mortgage assets grew by approximately 15 percent annually over the same period.[33] Pension funds, as well, increased real estate assets from 5 percent in 1965 to 17 percent of total assets by 1976. By the early 1980s, large public sector funds, which were advised by chartered surveyors and others, invested 30 percent of funds in real estate.[34] Prior to 1979, pension funds collectively invested 5 percent of portfolios abroad, which increased to approximately 16 percent after 1979 with the liberalization of capital export tax controls.[35]

The prevalence of inflated property bond values and portfolio funds during the 1971–4 period led institutional investors to establish stricter and more conservative investment strategies.[36] Chartered surveyors developed systematic criteria in creating research, appraisal and asset management programs for evaluating foreign property purchases. These programs encompassed a broad array of disciplines – estate management, appraisal, asset management, investment sales and purchases, and financial services.[37] Firms appeared to achieve competitive advantage by establishing systematic investment guidelines for different markets and different types of real estate products.[38] Regular market valuation for property valuations first became common in the UK in the mid-1940s for retail assets, such as Marks & Spencer's properties – appraised by

Hillier, Parker, May & Rowden.[39] Major institutional portfolio valuations were not performed consistently on an annualized basis until the late 1960s, such as in 1969 by UK chartered surveyor Debenham, Tewson & Chinnocks for the Royal Exchange Assurance–Guardian Assurance merger.[40] This marked the origins of modern real estate benchmarking and real estate financial services. Not until the late 1970s, however, did most leading chartered surveyors develop systematic performance measurements for institutional portfolios.

Performance measurements introduced during the mid-1970s and early 1980s enabled fund managers and institutions to evaluate real estate yields relative to other investment vehicles, notably equities. In the high-inflationary, slow-growth climate of 1974–5, institutional funds abandoned joint venture development projects and equity property investments in both domestic and foreign markets. In the early 1980s, growing usage of benchmark evaluations prompted UK pension funds to implement more rigorous asset allocation strategies and reduce fixed income and equity real estate investments from 18.3 percent of portfolios in 1980 to 12.1 percent in 1988.[41] In 1990 the British National Coal Board's pension fund entirely liquidated its $1 billion portfolio after eight years in the US market.

The diffusion of portfolio fund management skills from the UK to Germany and the US occurred over a period of several decades, because widespread market use appeared in the major urban markets around Frankfurt and Munich, and New York, Chicago and Washington, DC, only when insurance funds were interested in or legally able to invest in property. By the mid-1960s, German insurance and pension funds were the primary sources of equity and long-term debt of commercial properties in domestic markets.[42] Over time, German advisers informally observed UK chartered surveyors who were advising UK insurance funds investing in Munich and Frankfurt (such as JLW, Weatherall, Green & Smith, and Hillier, Parker, May & Rowden). They casually acquired knowledge about other firms' portfolio management services – services that German advisers subsequently used to manage the domestic portfolios of German open-end funds as well as potential investments in the major European capitals of Paris, London and Madrid.[43] UK advisers and the largest private German property companies (such as DIVAG and Fuender), by contrast, managed the majority of closed-end foreign and real estate funds.[44]

A similar diffusion process occurred in US markets where UK advisers and insurance funds were active – New York, Chicago and Washington, DC. Institutional portfolio management services were virtually nonexistent in the US until 1975, once the 1974 Employment Retirement Income Security Act (ERISA) came into effect. ERISA included asset allocation guidelines for US pension fund investments, including real estate. While insurance funds had been investing in real estate and property-backed mortgages since the mid-1930s – constituting about 3 percent and 8 percent of total assets respectively

– ERISA and the maturation of US real estate markets after the recession and high-inflationary period of the early 1970s elevated portfolio management services to the core business.[45] Professional techniques combined asset management and financial services, which had been introduced to the US real estate market by chartered surveyors and US banks and accounting firms.

The size and depth of US markets enabled pension and insurance funds to achieve adequate diversification by investing exclusively in domestic assets through the early 1980s.[46] Because pension funds tended to view "value creation" in the context of selected, long-term contractual relationships, the cultural compatibility of fund and adviser was an important criterion.[47] Only the very largest pension funds invested a small portion of their portfolios in overseas fixed-income investments, about 2 percent, and even less in foreign real estate. US real estate advisory firms competed directly with the major commercial banks that managed large pension funds and advised banking clients (such as BankAmerica) on real estate investment, orienting their practices to appraising and managing domestic real estate assets as well as targeting investment properties for US and foreign funds active in home markets.[48]

Eastern Air Lines Variable Benefit Retirement Plan for Pilots was one of the pioneer US funds to invest in foreign real estate when it began acquiring residential properties in London in 1984, assisted by UK estate managers.[49] By the late 1980s, prompted by the weaker performance of US equities and armed with international portfolio investment index surveys, US pension funds began to invest increasing amounts of capital in European markets as a means of simply diversifying and hedging the ups and downs of the US economy and domestic markets.[50] By 1987–8, overseas fixed-income assets, which included property, accounted for approximately 4 to 5 percent of pension fund portfolios.[51]

US and UK real estate advisers sought to introduce an international portfolio fund benchmarking system that encompassed key markets and property classes for assisting global clients. By 1990, however, the effort had failed because of logistic obstacles to uniform indexing of individual portfolios and funds: US investors questioned the technical accuracy and uniformity of UK indices, and German and Japanese financial institutions prohibited publication of proprietary financial performance data on managed insurance and pension funds.[52]

Japanese advisers came to establish portfolio investment guidelines in 1985–6, simultaneously with the surge in the country's cross-border real estate investment activities.[53] Because corporate pensions were managed by trust and insurance companies, which were linked with the *keiretsus*, real estate subsidiaries simply incorporated portfolio services in the scope of corporate services, domestic and abroad. Japanese life insurance companies, which were prohibited from entering non-life insurance businesses, aggressively entered foreign real estate by acquiring interests in foreign firms involved in financial and real estate advisory services. In 1987 Nippon Life bought 13 percent of Shearson Lehman Brothers of the US, and Yasuda Mutual Life acquired 18 percent of the Paine Webber Group.[54] Foreign advisers counseled Japanese funds on property purchases in home markets, while domestic advisers managed the overall portfolio of international assets.

Since the creation of real estate portfolio fund management services by UK chartered surveyors in the mid-1920s, real estate advisory firms which gained competitive advantage among international pension and insurance funds were distinguished by a solid national practice – or European practice, in the case of UK firms – as well as in-depth knowledge of multiple markets, systematic appraisal and asset management skills, and, ideally, a coordinated worldwide network of offices.

International corporate real estate services

The ultimate objective of international corporate real estate services since its origins in Japan around 1937 was for property advisers to achieve the lowest systemwide costs for corporate clients across widely dispersed regions, cultures and varying price and tax structures.[55] As discussed in Chapter 2, Japanese holding companies were the first multinational investors to capitalize on the advantages of real estate advisers in the interest of pursuing cross-border trade and managing corporate real estate assets, domestically and abroad. Multinational, corporate-wide systems became especially widespread in the post-World War Two decades of the 1940s and 1950s, and advanced in the 1966–70 period when total outward direct investment rose by 200 percent, from $1.2 to $3.6 billion, most focused in US markets.[56]

Even while the largest Japanese group companies and leading European and US multinationals created internal property functions or retained corporate real estate services for owned and leased assets, the function still remained incidental to foreign expansions down to the early 1980s. Affiliated professional services that managed corporate cross-border transactions dominated international corporate real estate services and technical innovations. Multinational investment banks and securities firms in the US and UK and European merchant banks (such as Goldman Sachs, Merrill Lynch International, Salomon Brothers, S.G. Warburg and Nomura Securities) and international accounting firms (such as Arthur Andersen and Price Waterhouse) developed internal real estate divisions, recognizing that property services could be an important source of fee-based revenue in cross-border mergers, acquisitions and operational investments.[57] By cross-selling multiple services linked with international public securities and capital markets and foreign tax management and investment strategies, the banks and accounting firms constituted formidable competition with standard real estate advisory firms.

Japanese corporations achieved worldwide leadership in corporate real estate services because they recognized the critical role that corporate facilities and resources played in establishing new overseas operations or joint ventures with foreign partners.[58] Japanese holding companies recognized the inherent balance-sheet "value" of corporate property assets decades before US and European multinationals, primarily because property was a key element in Japan's interlocking economic structure. Corporations owned one-quarter of the land in the domestic market, while resident households owned 68 percent. Because Japan's public companies were priced for stock purposes based on the market value and cash yield of real estate assets, corporate property advisers appraised and adjusted the value of both operating and undeveloped properties on an annual and semi-annual basis. Escalating property valuations were used to finance additional investments in public markets, a practice which became widespread in US leveraged buyouts in the second half of the 1980s.[59]

Another important factor in serving multinationals: Japan's Mitsubishi Estate Company was the first property service firm among the focal countries to introduce an international structure (in 1937). By heritage rather than innovation, Japanese advisers operated within the group company's hierarchical structure that centered around efficient intercompany coordination across several nations. The real estate subsidiaries of Mitsubishi, Mitsui and Sumitomo shared in the pooled resources of the interlocking families of companies throughout the world, including market intelligence, technical skills, labor and capital. During the 1960–84 period, when Japanese outward direct real estate investment remained at low levels of approximately 1 to 2 percent of total outward direct investment, Japanese advisers served domestic clients in foreign markets at minimal risk, efficiently entering and exiting other countries because of the *keiretsu*'s established operations and reputation. After 1985, when Japanese groups increased capitalization levels in affiliated real estate service firms to expand operations in foreign markets, property firms moved expeditiously through global intercompany mechanisms.[60]

While development and corporate asset management services were a core product of Japanese real estate firms since their founding in 1937 – Mitsubishi Estate Company was the first – strict limitations on communication between Japanese and Western European enterprises until the 1980s blocked diffusion and the cross-border transfer of property skills. Instead, corporate services in the UK beginning in the mid-1960s, in the US in the late 1970s, and in Germany in the early 1980s, emerged out of home market conditions in response to corporate demand in foreign trade.

In the UK, corporate real estate services emerged concurrently with the post-World War Two redevelopment of Europe. The high-inflationary 1973–5 period marked a turning point for property-intensive corporations and created the demand to seek alternative, low-cost funding vehicles to raise cash for operations. Chartered surveyors responded by developing innovative funding structures, primarily promoting the widespread use of sale-leasebacks as well as the income-producing value of owned land.[61] To liquidate the residual value of corporate-owned buildings and factories, corporations sold property portfolios to insurance and pension funds (predominantly) and leased back the facilities for their own use. UK investors tended to take an equity interest in property during inflationary periods, rather than high, fixed-term interest loans or debentures, and corporations removed real estate assets from operating statements and added sales proceeds to income.[62] The first modern sale-leaseback in the US occurred in 1984, when investment banker Goldman Sachs arranged a sale-leaseback for Security Pacific National Bank on its $300 million headquarters, having adopted the technique from its London office.[63]

Until the late 1970s, most US real estate advisory firms committed resources to domestic markets, despite a market environment in which expanding multinationals were among the largest clients. With few exceptions, US advisers were slow to recognize opportunities to develop international asset and investment management services – notably because about one-third of US multinationals actively managed foreign real estate investment from central headquarters and the majority retained real estate brokers in foreign markets to execute individual transactions. Research for this book indicated that, until about 1978–9 and into the early 1980s, most US corporations also remained equally ignorant about the value, operating performance and strategic management of owned and leased property.[64] A clear shift in perspective occurred during the 1982–3 recession when poor balance-sheet performance increased corporate demand for proactive management of real estate assets and transactions. Rising foreign merger and acquisition activity in the 1983–8 period, as well as an increase in hostile takeovers, also motivated corporations to tap into the value of owned real estate in corporate transactions.[65]

Domestic investment banks, having long-standing relationships with corporate clients as well as international practices and direct knowledge of foreign property markets, were well-positioned to advise corporations on real estate matters. This competitive advantage prompted US real estate advisers to acquire advanced capabilities in corporate advisory services, and to introduce systematic valuation techniques and multiregional asset management programs to enable corporate clients to capitalize on real estate by reducing occupancy costs and leveraging the value of owned assets.[66] US real estate advisory firms figured prominently during the 1983–8 period in devising corporate capitalization strategies to fend off hostile takeovers as well as cross-border mergers and acquisitions, which encompassed over $110 billion of real estate assets.[67]

After 1983, US investment banks and real estate advisers were the primary sources of innovative corporate finance techniques: these included cross-border sale-leasebacks, participating corporate facilities leases, and wraparound "operating" leases.[68] With the rise in foreign investment in US markets during the 1983–90 period, which accounted for 8.4 to 10.7 per cent of total inward direct investment, US advisers enjoyed a prosperous investment climate to introduce innovative services. UK chartered surveyors, too, acquired the technical expertise and marketing skills for valuations and asset management in corporate mergers and acquisitions, responding to growing competition from US advisers and international investment banks. In Germany, public and private German corporations controlled the majority of commercial land and buildings, and corporate real estate services encompassed building management and project finance as well as agency and estate management.[69] Since the late 1950s, developers and builders had advised corporations and invested equity in corporate development. By the early 1980s, growing competition among real estate advisers forced firms to distinguish themselves with development services and to acquire project and asset management capabilities to gain competitive advantage with corporations against specialized builders.[70]

The 1989 downturn in real estate markets worldwide, and the resulting devaluation of corporate assets, prompted corporate managers in each of the focal countries to seek new strategies to reduce long-term facilities costs and to establish more efficient management standards for owned and leased property. In all four nations, managers and advisers developed performance benchmarks to achieve uniform operating standards and efficiencies throughout multiregional and multinational companies.[71] In the US and Europe, several corporations were able to improve operating results by downsizing in-house real estate departments and outsourcing to property advisers and asset managers.[72]

International financial and investment banking services

US and Japanese government regulations during the early 1960s separated property finance from commercial and industrial financial activities. This division of complementary functions fueled the growth of investment banking services to provide a bridge between real estate capital sources (both domestic and foreign) and property and non-property companies seeking debt and equity funds for property investments.[73] Leading European and US investment banks, merchant banks and commercial banks, which dominated world capital markets, were mostly responsible for introducing innovative financial structures and funding mechanisms in foreign markets down to the early 1980s. Financing innovations for property acquisitions, refinancings and new development created the service technology and cross-border networks ultimately adopted by real estate advisory firms after 1981.

Europe was the site of the earliest innovations. Following the unprecedented rise of German foreign direct real estate investment in 1959–61, German banks, notably Deutsche Bank, pioneered the use of long-term equity financing and participating debt finance for real estate in 1963 and 1965 respectively. Participating debt and equity loans were most appealing to pension and insurance funds in domestic and foreign investments because yields on capital investment tended to be higher. These popular funding structures subsequently spread across Europe and into US markets, becoming a central feature in cross-border property investment throughout the 1970s and 1980s.[74]

Since the early 1960s, full-line banks such as Deutsche Bank, Commerzbank and Dresdner Bank of Germany, and the investment bank of S.G. Warburg in the UK, were among the leading agents in each nation's foreign real estate investment activities, and also among the largest lead managers in the international Eurobond market.[75] Germany's largest banks, notably Deutsche Bank, pioneered the prevailing mechanisms in cross-border property finance and investment banking services during the 1965–75 period, funding structures designed for acquiring assets for corporate and institutional investors. The largest German bank funds investing in major US and European markets – Washington, DC, New York City, Chicago and London – tended to retain domestic advisers most familiar with these local markets, such as CB Commercial, Cushman & Wakefield, LaSalle Partners, Goldman Sachs, Jones Lang Wootton and Richard Ellis, thereby unintentionally promoting the cross-border transfer of investment banking criteria and property investment services.[76] Even though UK banks never came to dominate international real estate finance – either in the volume of outward investment or in service innovations – such British institutions as S.G. Warburg, Lloyds Merchant Bank and Baring Brothers were important contributors to the innovation process due to their close associations with leading chartered surveyors.

More than a decade passed before significant advances in international financial services occurred in the early 1980s, subsequent to financial market deregulation in New York City and Tokyo, and to a lesser extent in Frankfurt and Paris. Intensified competition among the world's major investment banks catapulted real estate financial services, and particular firms such as Goldman Sachs, Morgan Stanley and Salomon Brothers, from a cross-border business between individual nations to a global industry. Between 1981 and early 1987, the center of innovation in real estate financial services shifted from Germany to the US, specifically from Deutsche Bank to the leading investment banks headquartered in New York City. Concurrently, foreign direct real estate investment in US markets rose to unprecedented levels, increasing from 8.2 percent of total direct investment in 1981 to 10.7 percent in 1985, and 8.6 percent in 1987. US investment banks also occupied four of the top six positions in the league of Eurobond lead managers in 1981 and all of the top five positions in 1985, evidence of dominance in multinational capital investment services.[77]

The same five leading banks in 1985 were also among the top advisers of the largest cross-border mergers and acquisitions in 1988, transactions which typically involved real estate valuations that encompassed a significant number of diverse properties.[78] Deutsche Bank, for example, which had built an international property client base since its earliest years in corporate finance in the nineteenth century, commenced systematic property valuations of US and European commercial portfolios in 1989, retaining multiple international real estate advisory firms (including Arthur Andersen, Coldwell Banker and Jones Lang Wootton) to perform overlapping, checks-and-balance advisory and valuation functions.[79] Standard appraisals for individual properties were periodically evaluated in the context of comprehensive corporate and multinational strategies to determine corporate asset book values and debt and equity exposures through different economic cycles in major national–metropolitan markets, such as New York, London and Mexico.

The prominence of globalized financial services in domestic and foreign real estate investment after 1981, as well as the competitive advantage held by international investment banking houses in major real estate markets, prompted real estate advisory firms in the US, UK and Germany to diversify into financial services. The most immediate challenge came from major investment banks, which competed favorably for the advisory business of real estate services firms' existing clientele.[80] Extensive research capabilities, financial and real estate expertise, august reputations among investors worldwide (particularly publicly-traded multinationals), and strategic links to capital sources, sustained investment banks' competitive advantage in developing innovative financing techniques – multinational bank syndicates, corporate commercial paper, Eurobonds, LIBOR-rated bonds, and foreign equity and debt investment structures.[81]

National real estate advisory service firms relied on both formal and informal professional relationships with US investment banks to acquire knowledge about financial structures and foreign capital sources. While most real estate service firms maintained an independent advisory role, two US firms distinguished themselves as both financial advisers and property finance principals, or portfolio agents – Eastdil, founded in 1967, and JMB Realty Corporation, founded in 1969. Eastdil specialized in investment banking via offshore capital sources, notably in the Pacific Rim, while JMB focused on syndicated equity and debt packages, predominantly among major life insurance and pension funds – Aetna, CBS, Inland Steel, Xerox and Chrysler, for example.[82] The success of Eastdil and JMB during the high-inflationary period of the mid-1970s was instrumental in increasing the demand from domestic and foreign investors for technical (fee-based) and agency (commissioned-based) real estate services. They also helped to expand real estate investment banking and financial services beyond the exclusive realm of international investment banks.[83]

The real estate advisory firms researched for this book indicated that, following the turbulent economy of the late 1970s and the worldwide recession during 1979–81, public and private investors, domestic and foreign, looked to invest long-term ("patient") equity into appreciating US real estate assets, income-producing property that yielded fixed and preferred returns. Investors sought flexible financing mechanisms that minimized risk through fixed rates of return and captured long-term capital appreciation by preferred partnership positions. Cushman & Wakefield of the US and Jones Lang Wootton of the UK, for example, assisted investment and commercial bankers at Goldman Sachs, Salomon Brothers, Citicorp and others, tailored debt and equity structures for individual transactions, and executed cross-border capital alliances to fund land acquisition, real estate development and long-term ownership. In the US and UK, the national insurance companies and pension funds remained the primary source of long-term debt and equity finance through the early 1980s when leading banks, such as Morgan Grenfell and S.G. Warburg in the UK, and First Boston and Goldman Sachs in the US, emerged as important sources of long-term debt for developers, multinationals and foreign investors.[84] The investment banks and insurance companies competed for funding deals on the basis of property services, finance fees and equity participation. A qualitative factor for the investor/developer seeking a venture partner was the quality of the business relationship. Quantitative factors included the quality of the advisers' property and financial services, the amount of equity participation offered, and the overall fee structure proposed to complete a debt/equity investment. In many instances, such as the 1987–8 development of Goldman Sachs International headquarters in the City of London, the equity principals also acted as the adviser for investment partnership.

In another transaction, Jones Lang Wootton assisted in formulating a mixed debt/equity structure in 1982 for the first phase of Broadgate, also in the City of London. The managing partners, Rosehaugh/Greycoat, secured debt financing for the real property, backed by the syndicate's equity investment, in the joint venture development company. Jones Lang Wootton was instrumental in managing the newly created investment syndicate of insurance and pension funds and corporate investors designed to raise equity for the Rosehaugh/Greycoat project through subscription shares in the project-specific development company. The syndicate also secured through debenture guarantees short-term debt to fund construction costs. Within five years, the project was built, fully leased, and generating positive cash flow. In 1987 the development partnership sold its shares to a managing building owner, a sale which returned the partners' original principal investment plus a profitable capital return.[85]

Participating debt represented another prevalent form of debt/equity financing by international pension and insurance funds after the early 1980s. Widely used and promoted by leading US investment banks such as Goldman Sachs, Morgan Stanley, Salomon Brothers and JMB Realty, participating financing combined traditional lending with equity participation – either in a portion of operating cash flow and/or a preferred return at the time of a capital event – sale or refinancing.[86] Another creative debt/equity combination, bordering on securitization, was developed in 1985–6 by Goldman Sachs of the US for Billingsgate City Securities of the UK, a scheme which involved a conventional company issuing two classes of share capital – ordinary shares and preferred share (the latter quoted on the Luxembourg Stock Exchange) supplemented by a deep-discount first mortgage bond. US and European shareholders participated in 30 percent of the Billingsgate development project's operating income and capital appreciation while having no direct ownership in the property.[87]

International bank syndicates (which real estate advisory firms often assisted in organizing and which totaled $20 billion in US assets in 1984 alone) also encouraged cross-border innovation and provided a productive environment for the diffusion of concepts and services.[88] In-house and retainer property advisers guided international banks (e.g. Citicorp and BankAmerica in the US, and Morgan Grenfell and N.M. Rothschild in the UK) with direct financings and international loan syndicates, such as the $5 billion Canary Wharf in London's Docklands development funding led by Morgan Stanley International, Citibank, Chemical Bank, Canada's four largest commercial banks, and J.P. Morgan.[89]

The New York City offices of UK and German investment banks active in US real estate markets during the 1980s, as well as the London offices of New York investment houses in Europe, transported acquired skills and techniques to European markets.[90] The UK's oldest merchant bank, Barings, acquired the real estate investment fund division of Landauer in 1989, renaming it Barings Institutional Realty Advisors. Barings Asset Management group also entered Japan, seeking to gain access to domestic capital for European and US property investments. Its former national partner in Japan, UK real estate adviser Hillier Parker, formed a new alliance with Japan Pacific Partners Ltd to advise US and European enterprises seeking Japanese investments and Japanese investors entering US markets.[91] Because British banks were less willing to lend to and invest in property after 1988, Barings and other leading UK advisers and bankers further internationalized financial services and turned to foreign capital funding sources.[92]

Japanese commercial banks were the principal targets, which had originally introduced commercial paper financing to domestic markets in 1958–9. In their capacity as investors and established institutional fund managers, Japan's commercial banks were the single largest source of real estate capital during the property boom of 1986–8, and effectively financed the nation's foreign investment surge.[93] However, they did not introduce new investment techniques and financial services, instead adopting those of US banks (on which they had the results of extensive research). In 1987 the MOF and Bank of Japan curtailed real estate lending by commercial banks in the face of rising volumes of nonperforming loans, and Japan's major investment banks stepped in.[94] Japanese investment banks, entering the international marketplace at a relatively late date and in the face of declining foreign investment, competed for the real estate financial services business of US and UK banks and property advisers. A few Japanese financial services firms, including Orix, Nomura

Securities and Sumitomo, entered cooperative agreements with or acquired equity interests in foreign real estate advisory firms, primarily in the US and UK. Nomura Securities, for example, which had a growing domestic real estate services practice, sought to capitalize on the two-fold rise in Japanese foreign direct real estate investment during 1985–6. In 1989 the Japanese securities firm acquired a 50 percent interest in Eastdil, the premier US real estate financial services firm of the 1970s. Nomura offered an entree to capital-rich Japanese investors and reinforced Eastdil's skills in innovative financial structures.[95] By the late 1980s, technical innovations that moved through international markets during 1982–7 were commonplace and appeared less critical to domestic and foreign property investment. Instead, international firms indicated that they now competed on the basis of established investor–client relationships and the ability to bring together compatible financial partners in cross-border investments. By 1990 financial services of real estate advisers and investment bankers focused on defining clients' investment criteria and the terms of the relationship with a foreign partner or in a foreign market.[96]

Public capital and securitized investment services

The capital-intensive real estate investment surge of the 1980s ended abruptly in late 1989–early 1990: Japanese investors pulled back from real estate loans and acquisitions; German funds slowed foreign investments to capitalize on expanded domestic opportunities; and US and UK investors restrained new investments in property assets in the face of a rising number of nonperforming assets. Real estate securities experienced marked growth and a capital expansion in the early 1960s in national markets in the UK, US and Germany, and became quite prevalent again after 1989.

Historical public-markets data suggest that securitized commercial property demand rose during periods when the availability of real estate investment capital diminished. In each of the focal countries, public markets tended to prevail as sources of real estate funding during periods of low/negative investment yields (i.e. the UK in 1967–71); a proportionate decline in inward investment flows (i.e. the US in 1987); turbulence in domestic real estate markets (i.e. Japan in 1965–70); and less willingness to lend or invest by traditional sources (i.e. the UK, 1963–7). Securitized investment carried higher upfront costs than direct debt and equity investments, yet appealed to investors during down-cycles in economic growth and property markets because of the liquidity and minimized risk (and return) of pooled assets.[97] By converting assets into tradable paper securities, unit shares provided greater liquidity, current cash flow potential, and, most important, risk-sharing portfolios – whether for a single property or for multiple assets and markets.

But commercial equity and debt issues historically were more difficult to package and sell in bulk on public markets, as characteristically they were structured with varying terms to reflect varying levels of risk – in contrast to the standardized structure of residential mortgage-backed securities, from which they originated. Anecdotal evidence suggested that investor demand for securitized real estate in the US, UK and Japan ebbed and flowed relative to the rise and fall, respectively, of private real estate capital markets as well as the availability of bank and insurance debt and equity funds.[98]

Real estate advisers tended to be reactive, rather than proactive, to investor (or client) demand for securitized investment services, responding to the strength/weakness of public securities markets and national capital availability. Public property companies listed on the London market experienced significant growth after 1958, as insurance companies and pension funds recorded losses and reduced property funding commitments.[99] In 1970 the first insurance property bond fund merged with a publicly quoted property investment company, known as Fordham Life and General Assurance Company, which raised concerns about conflicts of interest and the financial risks of overlapping investment markets.[100] Yet property unit trusts, or PUTs, established in 1966 and backed by real estate assets rather than the reputation of particular firms, generated only moderate interest from investors. PUTs constituted only about 5 percent of equity investment in domestic real estate during the late 1960s and early 1970s. Related advisory services were simply integrated into the mainline practice of real estate advisory firms – appraisal, estate management, investment sales and research. The high-interest rate environment of the mid-1970s reduced the attractiveness of equity securities as a source of real estate investment capital; they would not re-emerge for more than a decade.[101]

The US market was eminently familiar with residential securities, the primary source of government-insured mortgage funds since the 1940s. In 1960, US investment banks and real estate advisers successfully lobbied for the creation of real estate investment trusts (REITs), tax-exempt investment vehicles designed to increase the supply of mortgage capital. REITs were structured similarly to tax-exempt business trusts or property holding companies for corporate facilities, and inspired by the success of the domestic market in securitized residential mortgages – rather than by the commercial experience in the UK. During the first decade, REITs sold only equity securities and shares of beneficial interests in other REITs.[102]

The recession and high-inflationary environment of 1976–7, however, prompted bankers and advisers to develop lower cost debt vehicles accessible to a broader spectrum of investors. In response, BankAmerica issued the first commercial mortgage-backed security in 1977 in the US.[103] REITs gained widespread favor among domestic investors and large institutional funds during the late 1970s and early 1980s, but attracted modest investment capital from abroad.[104] When inward direct real estate investment rose to over 10 percent of total foreign investment during 1981–2, US real estate companies and property funds largely shifted away from REITs with offshore investment funds in abundance. In addition, critics argued that real estate advisers had overvalued the income potential and market value of assets. As domestic investors and property companies shifted to direct, private investment markets during the 1980s, publicly traded REIT yields declined, posting the worst performance during the decade in 1989–90.[105] During the 1990s, the US exploded with office, retail, industrial and other REIT formation. Firms managed by Sam Zell and Bill Sanders were national leaders in the consolidation of property portfolios.

In Germany, rigorous property finance laws dating back to 1900 limited the number of institutions permitted to issue public mortgage bonds, principally public-sector commercial banks, and allowed only real estate advisory firms experienced in domestic lending laws to appraise property portfolios. The first, Grundbesitz-Invest, established in 1970, was controlled entirely by Deutsche Bank and included seventy-three properties across Germany by 1990.[106] The largest among the top twelve open-end property funds, DEGI, was 65 percent controlled by Dresdner Bank, which, through the offices of its in-house real estate advisory group, encompassed 110 geographically diversified commercial properties.[107]

High-quality German funds, which attracted up to 70,000 domestic and foreign investors by 1990, set the standards that financial institutions in the US, UK and Japan sought to achieve in the late 1980s. With falling property values worldwide, institutional and private investors required flexibility through liquid equity investments, at home and abroad, and holders of real estate debt and equities looked to convertible securities for nonperforming assets. In Japan, for example, the MOF encouraged commercial banks – Nomura, Saiwa, Nikko and Yamaichi – to convert mortgage portfolios into equity securities. Yet Japan's mature secondary mortgage residential market had little appetite for commercial mortgage-backed securities.[108] Even so, in 1990 Goldman Sachs International and Daiwa Real Estate advisers established an alliance to sell large-scale commercial securities packages to Japanese and foreign investors.[109]

International portfolios of securitized commercial properties were the most recent innovation in cross-border investment in 1990, and real estate advisers and commercial and investment banks had only begun to test their acceptance in global capital and Eurobond markets. While such fundamental skills in research, valuation, asset management and finance are required, competitive advantage depends on innovative transactional techniques and capabilities, as well as on knowledge of multinational real estate and public securities markets.[110]

Competitive advantage in innovation

UK and Japanese real estate advisers enjoyed a distinct advantage in the international marketplace because of each nation's economic culture, which emphasized a self-defined and long-standing multinational stature. Individual firms tended to cultivate business strategies that coordinated allied technical functions and different investor groups, especially over wide-ranging geographic areas. Such multifunctional and multiregional practices were expensive to imitate in a relatively short period. A high degree of commitment to an organization, especially among Japanese firms, also encouraged trust among different (and sometimes competing) functions internally and decreased the need for hierarchical supervision, thus increasing the flow of communication, cooperation and innovation.

Throughout the period between 1960 and 1997, the comparatively open structure of the property services profession, and its multifunctional disciplines, attracted competition from niche firms in investment banking, accounting, appraisal and corporate finance. Such firms as Eastdil, Goldman Sachs, Nomura Securities, Price Waterhouse and Deutsche Bank were organized for constant research and innovation because of their specialized focus. The concentration of various types of investors in international markets also encouraged innovation to respond to their specialized demands.[111] In turn, this increased breadth heightened the value of multiregional coordination as well as local market/investor responsiveness.

Was a strategy of global integration anathema to local responsiveness? Japanese and German firms tended to emphasize centralized, product-oriented structures, which were ultimately less efficient for the innovation process.[112] In US and UK firms, which excelled in developing decentralized organizations that emphasized local-to-global production, local specialists were the primary sources of innovation.[113] International accounting, construction and corporate relocation firms that incorporated real estate advisory services into their businesses after 1975 tended to promote a centralized, product-oriented management structure, and acquired innovative services and technical skills from the marketplace rather than developing them internally.

Historically, real estate advisory service firms reacted to changes in markets and competitors' strategies rather than invest proactively in systematic research and the development of innovations. Strategic planning (based on market knowledge and analytical forecasts) remained a low priority, except among Japanese advisers who benefited from the umbrella support of parent holding companies.[114] Even so, local market knowledge throughout the thirty-seven-year period was the core of developing new skills and the basis for counseling investors on market risks, tax impacts and the cultural practices of nations and regions.

Notes

1 A.D. Chandler, Jr., defined the move into new functions as vertical integration and the development of new products as diversification, in *Strategy and Structure: Chapters in the History of American Industrial Enterprise* (Cambridge, MA: MIT

Press, 1962), p. 14. Also see R.W. Jones and F. Ruane, "Appraising the Options for International Trade in Services", *Oxford Economic Papers*, vol. 42, no. 4 (Oct. 1990), pp. 672–87, which argued that "opening up trade in either the service factor or the service product will improve economic welfare" (p. 686).

2 Chapter 2, Table 2.1.

3 Chapter 2, Table 2.3. J.S. Metcalfe and M. Gibbons, "Technology, Variety and Organization: A Systematic Perspective on the Competitive Process", in *Research on Technological Innovation, Management and Policy*, ed. R.S. Rosenbloom (London: JAI Press, 1989), pp. 154–8, 190.

4 P.A. Geroski argued that active markets generated more innovations and investment activity with higher total returns than less active ones, and that high import levels strengthened competition and productivity, in "Entry, Innovation and Productivity Growth", Working Paper Series No. 53, Centre for Business Strategy (London Business School, August 1988), pp. 20–1.

5 R. McLean III, Director of corporate real estate for Cushman & Wakefield, US, discussed the manner in which economic and market shifts gave rise to demand for innovative real estate advisory services in the 1970s and 1980s, in *Focus*, no. 952 (24 June 1987).

6 M. Casson argued that a nation's comparative advantage in innovation attracted the best professionals, whether in finance or the sciences, in *Global Research Strategy and International Competitiveness* (London: Basil Blackwell, 1991), pp. 77–9.

7 A. Baum and A. Schofield, "Property as a Global Asset", Working Papers in European Property, Centre for European Property Research (University of Reading, March 1991), p. 67.

8 Because national statistics for inward and outward direct real estate investment did not specify types of investors, this analysis relied on anecdotal assertions by market analysts and participants and historical accounts about real estate markets in the US, UK, Germany and Japan, as well as assertions by market analysts and industry participants, to determine each sector's relative contribution to cross-border investment activity and specific innovations at particular points in time.

9 A.D. Chandler, Jr., *Scale and Scope: The Dynamics of Industrial Capitalism* (Cambridge, MA: Belknap Press of Harvard University Press, 1990), p. 41. The structure and diseconomies of multimarket, multidiscipline investment banking firms were similar to real estate service firms, in I. Walter and R.C. Smith, *Investment Banking in Europe: Restructuring for the 1990s* (Oxford: Basil Blackwell, 1990), p. 136; also in G.J. Stigler, *The Organization of Industry* (Chicago: The University of Chicago Press, 1968), p. 99.

10 I have found no evidence of this cited in the literature on real estate advisory services, yet the research on the forty firms and the four case studies indicated a strong relationship between trade barriers and the international transfer of skills and knowledge.

11 Since 1986 the Group of Negotiations on Services at GATT in Geneva has begun to address cross-border trade interests of consultancy and construction services, principally focusing on developing countries. See D. Liston and N. Reeves, *The Invisible Economy: A Profile of Britain's Invisible Exports* (London: Pitman Publishing, 1988), p. 216.

12 C.K. Prahalad and Y.L. Doz, *The Multinational Mission: Balancing Local Demands and Global Vision* (New York and London: The Free Press, 1987), pp. 57–8.

13 Specific issues that a constitution for international trade in services might address were outlined by J.H. Jackson, in "Constructing a Constitution for Trade in Services", *The World Economy*, vol. 11, no. 2 (June 1988), pp. 187–202.

14 Based on research results of the forty firms and the four case studies. H.G. Grubel affirmed that certain service innovations derived from specific demand conditions, contending that services were consumed as they were produced in "All Traded Services Are Embodied in Materials or People", *The World Economy*, vol. 10, no. 3 (Sept. 1987), p. 319.

15 The experience of real estate advisory service firms reinforced G.B. Richardson's argument that "a firm has to settle down and 'digest' large expansions before it can successfully carry out others; otherwise, 'managerial diseconomies' would result from rapid expansion in widely dispersed markets", in *Information and Investment: A Study in the Working of the Competitive Economy* (Oxford: Clarendon Press, 1990), p. 59.

16 M. Casson argued that firms gained competitive advantage by capitalizing on proprietary technology or a superior business strategy, in *Enterprise and Competitiveness: A Systems View of International Business* (Oxford: Clarendon Press, 1990), pp. 86–7.

17 Leading international investment banks, whose principal focus was stock brokerage and securities, intermittently subsidized real estate departments to provide full-service support to corporate clients, including Deutsche Bank, Credit Suisse First Boston, Nomura Securities, Morgan Guaranty, Morgan Stanley, Salomon Brothers, S.G. Warburg, and Paribas. S.L. Hayes III and P.M. Hubbard, *Investment Banking: A Tale of Three Cities* (Boston: Harvard Business School Press, 1990), pp. 85–8. For an account of the international accounting profession's real estate-related services, see C. Rassam and D. Oates, *Management Consultancy: The Inside Story* (London: Mercury Business Books, 1991).

18 As documented for manufacturing by A.D. Chandler, Jr., innovations through joint production transformed existing industries and created many new ones, in *Scale and Scope: The Dynamics of Industrial Capitalism* (Cambridge, MA: Belknap Press of Harvard University Press, 1990), p. 21.

19 This finding conflicts with the conclusions presented by H.O. Armour and D.J. Teece, "Vertical Integration and Technological Innovation", *The Review of Economics and Statistics*, vol. 62, no. 3 (Aug. 1980), p. 470.

20 Virtually no published research on the profitability and sources of revenues exists for investment banks and real estate advisory services, yet the author's direct experience over the 1982–93 period (with Arthur Andersen, Goldman Sachs & Co., Jones Lang Wootton and Morgan Stanley) suggested that Goldman's and Morgan Stanley's ability to take an equity position in collaborative projects and with the ability of Arthur Andersen and Jones Lang Wootton to not participate, respectively, produced higher profits for Goldman Sachs and Morgan Stanley.

21 O.E. Williamson argued for diversification until managerial diseconomies set in, in *Markets and Hierarchies: Analysis and Antitrust Implications*, (New York and London: Free Press, 1975), p. 82; M.E. Porter and V.E. Millar argued the benefits of specialization, in "How Information Gives You Competitive Advantage", *Harvard Business Review* (July–August 1985), p. 151.

22 On this general point, see G.B. Richardson, *Information and Investment: A Study in the Working of the Competitive Economy*, (Oxford: Clarendon Press, 1990), p. viii.

23 L. Hannah, "International Perspectives on Competition and Regulatory Change in Pension Fund Asset Management", in *Pension Asset Management: An International Perspective*, ed. L. Hannah (Homewood, IL: Richard D. Irwin, 1988), pp. 1–13.

24 *Ibid.*, p. 6.
25 P. Scott, "Financial Institutions and the British Property Investment Market, 1850–1980." Unpublished DPhil thesis (Oxford University, 1992), pp. 97–8.
26 *The Economist* (30 March 1963), p. 1291; (28 January 1967), p. 356; (18 March 1972), p. 8; N. Morris, "Competition, Regulation, and Deregulation in Pension Fund Portfolio Management: The Case of the United Kingdom", in *Pension Asset Management: An International Perspective*, ed. L. Hannah (Homewood, IL: Richard D. Irwin, 1988), pp. 71, 75.
27 *The Economist* (5 November 1966), p. 610; (2 March 1968), p. 61; (6 July 1968), p. 69; (25 July 1970), p. 81; (11 September 1971), p. 93; (18 March 1972), p. 8; (23 September 1972), pp. 100–1; (8 September 1973), pp. 70–1. Property bond fund investments increased more than three-fold from December 1970 to September 1972, from £80 million to £300 million.
28 S.L. Barter, ed., *Real Estate Finance* (London: Butterworth, 1988), pp. 10–11.
29 P. Scott, "The Hammerson Investment & Development Corp., PLC", in *International Directory of Company Histories*, vol. IV, ed. A. Hast (London: St. James Press, 1991), pp. 696–7.
30 P. Scott, "MEPC PLC", in *International Directory of Company Histories*, vol. IV, ed. A. Hast (1991), pp. 710–12.
31 *The Economist* (10 June 1961), p. 152.
32 *The Economist* (12 September 1970), p. 91; (19 September 1970), p. 104.
33 "Are Investment Policies Changing?", *The Economist*, (22 July 1961), p. 381; A. Baum and A. Schofield, "Property as a Global Asset", Working Papers in European Property, Centre for European Property Research, University of Reading (March 1991), pp. 37–8; Royal Institution of Chartered Surveyors, *Finance in Property* (London, October 1977), p. 23.
34 J.N. Gordon, "Property Performance Indexes in the United Kingdom and the United States", *Real Estate Review* (Summer 1991), p. 34. UK pension funds with major real estate investment included National Coal, British Telecom, Electricity Supply, Post Office, and the British Railways Board, in S.L. Barter, ed., *Real Estate Finance* (London: Butterworth, 1988), p. 3.
35 L. Hannah, "International Perspectives on Competition and Regulatory Change in Pension Fund Asset Management", in *Pension Asset Management: An International Perspective*, ed. L. Hannah (Homewood, IL: Richard D. Irwin, 1988), p. 10; RICS, *Finance in Property*, p. 23.
36 *The Economist* (25 September 1971), pp. 106–7; (23 September 1972), pp. 100–1.
37 M. Mallinson, "Equity Finance", in S.L. Barter, ed., *Real Estate Finance* (London: Butterworth, 1988), pp. 66–9, 78–9. Also see R. Sobel, *Trammell Crow, Master Builder: The Story of America's Largest Real Estate Empire* (New York: John Wiley & Sons, 1989), pp. 133–4, on a Paris project guaranteed by two British pension funds; and E.L. Erdman, *People & Property* (London: B.T. Batsford Ltd, 1982), p. 73, on a Knightsbridge, London project sold to the BP Pension Fund.
38 UK chartered surveyors active in foreign markets also took on foreign institutional clients investing in the UK, thus becoming international channels for cross-border investment.
39 See P. Scott, "Learning to Multiply: The Property Market and the Growth of Multiple Retailing in Britain, 1919–39", *Business History* 36, No. 3 (1994), p. 23, n. 51, n. 63.
40 H. Barty-King, *Scratch a Surveyor*, (London: William Heinemann Ltd., 1975), p. 249.

41 A. Baum and A. Schofield, "Property as a Global Asset", Working Papers in European Property, Centre for European Property Research (University of Reading, March 1991), pp. 36–9; M. Mallinson, "Equity Finance", in S.L. Barter, ed., *Real Estate Finance* (London: Butterworth, 1988), p. 40; "U.K. Funds Still Shunning Real Estate, Fixed Income", *Pensions & Investments* (1 October 1990). Two UK performance measurement services are World Markets Co. and Combined Actuarial Performance Services (CAPS).

42 Property investment stemmed from the Insurance investment law no. 54. See S. Cowan, *The Guide to European Property Investment* I (London: Waterlow Publishers, 1989), pp. 8–9, 8–14 through 8–19; *The Economist* (22 December 1984), pp. 24–63.

43 Private company reports and public corporate statements, Jones Lang Wootton; Weatherall, Green & Smith; Hillier, Parker, May & Rowden; and the Zadelhoff Group (DTZ Debenham Thorpe).

44 Up until 1990, the German government prohibited open-end institutional funds from investing capital in foreign properties. Moreover, Germany's tax structure limited the growth of large, externally invested funds. See "New Briefs", *National Real Estate Investor* (July 1991), p. 16; Jones Lang Wootton, *JLWorld*, unpublished corporate brochure (May 1991), p. 19; and L. Hannah, "International Perspectives on Competition and Regulatory Change in Pension Fund Asset Management", in *Pension Asset Management: An International Perspective*, ed. L. Hannah (Homewood, IL: Richard D. Irwin, 1988), p. 1.

45 Assets and earnings rate of US life insurance companies, 1955–90, American Council of Life Insurance files, Washington, DC.

46 D.A. Love, "U.S. Pension Fund Asset Management", in *Pension Asset Management: An International Perspective*, ed. L. Hannah, (Homewood, IL: Richard D. Irwin, 1988), pp. 65–6.

47 See Chapter 3, pp. 124–5, Chapter 4, pp. 138 and 141, and Appendix D, p. 331, for definition of the concept of "value creation".

48 BankAmerica, for example, advised CALPERS, California's largest state pension fund, on mortgage lending and real estate investments through the US and the UK. The pension funds of General Motors Corporation and AT&T (prior to the break-up) were advised by major investment banks in structuring a $685 million participating loan to Taubman Realty Group; see *Washington Post* (21 June 1991), p. H1. LaSalle Partners, Chicago real estate advisors, typically managed property investments for pension fund clients; see "LaSalle Partners' Mike Bell: Sharp-Eyed Insights from the Service Provider Side", *Site Selection* (December 1990), p. 1357.

49 H. Rosenberg, "Will U.S. Pension Funds Go Global?", *Institutional Investor* (March 1989), p. 123.

50 "Pension Funds Off Target", *World Property* (March 1990), p. 42; G.F. Blundell and C.W.R. Ward, "Property Portfolio Allocation: A Multi-Factor Model", *Land Development Studies* (May 1987), pp. 145–56; J. Lewis, "MPT Comes to Real Estate", *Institutional Investor* (February 1990), pp. 153–60.

51 See *Pension Funds and Their Advisors 1990/91: The Blue Book of the Global Pension Fund Industry* (Tiburon, CA: Global Info-Net Inc., 1990), which publishes statistical data on how and where the major funds from ten countries, including the four focal countries, invest their assets. Also, discussion of pension fund real estate investment and future outlook, in "Future Opportunities for Pension Fund Investment in Real Estate", proceedings of a Seminar at the Center for Real Estate Development, Massachusetts Institute of Technology (3 December 1984); and L. Hannah, "International Perspectives on Competition and Regulatory

Change in Pension Fund Asset Management", in *Pension Asset Management: An International Perspective*, ed. L. Hannah (Homewood, IL: Richard D. Irwin, 1988), pp. 2, 9.

52 In the US, the Frank J. Russell Company/MCREIF Property Index is the most widely used valuation benchmark. In addition, Jones Lang Wootton, Cushman & Wakefield/Healey & Baker, Landauer, and Morgan Stanley International publish international real estate market reports. D.J. Kostin, "An Initial Benchmark Portfolio for Global Office Building Investments", Bond Market Research pamphlet, Salomon Brothers (4 October 1989), p. 2; J.N. Gordon, "Property Performance Indexes in the United Kingdom and the United States", *Real Estate Review* (Summer 1991), p. 40; M. Hay and P. Williamson, *The Strategy Handbook* (Oxford: Basil Blackwell, 1991), pp. 16–18.

53 This also coincided with the Japanese Ministry of Finance's initiative to increase the amount of assets allocated to foreign investments. Prior to 1986, MOF limited foreign assets to 10 percent of pension trust funds; after 1986 the limit was raised to 25 percent. The maximum limit for real estate investments was set at 20 percent of total assets; see N. Terada, "Pension Fund Portfolio Management in Japan", in *Pension Asset Management: An International Perspective*, ed. L. Hannah, (Homewood, IL: Richard D. Irwin, 1988), p. 167.

54 D. Ostrom, "Japanese Insurance Companies", *Japan Economic Institute Report* (12 August 1988), no. 31A.

55 The cost efficiencies sought by multinationals in foreign facility transactions and property investments attempted to alleviate what R.H. Coase described in "The Nature of the Firm" (first published in *Economica*, n.s., 4, November 1937) as "the costs of organizing and the losses through mistakes will increase with an increase in the spatial distribution of the transactions organized, in the dissimilarity of the transactions, and in the probability of changes in the relevant prices", p. 25. Also see C.K. Prahalad and Y.L. Doz, *The Multinational Mission: Balancing Local Demands and Global Vision* (New York and London: The Free Press, 1987), p. 41.

56 The leading Japanese international corporate real estate services firms were subsidiaries of the large holding companies, including Mitsubishi Estate Company Ltd (est. 1937), Mitsui Real Estate Development Co., Ltd (est. 1941), and Tokyu Land Corporation (est. 1953).

57 S.L. Hayes III and P.M. Hubbard, *Investment Banking: A Tale of Three Cities* (Boston: Harvard Business School Press, 1990), pp. 278, 333–4; M. Stevens, *The Big Six: The Selling Out of America's Top Accounting Firms* (New York: Simon & Schuster, 1991).

58 Even though Japanese corporations frequently retained foreign financial advisors to negotiate financial transactions, in real estate-related matters they ultimately relied on real estate subsidiaries for counsel on corporate assets. One example is the Toshiba–Westinghouse joint venture, in which each partner divided ownership of corporate assets in a ratio of 50.1 percent/49.9 percent respectively, including the Westinghouse facility in the US where the new joint corporation is housed. For a discussion of corporate real estate's role in foreign expansion, see S. Goldenberg, *Hands Across the Ocean: Managing Joint Ventures with a Spotlight on China and Japan* (Boston: Harvard Business School Press, 1988), pp. 80, 139.

59 L.S. Bacow, "The Tokyo Land Market: An Essay", Working Paper Series No. 26, Center for Real Estate Development (Massachusetts Institute of Technology, October 1990), pp. 10–11; and M.A. Hines, *Investing in Japanese Real Estate* (New York: Quorum Books, 1987), p. 19.

60 Xerox, Disney Corporation and IBM were the largest US multinationals to establish corporate real estate service affiliates, as were Smith Kline Beecham in the UK and Siemens in Germany. Japanese firms never entered a global network affiliation; these were sponsored by US and European corporations.

61 British Rail created a separate property company, advised by chartered surveyors in planning joint development projects on large land parcels; see *The Economist* (14 July 1973), p. 77; C.G. Powell, *An Economic History of the British Building Industry, 1815–1979* (London: Methuen, 1982), pp. 176–83.

62 S.L. Barter, ed., *Real Estate Finance* (London: Butterworth, 1988), pp. 119–20; The Royal Institution of Chartered Surveyors, *Finance in Property* (London: October 1977), pp. 3, 16. For recent practices, see V. Houlder, "How Under-Used Assets Can Be Exploited", *Financial Times* (17 May 1991).

63 C.A. Manning, "Getting Things Done: The Economics of Real Estate Decisions", *Harvard Business Review*, no. 6 (November–December 1986), p. 12. Union Carbide structured a sale-leaseback of its Connecticut headquarters as an anti-takeover defense, and Amoco Corp. established a real estate fund of its prime property assets for the same reason; cited in M.A. Hines, *Global Corporate Real Estate Management: A Handbook for Multinational Businesses and Organizations* (New York: Quorum Books, 1990), pp. 3, 15–18, 30; A.M. Berman, R.J. Jinnett and R.A.N. Cudd, "Strategic Use of Real Estate Against the Hostile Takeover Bid", *The Real Estate Finance Journal* (Winter 1989), pp. 1–2.

64 S. Zeckhauser and R. Silverman, "Rediscover Your Company's Real Estate", *Harvard Business Review* (January–February 1983), pp. 111–17.

65 For a chronicle of growing recognition by US corporations that real estate assets were an important financial resource, see C.A. Manning, "Getting Things Done: The Economics of Real Estate Decisions", *Harvard Business Review*, no. 6 (November–December 1986), p. 12. For an analysis of US and European mergers and acquisitions, 1983–8, see I. Walter and R.C. Smith, "European Investment Banking: Structure, Transactions Flow and Regulation", in *European Banking in the 1990s*, ed. J. Dermine (London: Basil Blackwell, 1990), pp. 115–25.

66 US corporations appraise real estate assets at book value (original cost less depreciation), rather than market value; this valuation technique increases corporations' vulnerability to takeovers in strong real estate markets by understating the value of owned assets; see R.K. Brown, "Competitiveness, the CEO and Real Estate Decisions", *National Real Estate Investor* (October 1987), p. 54; H. Nourse, IDREC report, p. 6.

67 Between 1983 and 1988, total cross-border mergers and acquisitions rose from 16 percent to 43 percent of all transactions worldwide, most hosted by US and European buyers and sellers. Real estate assets represented approximately 25 percent of corporate value (a conservative estimate); in the US, $172.6 billion of international mergers and acquisitions occurred, most of which were sponsored by European buyers and sellers; outside of the US, transactions valued at $294 billion were executed; see I. Walter and R.C. Smith, *Investment Banking in Europe: Restructuring for the 1990s* (Oxford: Basil Blackwell, 1990), pp. 45–8.

68 M.G. Star, "Financing Arranged for Office", *Pensions & Investments* (17 September 1990); K.C. Knutsen, "The Impact of Real Estate on Operations and Financial Statements: Sale-Leaseback Transactions", *Site Selection* (November 1990), p. 27 (1409); W.T. McGrath, "Unwrapping Leasehold Equity: An Introduction to the 'Wraparound Lease'", *Real Estate Review*, vol. 19, no. 4 (Winter 1990), pp. 23, 26–7; R. Waters, "Goldman Sachs Heads Towards a Half-Way House", *Financial Times* (12 June 1991); A.M. DiSciullo and J.B. Wood, "Financing Real Estate

Development Through Participation Leases", *Real Estate Review*, vol. 20, no. 4 (Winter 1991), p. 30.

69 Only the largest German corporations recognized the value and practice of corporate real estate services, including VEBA, Volkswagen, VIAB, BASF and some of the largest transport companies.

70 D.J. Kostin, "German Real Estate Market: An Introduction for Non-German Investors", report for Salomon Brothers (New York, April 1991), p. 23; S.E. Roulac, "The Globalization of Real Estate Finance", *The Real Estate Finance Journal*, vol. 4, no. 2 (1987), p. 44. German corporations also preceded major UK and US companies in developing internal real estate functions, established to manage corporate property assets at home and abroad; see L. Liston, "Peter Ball of Philips: Advocate for Asset Management", *Site Selection Europe* (March 1992), p. 6.

71 R.K. Brown, "Competitiveness, the CEO and Real Estate Decisions", *National Real Estate Investor* (October 1987), p. 54; M.J. Joroff, "Corporate Real Estate 2000: Management Strategies for the Next Decade", Industrial Development Research Foundation, (Washington, DC: 1992).

72 G. Schuck, "Outsourcing in the 1990s: Managing Corporate Real Estate Consultants", Working Paper No. 33, Massachusetts Institute of Technology, Center for Real Estate Development (June 1991); J. Lyne, "The Out-Sourcing of Real Estate: Entrenched, Growing and Controversial", *Site Selection* (February 1991), pp. 50–8; L. Kimbler, "Corporate Real Estate Outside Services Survey", unpublished presentation at the Industrial Development Research Council Conference (Fall 1991); L. Liston, "Peter Ball of Philips: Advocate for Asset Management", *Site Selection Europe* (March 1992), pp. 6, 8; *Wall Street Journal* (4 June 1992), p. B1.

73 See D. Liston and N. Reeves, *The Invisible Economy: A Profile of Britain's Invisible Exports* (London: Pitman Publishing, 1988), pp. 48–9, for national regulations governing financial institutions in the focal countries.

74 In the UK, British investment banks were among the principal managers of institutional funds, the primary sources of long-term real estate credit.

75 For a ranking of lead managers in Eurobond markets, 1969–87, see G. Dufey, "The Role of Japanese Financial Institutions Abroad", in *Japanese Financial Growth*, ed. C.A.E. Goodhart and G. Sutija (London: Macmillan, 1990), p. 149.

76 Public corporate reports and private company files, confirmed by author via direct interviews.

77 During the 1981–7 period, Deutsche Bank dominated international real estate finance, ranking fourth among Eurobond lead managers in 1981, sixth in 1985, and third in 1987; see G. Dufey, "The Role of Japanese Financial Institutions Abroad", in *Japanese Financial Growth*, ed. C.A.E. Goodhart and G. Sutija (London: Macmillan, 1990), p. 149.

78 *Ibid.*, Table 9.3 (reprint from *Euromoney*, March 1989).

79 Deutsche Bank, "Deutsche Bank – A Brief History", (Frankfurt am Main, December 1989); Arthur Andersen Real Estate Services Group, USA, confidential corporate reports.

80 M. Wilkins, *The Maturing Multinational Enterprise: American Business Abroad from 1914 to 1970* (Cambridge, MA: Harvard University Press, 1974), pp. 393–5; S.L. Hayes III and P.M. Hubbard, *Investment Banking: A Tale of Three Cities* (Boston: Harvard Business School Press, 1990), pp. 251–63; R. Volhard, D. Weber and W. Usinger, eds, *Real Property In Germany: Legal and Tax Impacts of Development and Investment* (Frankfurt: Fritz Knapp Verlag, 1975, 1991), pp. vii,

74–81; and P. Kavanaugh, "Levy, Younce, Roth Ease U.S. Firms' Entree Into Europe", *Commercial Property News* 16 April 1991, p. 27.

81 P.D. Kazilionis, "Real Estate Finance", in *The Investment Banking Handbook*, ed. J.P. Williamson (New York: John Wiley & Sons, 1988), pp. 176–8; "Bankers Trust Co., On the Move in Tokyo", *Euromoney* (February 1988), pp. 40–3; S.L. Barter, ed., *Real Estate Finance* (London: Butterworth, 1988), pp. 14–16; Ian Flanagan, Chairman, Landauer Associates, interview with author (London: 30 July 1991).

82 P. Kavanaugh, "Levy, Younce, Roth Ease U.S. Firms' Entree Into Europe", *Commercial Property News* 16 April 1991, p. 26; J. Martin, "JMB Realty Corporation", in *International Directory of Company Histories* IV, ed. A. Hast (London: St. James Press, 1991), pp. 702–3.

83 Eastdil's partnership with The Nomura Group of Japan, 1986, broadened the geographic scope and active participation of real estate advisory service firms in foreign capital markets.

84 *The Economist* (3 April 1976); Royal Institute of Chartered Surveyors, Finance in Property (London: Royal Institute of Chartered Surveyors, October 1997), pp. 23–5; *The Economist* (11 September 1976); R.J. Wolfe, "Debt Finance", in *Real Estate Finance*, ed. S.L. Barter (London: Butterworth, 1988), pp. 83, 96.

85 S.L. Barter, *Real Estate Finance* (London: Butterworth, 1988), pp. 21–3.

86 D. Bramson, "The Mechanics of Joint Ventures", in *Real Estate Finance*, ed. S.L. Barter (London: Butterworth, 1988), pp. 139–49.

87 D. Hughes, "Necessity is the Mother of Invention", *Accountancy* (April 1987), p. 118.

88 D. Lake, "Japan and Mortgage-Backed Securities", *World Property* (March 1990), p. 34.

89 N. Barsky, "Olympia & York, New York City Set Restructuring of Firm's Property Taxes", *Wall Street Journal* (22 May 1992), p. A3; L. Light, "Even the Reichmanns are Feeling the Pinch", *Business Week* (8 October 1990), pp. 128–9; W. Claiborne and K. Day, "A Dynasty of Control", *The Washington Post* (26 April 1992), p. H1; W. Claiborne and K. Day, "Bank Experts Differ on Impact of Surprise Bankruptcy Filings", *The Washington Post* (16 May 1992), p. C1; G. Frankel, "Futuristic London Project Threatened", *The Washington Post* (24 May 1992), p. A39.

90 For example, Natwest Bankcorp, the US subsidiary of a UK clearing bank, was heavily committed to loan syndicates in US property, which, in the 1990–1 market downturn, produced $1.3 billion of losses; see "British Bank Is Hit for $352 million Loss in America", *The European* (1–3 February 1991).

91 Barings annual report (1989); Ian Flanagan, Senior Partner of Hillier Parker, interview with author (London: 30 July 1991).

92 S.L. Barter, ed., *Real Estate Finance* (London: Butterworth, 1988), p. 18.

93 Japanese partners played a major role in foreign markets, facilitating the growth of real estate investment banking services worldwide.

94 In 1987, Japanese investment banks represented five of the top ten lead managers in Eurobond placements. G. Dufey, "The Role of Japanese Financial Institutions Abroad", in *Japanese Financial Growth*, ed. C.A.E. Goodhart and G. Sutija (London: Macmillan, 1990), p. 149. *The Economist* (28 May 1988), p. 609; G.A. Goodman, "Pacific Basin Investment in U.S. Real Estate: An Overview for the Professional Adviser", *Real Estate Finance Journal*, vol. 5, no. 3 (Fall 1988), p. 54; H. Mitani, "Capital from Japan, Part II: Gaining Access to Japanese Investors", *Real Estate Finance Journal*, vol. 4, no. 4 (Winter 1988), pp. 19–25; A.H. Levy, E.M. Marks and J.B. Weller, "Convertible Mortgages Lure Creative

Investors and Owners", *Real Estate Review*, vol. 18 no. 4 (Winter 1989), p. 30; T. Shale, "Clipping the Wings of Japan's High Flyers", *Euromoney* (June 1990), pp. 70–2.

95 S.L. Hayes III and P.M. Hubbard, *Investment Banking: A Tale of Three Cities* (Boston: Harvard Business School Press, 1990); Eastdil Realty Corporate services brochure (New York: 1990–1).

96 S.L. Barter, ed., *Real Estate Finance* (London: Butterworth, 1988), pp. 17–18; *Chartered Surveyor Weekly* (18 July 1991), p. 11.

97 Higher costs of asset-backed securities were due to the need for prospectuses, advertising, appraisers, lawyers, accountants, brokers' fees and underwriters.

98 S.L. Barter, ed., *Real Estate Finance* (London: Butterworth, 1988), p. 23; R.J. Wolfe, "Debt Finance", in S.L. Barter, ed., *Real Estate Finance* (London: Butterworth, 1988), p. 38; T.J. Jenkinson, "Initial Public Offerings in the United Kingdom, the United States, and Japan", *Journal of the Japanese and International Economies*, vol. 3, no. 4 (December 1990), pp. 428–49.

99 *The Economist* (16 January 1963), p. 348; (14 September 1963), p. 946; (11 November 1967), p. 638; (28 September 1968), pp. 77–8.

100 *The Economist* (1 August 1970), p. 60.

101 RICS, *Finance in Property*, pp. 23–4.

102 *The Economist* (18 March 1972), p. 8; M.A. Hines, *Marketing Real Estate Internationally* (New York: Quorum Books, 1988), pp. 158, 163.

103 UK investors might have taken advantage of persistent differences between US and UK markets, and invested in US REITs, but this did not occur. In the US and UK, demand for real estate securities was uneven and highly localized in national markets until the late 1980s. See P.A. Geroski and S. Toker, "Picking Profitable Markets", Centre for Business Strategy, London Business School (November 1988).

104 By 1987 the US commercial securities market was valued at over $600 billion. W. Kay, "Bringing Security to Hearth and Home", *Euromoney* (December 1987), pp. 159–60; T.S. Schubert, "Publicly Traded Real Estate and the Myth of Inherent Appreciation", *The Real Estate Finance Journal*, vol. 7, no. 3 (Fall 1990), p. 58.

105 *Ibid.*, pp. 53–7.

106 Grundbesitz-Invest (Deutsche Grundbesitz-Investmentgesellschaft mbH), Deutsche Bank, custodian, annual reports, 1970–90.

107 D.J. Kostin, "German Real Estate Market: An Introduction for Non-German Investors", report for Salomon Brothers (New York, April 1991), pp. 22–3; J. van den Bos, "JLW Signs up to Manage German Buying Spree", *Chartered Surveyor Weekly* (31 January 1991), p. 7.

108 *The Economist* (24 September 1988), p. 565; A.J. Alletzhauser, *The House of Nomura* (New York: Arcade Publishing, 1990), p. xi. Assessments of 1990 Japanese securitization in Kenneth Leventhal & Co., "Japanese Capital Flows: Availability and Constraints", unpublished report (1992); S.L. Barter, ed., *Real Estate Finance* (London: Butterworth, 1988), pp. 23–6.

109 D. Lake, "Japan and Mortgage-Backed Securities", *World Property* (March 1990), p. 34.

110 Goldman Sachs & Co. reports (1990); confirmed by author in interview with Richard Moore, Vice President (April 1993).

111 The specialized demands of different investor groups in the four focal countries are assessed in the case studies in Chapter 6.

112 These findings are based on the profiles of firms reviewed in Chapter 4 and the case studies analyzed in Chapter 6, and reinforce Chandler's thesis that

exploitation of economies of scope (product innovation and diversification) first required an administrative structure that exploited economies of scale (markets), as witnessed by Jones Lang Wootton's organizational evolution, early investment in market coverage kept an enterprise more innovative. See also A.D. Chandler, Jr., *Scale and Scope: The Dynamics of Industrial Capitalism* (Cambridge, MA: Belknap Press of Harvard University Press, 1990), pp. 169, 218.

113 M. Wilkins contended that the most profitable US multinational corporations gave equal weight to product divisions and regional operating subsidiaries, in *The Maturing Multinational Enterprise: American Business Abroad from 1914 to 1970* (Cambridge, MA: Harvard University Press, 1974), pp. 382–3. However, reinforcing the experience of real estate services, J.W. Lorsch and P.R. Lawrence concluded that product innovation required an organizational environment in which market and technical specialists were able to coordinate their research with other geographic and product divisions, in "Organizing for Product Innovation", *Harvard Business Review* (January–February 1965), pp. 109–22.

114 Japan's four largest banks – Mitsui, Mitsubishi, Yamaichi and Daiwa – created separate research institutes to develop in-depth analyses of economic trends, alternative financial forecasts, demographic studies and theoretical models on equity and debt markets. See A. Baum and A. Schofield, "Property as a Global Asset", Working Papers in European Property, Centre for European Property Research (University of Reading, March 1991), p. 56.

6

REAL ESTATE ADVISORY SERVICE FIRMS FROM THE FOCAL COUNTRIES

Four case studies

A closer look at four major players

This chapter presents a comparative analysis of the international expansion strategies and the resulting corporate structures of four real estate advisory service firms based one in each of the four focal countries. These companies were among the leading domestic real estate advisory firms to capitalize on the growth of both national and foreign real estate markets between 1960 and 1997 (Table 6.1). Each firm invested substantial capital to diversify its core advisory services in response to the rise of cross-border direct investments in the domestic market and abroad. Moreover, each enterprise developed specific strategies for domestic and global expansion to deepen the firm's penetration of rapidly growing international corporate, development and investment markets, as outlined in the top-ten profiles in Chapter 4.

The case studies provide factual evidence that international real estate advisory service firms initially cultivated and achieved a solid reputation in their home nations by diversifying services and operations to exploit the domestic economy's growing financial and real estate markets. Each responded to foreign direct investment by existing and prospective multinational clients through some form of combination or consolidation (Figure 6.1). Privately-owned service enterprises that were governed by conservative financial stewardship gained competitive advantage by financing service diversification and geographic expansion with retained earnings as well as by infusions of domestic and foreign capital from equity partners or shareholders. Simultaneously they formulated an integrated and multidepartmental structure that centralized corporate entrepreneurial control and decentralized operational management at the local level.

The collective historical profiles presented in Chapter 4 indicated that growth in personnel and foreign operations and innovation in services occurred concurrently with the rise in real estate markets worldwide and cross-border investment activity. Was a strategy of service diversification a necessary precondition to successful geographic expansion and internationalization by these firms?

Table 6.1 Size of firms before and after implementation of international strategy

Before–1960	*Employees*	*Offices*	*National Markets*
Cushman & Wakefield	50	2	1
Jones Lang Wootton	80	4	2
Müller	6	1	1
Orix	0	0	0
Midpoint–1975	*Employees*	*Offices*	*National Markets*
Cushman & Wakefield	275	24	1
Jones Lang Wootton	2,000	20	9
Müller	56	5	2
Orix	0	0	0
After–1997	*Employees*	*Offices*	*National/Regional Markets*
Cushman & Wakefield	1,750	65	10[a]
Jones Lang Wootton	3,735	72	27[a]
Müller	190	12	5
Orix	402	10	3

Sources: Private company reports and documents; interviews with executives of Cushman & Wakefield, Jones Lang Wootton, Müller and Orix; company documents.

Note:
[a] Worldwide

A.D. Chandler, Jr. and R.H. Coase[1] concluded from their research of industrial enterprises that a diversified firm might choose alternative ways and vehicles to expand abroad. Does the evidence which follows indicate measurable economic or other administrative benefits for internalized expansion, collaboration or acquisition? Each of the case studies represents one or more of these strategies, the respective choice a result of organizational perceptions based on different professional service skills, ambitions and domestic performance.[2] The choice of how much a firm grew in size and complexity, Coase argued, depended on the capabilities and risk tolerance of the "entrepreneur" or corporate management.[3] There were the costs and marginal benefits of buying additional services (or products) in the market versus the costs of administration and management. For these real estate advisory service firms, the complexity and costs of managing several offices over widely dispersed

136

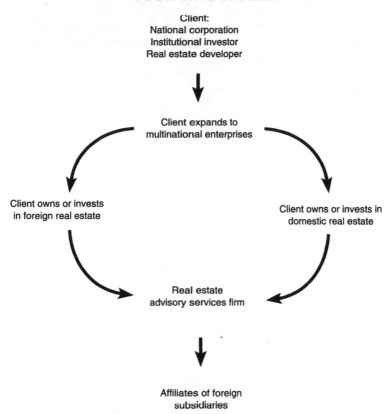

Client:
National corporation
Institutional investor
Real estate developer

Client expands to
multinational enterprises

Client owns or invests
in foreign real estate

Client owns or invests in
domestic real estate

Real estate
advisory services firm

Affiliates of foreign
subsidiaries

Figure 6.1 Globalization of real estate advisory services: growing inward–outward
direct investment

regions and different cultures, balanced against the coordination of disparate
departmental services and clients, proved to be the greatest challenges. The
case studies were designed to demonstrate how effectively and profitably each
firm met these challenges.

The analytical framework for evaluating the factors that promoted or
hindered globalization by real estate advisory firms drew from the standard
literature on economic and business history, principally Chandler's systematic
analyses of American industrial enterprises. The analysis highlights relevant
comparisons between accepted business theory and the actual experience of
these four real estate advisory service firms. Based on Chandler's thesis in
Strategy and Structure that a "new strategy required a new or at least refashioned
structure if the enlarged enterprise was to be operated efficiently",[4] the analytical framework for each case study was designed to evaluate the most
important factors in the internationalization of a professional services firm:

1   What was the firm's corporate expansion philosophy and history?
2   How did each firm broaden the scope of its business through geographic expansion and service diversification?
3   Did alliances and/or acquisitions play a central role in the firm's geographic and service diversification?
4   Did the executives of the four firms develop an ownership and management structure independently of one another, and was this structure developed explicitly to support the firm's service diversification and/or geographic expansion strategy?

Cushman & Wakefield of the United States was the nation's largest real estate advisory firm by 1990[5] and expanded domestically and abroad to a greater extent than any of its American competitors. Jones Lang Wootton of the United Kingdom remained the largest real estate advisory service firm worldwide and, more than any British competitor (domestically known as "chartered surveyors"), successfully expanded throughout the global marketplace. Müller of Germany became the largest and most prominent real estate advisory service firm in its home nation, yet, due to the fragmented nature of the German economy and domestic real estate markets, it lacked a uniform national reputation. However, Müller was among the first, and the most visible German real estate advisory firm to expand into the international marketplace. Finally, Orix of Japan was one of the first and most prominent independent, nontrading enterprises involved in international real estate advisory services.[6]

In the absence of published industry-wide data, an examination of the corporate growth strategies of these major players provides evidence that real estate advisory service firms most effectively expanded into foreign markets (1) in tandem with multinational clients expanding abroad, and (2) by implementing a multifunctional management structure that emphasized vertical integration, corporate identity, and central control.

Cushman & Wakefield, Inc.

Cushman & Wakefield, Inc. was founded in 1917 in New York City and became a national and international innovator in real estate advisory services over seven decades. It was the largest real estate advisory firm in the US by 1990, providing services to all segments of the real estate industry. Established by J. Clydesdale Cushman and Bernard Wakefield as a small real estate management firm, Cushman & Wakefield initially focused on property management and leasing of office buildings in midtown Manhattan.[7] The firm's size, structure and function changed little over the first forty years; after 1960, however, Cushman & Wakefield grew more than five-fold. In 1990 it stood at 2,800 employees worldwide, with fifty-three offices in twenty states across America and twelve affiliate offices in eight European countries.

The firm's clientele and services divisions expanded in response to the more sophisticated needs of domestic, multinational and foreign clients, and a more complex property market – both at home and abroad. Cushman & Wakefield expanded the scope of services to include new professional disciplines and new geographic markets (Table 6.2).

Historically, the firm maintained a conservative policy of controlled growth. Domestic expansion was led by flagship projects and targeted to perceived market opportunities, both short- and long-term. This corporate strategy paralleled the firm's financial management: it had never borrowed to expand into new markets or to upgrade innovative technology; it had never been in debt; and its domestic growth throughout the continental US was either in tandem with major clients or in response to accessible client opportunities in growing employment and real estate markets. Since the company's founding in 1917, Cushman & Wakefield financed a majority of domestic and international expansions and service-line diversifications with retained earnings generated by ongoing client engagements.[8]

Geographic expansion

Cushman & Wakefield expanded its geographic scope independently of the scope of its service divisions (Table 6.3). It opened the first office outside New York City in the late 1950s, when San Francisco-based Bank of America – also a New York client – retained the firm to advise it on building and leasing a new world headquarters. Because the City of San Francisco pressured Bank of America to retain a local firm, Cushman & Wakefield promptly decided to open a San Francisco office, staffed by experienced people from the New York office as well as local professionals.

Throughout the 1960s, the company opened offices in other US cities as it secured new clients or new engagements for existing national clients. By 1970, Cushman & Wakefield operated twenty offices nationwide, gaining a national reputation with each successive move. In the late 1970s, for example, First International Bank of Dallas, Texas retained Cushman & Wakefield to represent the bank in leasing new headquarters offices. Cushman & Wakefield had no local presence at the time and employed a leasing representative from the Dallas office of Tishman Realty & Construction Co., thereby continuing a long-held strategy of creating competitive advantage through localized knowledge and perceived market opportunities.[9] Then, as today, this strategy proved to be a profitable means of establishing immediate credibility in a new market.[10]

Service diversification

Throughout the 1980s, Cushman & Wakefield continued its national expansion by advising major clients on the development, leasing and management

139

of such premier projects as Sears Tower in Chicago, Arco Plaza in Los Angeles, the Tampa City Center in Florida, and the World Bank headquarters in Washington, DC. These flagship projects were complemented by other corporate headquarters buildings – for such multinationals as American Express, RCA, GTE Corporation and CBS Records – as well as hundreds of development consulting engagements for hotels, renovations, and interior tenant improvements. Even though development consulting projects across the country triggered Cushman & Wakefield's national expansion, brokerage services in office and commercial properties constituted the principal source of gross revenues and revenue growth throughout the 1960s, 1970s and 1980s (Table 6.4).

During the 1980s, commercial brokerage spawned the new industrial/technology brokerage group, once economies of scope and the division's profitability appeared to be assured. While industrial brokerage constituted a small share of the company's gross revenues during the 1970s and 1980s, the division contributed to international expansion by enabling the firm to capitalize on work for multinational clients which had overseas manufacturing facilities.

In 1980 the firm formally established the appraisal division and, in 1983, the financial services division. Both groups further diversified the firm's core services and broadened its national and international presence among institutional investors. In just five years (1975–80), the stock of inward direct investment in US real estate had grown from $0.8 billion to $6.1 billion.[11] As a "first mover"[12] among domestic competitors, Cushman & Wakefield secured long-term contracts from several domestic and foreign investment funds. Over the 1980–90 period the appraisal group and financial services, particularly, enabled the firm to capture a substantial share of the growing US real estate market.[13] The appraisal group, for example, advised such multinational corporations as IBM and domestic and foreign pension funds investing a significant portion of their portfolios in real estate assets. Because the funds' assets were located in numerous markets throughout the country, Cushman & Wakefield was able to advise institutional investors from both local and national perspectives in contrast to competing firms which had only regional practices or less coverage in major markets.

The financial services group also represented corporations, investors and institutional funds in a variety of capital funding and financing plans and transactions, domestically and abroad.[14] Moving beyond these core services to introduce more sophisticated financial services and respond to the unprecedented increase in cross-border direct investment in the 1980s, Cushman & Wakefield executives invested substantial capital in developing the firm's in-house expertise to assist foreign investors in targeting US property purchases. Senior management believed that the firm's competitive position would be enhanced by strengthening the skills of existing staff, rather than acquiring another firm and adjusting to the diseconomies of bringing two distinct

140

Table 6.2 Corporate profile of Cushman & Wakefield (1960–97)

Factors	1960	1970	1980	1997
Number of Employees				
Domestic	50	175	410	650
Foreign	0	0	0	1,100
Total	75	175	410	1,751
Number of Offices				
Domestic	2	20	28	53
Foreign	0	0	0	12a
Total	2	20	28	65
Alliances/Acquisitions				
Alliances	0	0	0	4
Mergers/Acquisitions	0	0	0	1
Total	0	0	0	5
Global Client Mix				
Manufacturing (%)	10	30	40	35
Services (%)	85	65	50	50
Government (%)	5	5	10	15
Sources of Revenue (%)				
Manufacturing (%)	20	20	30	30
Services (%)	75	75	60	60
Government (%)	5	5	10	10

Sources: Corporate documents and publications; author's interviews with Cushman & Wakefield executives.

Note:
[a] Worldwide affiliations

Table 6.3 Competitive scope, service diversification and geographic expansion at
Cushman & Wakefield (1960–97)

Competitive Scope	1960	1970	1980	1997
Services Scope[a]	Office brokerage Property management	Office brokerage Property management	Commercial brokerage[b] Industrial brokerage Property management Appraisal Financial services Development consulting	Commercial brokerage Industrial brokerage Management Appraisal Financial services Development consulting Research
Geographic Scope	United States	United States	United States	United States United Kingdom Belgium Channel Islands France Italy The Netherlands Spain Sweden Germany

Sources:
Unpublished private corporate documents; T. Sarowitz, "Evolution of a Real Estate Firm";
author's interviews with Cushman & Wakefield executives H.C. Carey and Richard Hollander.

Notes:
[a] Common terminology to define real estate advisory services is used for all four companies for
   purposes of consistency and comparative analysis; specific terms may depart from the
   company's terminology.
[b] Includes commercial office and retail space.

organizations together. This strategy reinforced the theories of Coase and
Williamson, notably that superior market performance is achieved by effective
management of vertical relationships, especially internally within the firm.[15]

As a result, Cushman & Wakefield's financial services group secured a superior position with foreign investors relative to its American competitors
during the 1980s. The financial services group also diversified into complementary advisory services for corporate and institutional clients, such as
monitoring institutional offshore funds and investor criteria on a systematic
basis, and representing US clients in securing debt and equity funds with
financial institutions in Europe and the Pacific Rim. Thus, by expanding its
service capabilities, the firm tapped into international real estate and financial

Table 6.4 Sources of revenue for Cushman & Wakefield (1960–97)

Services	1960	1970	1980	1997
Commercial Brokerage (%)	95	70	70	60
Industrial/Technology Brokerage (%)	-	10	10	10
Property Management (%)	5	15	15	15
Development Consulting (%)	-	5	5	5
Appraisal (%)	-	-	-	5
Financial Services (%)	-	-	-	5
Total (%)	100	100	100	100

Sources:
Unpublished corporate documents and industry publications; author's interviews with Cushman & Wakefield executives H.C. Carey and Richard Hollander; and T. Sarowitz, "Evolution of a Real Estate Firm".

markets, and concurrently expanded its geographic scope together with its base of national and multinational clients. One example of how service diversification reinforced geographic expansion is an engagement for the Greyhound Corporation of Phoenix, Arizona. Cushman & Wakefield introduced Greyhound to Deutsche Bank, Germany's largest bank and a client of long standing, to finance the transit company's new headquarters. This transaction marked the largest foreign debt or equity financing in the state of Arizona.[16]

Strategic alliances and service diversification

By 1985, in spite of advances in the domestic market, Cushman & Wakefield executives believed that its competitive position in cross-border real estate investment activity would be limited without an external alliance with a major player in international investment. With an eye to minimizing risk and opportunity costs,[17] in 1985 the firm entered into a non-equity alliance with Mitsubishi Trust & Banking Corporation, Japan's largest trust bank (Figure 6.2). The vertical alliance was undertaken to better position the firm in expanding into international financial markets. Through the exclusive joint agreement, which resulted in eleven transactions within the first eighteen months, Cushman & Wakefield advised Mitsubishi's clientele – corporations, private investors and pension funds – in seeking real estate investment opportunities throughout the US. In turn, Cushman & Wakefield had direct exposure to Mitsubishi's foreign clients and gained first-hand knowledge of the rigorous investment guidelines of Japanese nationals.

Mitsubishi chose to enter into the vertical alliance with Cushman & Wakefield because of the firm's national and growing international reputation and, importantly, because of its long-established experience in local US markets. One advantage stemmed from Cushman & Wakefield being the largest third-party property manager of commercial real estate in America.[18] The firm secured management contracts with an array of property owners – national and foreign life insurance companies, banks, pension funds and institutional investors. Property contracts emphasized market research and computerized asset management. In addition, multinational clients that owned facilities in both the US and Europe retained Cushman & Wakefield to provide uniform reporting and management standards via the firm's international office network. Few competitive real estate advisory firms active in the US and international markets could commit to such a uniform level of service.

Cushman & Wakefield's growing international reputation during the 1980s exemplified what Davis & Smales and Kay identified among companies worldwide: a national firm's success in expanding into international markets capitalized on its domestic market stature to establish a competitive foothold in foreign nations.[19] Cushman & Wakefield's executives maintained that the firm's ability to expand its client base domestically and abroad is ultimately tied to local expertise because real estate is a local business.

Alliances

- The Mitsubishi Trust & Banking Corporation, Japan, 1985
- Healey & Baker, United Kingdom, 1990
- MacKenzie Hill, 1993
- Asian Ventures

Mergers/Acquisitions/Joint Ventures

- RCA Corporation acquired Cushman & Wakefield, 1970
- The Rockefeller Group acquired 80 percent of Cushman & Wakefield private stock, 1976
- The Mitsubishi Estate Company, Ltd acquired 51 percent of The Rockefeller Group, 1989

Figure 6.2 Strategic alliances and acquisitions by Cushman & Wakefield

Sources: Author's interviews with Cushman & Wakefield executives; corporate documents and publications.

Ownership and management structure

Private ownership and capital investment from retained earnings enabled Cushman & Wakefield to respond promptly and decisively to current client needs and perceived market opportunities. This flexibility also reduced the firm's exposure and indebtedness, thereby enhancing its market position during downturns in the economy. Before 1970, Cushman & Wakefield's corporate stock was owned by senior executives and major financial partners. In 1970, with annual revenues of nearly $19 million and twenty offices nationwide, Cushman & Wakefield sold the company's privately-held stock to the communications conglomerate RCA. The real estate advisory firm initially welcomed the acquisition and capital infusion. For its part, RCA was one of several multinational conglomerates at the time that were diversifying into unrelated businesses, even though ownership of a real estate services firm provided no real advantages to the communications business. Within two years, diverging expansion strategies and management policies proved to be insurmountable obstacles between the two companies.[20] Most important, RCA dictated a systematic national expansion, while Cushman & Wakefield believed that moving with clients and market opportunities was the most effective, and profitable, strategy. During 1970–6, the firm's revenue growth stagnated while the number of nationwide offices and personnel increased. The result was unprecedented deficits.

The turning point in regaining profitable expansion came in 1976, when the Rockefeller Group, Inc. (RGI), then known as Rockefeller Center, Inc., acquired an 80 percent ownership position. The remaining 20 percent was retained by the firm's employees.[21] The Rockefeller Group owned and managed properties throughout the US and believed that Cushman & Wakefield still had a good reputation, despite six marginal years. RGI and Cushman & Wakefield executives reinforced the real estate advisory firm's national reputation by infusing fresh capital to strengthen professional capabilities in a broader range of disciplines.

Toward this end, senior management restructured the compensation policy for regional directors and office managers, shifting from commission to salary-plus-bonus, based on operational performance and the office's profitability. The intent was to trade off pure entrepreneurial competition internally for a more externally focused entrepreneurship that advanced Cushman & Wakefield's larger corporate identity. As Williamson documented through studies of trading companies, Cushman & Wakefield's executives decided that, to economize transaction costs over the long term and provide greater opportunity to deepen market penetration, they needed a hierarchical management structure in local offices, thus placing separate functional groups under common direction.[22] It was an expensive restructuring,[23] but since the late 1970s the rate of revenue growth for each of the sixty US offices exceeded the company's historical performance.[24]

RGI and Cushman & Wakefield executives also developed a new corporate management structure, which paralleled the changes in managers' functions and compensation. It also reflected the firm's national growth in both personnel and offices during the 1970s, and the diversification of the company's core services (Figures 6.3 and 6.4). The new structure essentially represented a mix of what Williamson termed the "peer group" and "simple hierarchy" forms of management.[25] The firm's executives recognized the need to implement a structure that emphasized both the team approach – for each office and throughout the company – and distinct lines of authority – from the local office, to the regional office, to national headquarters. To ensure quality control for the firm's multifunctional and multiregional services, the US-based offices, which numbered sixty in 1990, were realigned to report to six regional directors. The regional directors, in turn, now reported to the chief operating officer, who reported to the chief executive officer and president, both of whom resided in corporate headquarters in New York City.[26]

Overall management of each of the functional service groups was integrated within the larger regional structure. The service line directors, also located in corporate headquarters, were given both entrepreneurial and operational authority to work directly with the regional directors and chief operating officer, and report to the chief executive officer. With this structural change, each director was responsible for the financial and competitive performance of a core business group and managed the relationships with national and multinational clients. Taken together, the service line directors and the corporate officers constituted Cushman & Wakefield's board of directors. Together, they established corporate policy and the broader national and international competitive strategy.

International expansion and strategic alliances

Cushman & Wakefield's previous expansion strategy, which focused on service capabilities and established client relationships of local offices, formally moved beyond national boundaries in late 1989 to encompass an international scope. Senior management recognized the growing demand for real estate advisory services in Western Europe.[27] The most compelling factor was that a majority of the firm's tenants, many of whom were multinationals, were expanding their activities into Europe. A central management committee considered four European expansion strategies[28] and chose to pursue a joint initiative, in consideration of the financial risks the US-based firm faced in securing local clients in a foreign marketplace as well as access to foreign funds.[29] Cushman & Wakefield's primary competitor, London-based Jones Lang Wootton, had established offices throughout Europe and the US, and another competitor, London-based Weatherall Green & Smith, had followed

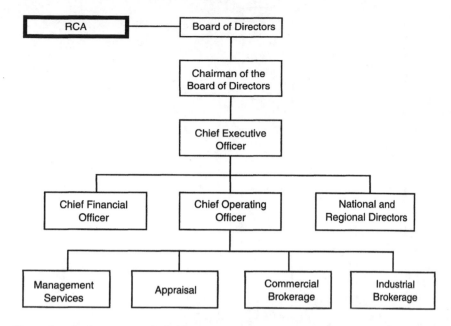

Figure 6.3 Cushman & Wakefield management structure (1975)

the British Petroleum Pension Fund and other British institutional clients in its expansion throughout Europe and the US.[30]

Even with an established reputation among its multinational corporate clients and European and Japanese institutional investors, Cushman & Wakefield's management committee believed – as Davis and Smales documented in their research of service corporations – that a local presence in both domestic and foreign markets was essential to attracting customers to the real estate advisory service firm.[31] Recognizing from its own US practice that cultural conventions played a central role in securing both domestic and foreign clients, Cushman & Wakefield decided that the risk inherent in international expansion would likely be reduced by forming an alliance with a reputable foreign firm that shared a similar business strategy.[32]

Cushman & Wakefield chose London-based Healey & Baker because it owned and operated twelve offices in eight European countries and because of the two firms' complementary strategies – commitment to employees, to market research, to multidisciplinary team efforts, and to long-term relationships with clients.[33] Moreover, Healey & Baker had a long history of centralized management and control by thirty-two equity partners.[34] Cushman & Wakefield valued Healey & Baker's 170 years of practice as respected British chartered surveyors and its successful penetration of several retail markets across Europe.[35]

In April 1990, the two companies formed a joint initiative, known as

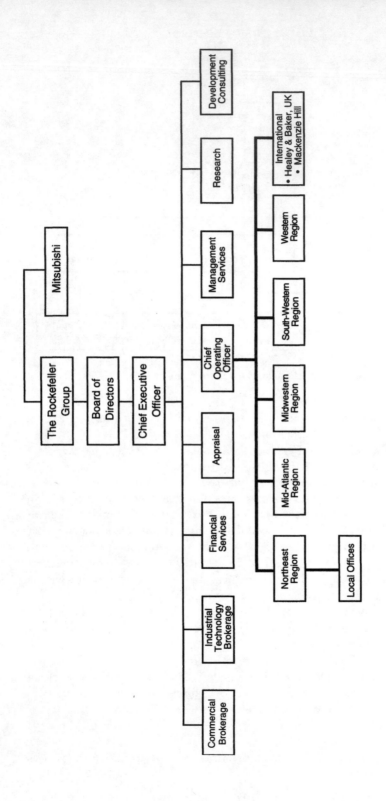

Figure 6.4 Cushman & Wakefield management structure (1997)

Cushman & Wakefield/Healey & Baker. Each firm moved a senior manager into the other's headquarters, yet consciously decided to maintain independent corporate control. No equity was exchanged, yet they did consult with one another on expansion plans, overall business strategy and multinational clients.[36] While Healey & Baker's core services were somewhat different to those of Cushman & Wakefield, notably its retail consulting and property management, both firms viewed these differences as an advantage in strengthening their respective knowledge of local markets. The allied partners explicitly sought to capitalize on the rise in cross-border activity and to compete successfully against such firms as the $3 billion Prudential Global Real Estate Investment Program, managed jointly by the London-based Jones Lang Wootton and the Prudential Company of America. Even so, neither Cushman & Wakefield nor Healey & Baker pursued a systematic integration whereby their individual corporate networks would be linked as one; instead, they chose to remain as two separate entities of one loosely interdependent system.[37] This strategy contrasted with those implemented by direct competitors Jones Lang Wootton and Orix.

In 1992, Cushman & Wakefield formed a joint venture with Grupo Comercial Inmobiliario (GCI), a major real estate brokerage firm in Mexico City; thereby making Cushman & Wakefield the first major US brokerage firm to establish a permanent office there.

The firm entered a similar venture in 1993 when it formed an alliance with Royal LePage, a large real estate service company in Canada with 400 brokers in eight cities. The arrangement called for the firm to provide real estate services to Royal LePage clients in the US, and for Royal LePage to provide the firm's clients with access to Canada.

In 1993 the firm formed a joint initiative with Mackenzie Hill, a major South American commercial real estate firm based in Sao Paulo, Brazil. The alliance provided the firm's clients with access to all markets in Brazil, Argentina and Chile, while Mackenzie Hill's clients were able to use Cushman & Wakefield for their real estate needs in the US, Mexico and Canada.

In 1994, Bell Atlantic named the firm its strategic alliance partner for a two-year period to provide corporate real estate services in the mid-Atlantic region of the US. The next year the firm was named strategic real estate services partner for GTE Corporation in its Eastern and Western Zones of the US, and Saks Fifth Avenue named the firm its national real estate services strategic alliance partner.

The culmination of these mergers was the establishment, in 1994, of Cushman & Wakefield Worldwide, an association of seven internationally known real estate providers:

- Cushman & Wakefield
- Healey & Baker
- Cushman & Wakefield/CGI

- Royal LePage
- Mackenzie Hill
- Cushman & Wakefield/SEMCO
- Marlin Land

In 1995, Cushman & Wakefield entered a joint venture with Marlin Land Corporation, a real estate services firm based in Hong Kong. According to the arrangement, the firm provided Marlin Land's clients with real estate services in the Americas, while Marlin Land provided services to the firm's clients in Asia. In addition, the two firms exchanged professionals from their offices in San Francisco and Hong Kong. The owners of Marlin Land included Cushman & Wakefield; Healey & Baker; the Shaw family; and Grosvenor Estate Holdings.

By 1995 the firm had thirty-nine offices in the US and operations through Cushman & Wakefield Worldwide in Europe, Canada, Mexico, South America, South Africa and Asia.

Cushman & Wakefield continued to use innovation to improve its business and gain competitive advantage. In 1996 it placed corporate policies and human resources information on an intranet readily available to approximately 2,000 employees in thirty-nine locations around the world. In addition, the firm uses the intranet for a client–server real estate application called Site Solutions and for its commissions-accounting system.

In 1996, the firm released the preliminary findings of a survey of top executives at 250 multinational companies in "The Cushman & Wakefield Report on Business Without Borders": over 90 percent believed their own business is expanding globally; almost 60 percent thought the expansion is rapid.

Jones Lang Wootton

Jones Lang Wootton is the largest real estate advisory service firm worldwide, with seventy-two offices in twenty-seven countries. The firm was founded in 1783 as a sole partnership in London, originally providing auctioneering and land surveying services. By 1840, it had expanded into estate agency for residential and commercial property owners, responding to the rapid rise of land development throughout England. The modern firm of Jones Lang Wootton was established in 1939, when chartered surveyors Jones Lang & Co. merged with Wootton & Sons (founded in 1892).[38]

Geographic expansion

Over the next twenty years, through the post-World War Two decades, the firm remained comparatively small, ranking among the mid range of chartered surveyors in the UK and limiting its activities to domestic clients. In 1958, when Jones Lang Wootton (JLW) opened the first foreign office in

Australia, the firm had eight partners and eighty employees. By 1970, however, JLW had expanded to 1,300 professionals, with 350 staff in Australia alone (Figure 6.5 and Table 6.5).

Two JLW partners initiated the move into Australia. They were introduced to the market by an existing UK client and perceived sufficient investment opportunities to open an office, even though Australia offered only a fledgling investment market at the time. The partners developed additional business and investment prospects, and introduced other UK clients, including major insurance companies, developers and investors.

In addition to its entry into Australia, the firm logically extended its investment and chartered surveyor practice across the English Channel to Belgium, opening an office in Brussels in 1965. From this base, JLW opened new offices during the 1960s and 1970s across Europe and the South East Asian and Pacific regions – New Zealand (1964), Belgium (1965), Ireland (1965), The Netherlands (1970), France (1972), Hong Kong (1973), Singapore (1973), Germany (1973) and Malaysia (1974).[39] Since the 1960s, the firm's principal expansion strategy – in both services and new markets – was to respond to the real estate activities of existing clients. Deliberate expansion into new markets enabled JLW to provide local expertise and an international perspective for those clients that sought advice across national boundaries (Table 6.6). A network of JLW-owned offices and JLW-trained staff, and a core of multinational clients, were the key elements of this strategy.

The first German office, for example, was established in 1973 when JLW was retained by two British-based clients, developer MEPC and institutional investor Pan-European Property Unit Trust (managed by Montagu Investment Fund), to advise them on their entry into the Frankfurt market.[40] The firm's international network provided a solid foundation for entering Germany, as it did in other new foreign markets. Seventeen years later, in 1990, Frankfurt-based developer BTG retained JLW specifically because of its established presence in twenty-five European cities. The real estate advisers acquired, managed, and leased the BTG office/warehouse development near the international airport, letting the space to international firms based in the US, Holland, the UK, Italy and Turkey.[41]

Having established a profitable network of offices across Europe and Asia, the firm's senior partners developed a global marketing plan by the mid-1970s. This plan centered around JLW's entry into the US to capitalize on the rise in cross-border direct real estate investment by British, Middle Eastern and Asian investors. The four-person office in New York City provided advisory services to existing and prospective foreign clients that were unfamiliar with the American market, as well as US management standards and appraisal techniques.

By the early 1980s, JLW enjoyed a superior position relative to its US competitors, including Cushman & Wakefield, because it offered direct access to several foreign investment markets and a broader array of core advisory services. In 1983, for example, JLW represented Prudential UK in the purchase of an 836,000-square-foot office building in Houston, Texas, and leased and managed the building for its British client.[42]

By the mid-1980s, the firm expanded its services beyond investment sales and purchases to include financial services for corporate clients and major pension funds.[43] Among the largest projects of this kind was a 1990 joint venture with Prudential Insurance Company of America and Japan Air Lines Development Group (a partnership of four Japanese companies): JLW advised on the 3.3 million-square-foot Hotel Nikko mixed-use development in Atlanta, Georgia, and arranged a financing package with a Japanese and a UK bank.[44] As of 1990, JLW had offices in four US cities, staffed by twenty partners and 100 professionals.[45]

In 1983, responding to the growing outflow of Japanese capital to major Western markets, JLW opened an office in Tokyo in an effort to tap into the rise in export capital. JLW had no previous experience with Japanese real estate investors, marking the first time in the firm's history that it had established a new foreign operation in the absence of a concrete business prospect. The Japan office was organized as a cooperative operation with JLW's three major regions in Europe, North America and the Asia–Pacific region. Its principal mission was to work with worldwide offices and clients to secure Japanese debt and equity funds for foreign real estate investments.[46] The Tokyo office was also established to advise JLW's corporate clients in Europe and the US on entering or expanding their operations in Japan.

Contrary to the firm's previous experience in establishing a foothold in a new foreign market – but similar to the experience of most service firms that entered the Japanese market without a cooperative venture agreement with a Japanese firm and no innovative technology to sell to an existing national[47] – JLW encountered substantial cultural barriers in building an advisory practice in Japan: language, business customs and access to major investors. With no Japanese client or affiliate to provide an entree, JLW discovered over time that the major trading companies were the linchpins of real estate export capital. It took JLW seven years, until 1990, to establish a competitive presence among Japanese companies engaged in cross-border real estate investment. For example, in 1989 JLW secured $92.5 million in debt financing from the Sumitomo Bank, Ltd, for the National Press Building, an office project developed by a Washington, DC, client.[48] In the same year, Kumagai Gumi UK, the British affiliate of one of Japan's largest contractors, retained JLW to represent it in acquiring, developing and leasing a prime commercial site and two adjacent freehold properties in downtown London.[49]

JLW opened an office in Berlin in 1989 to capitalize on new business opportunities in the fledgling market economies of former Eastern Bloc states and to establish a regional gateway to Hungary, Czechoslovakia, Poland and Eastern Germany. Privatization of property in these countries after 1989 inspired JLW to cultivate local expertise in legal and cultural matters for US, European and Japanese clients – manufacturers, hotels and developers – that were entering Eastern Europe through joint ventures. For example, a US-based development partnership headquartered in Washington, DC acquired a large commercial parcel in Warsaw in 1990. After evaluating the market and the property's competitive positioning, the group retained JLW's Berlin office to lease the 280,000-square-foot office building because of the real estate advisory firm's direct access to Western Europe, the US and Japan.[50]

Service diversification

JLW incrementally broadened its operations in response to new business opportunities presented by clients' cross-border expansion (Table 6.6). Unlike Cushman & Wakefield and several other real estate and financial advisory firms that expanded into foreign markets, JLW's senior management generally chose to expand under the firm's own name, capitalized by partner equity and JLW-trained personnel. Relocated senior managers would then hire local practitioners in each place. This strategy, while resulting in higher capital costs and longer lead times in such markets as Japan, enabled the firm to control the scope and value of professional services. The strict "Code of Conduct", instituted in 1986 and observed by all offices, was one measure of JLW's commitment to a unified standard of quality.[51]

JLW and other internationalizing real estate advisory firms tended to introduce new, innovative services at a rate approximately proportionate to the firm's rate of geographic diversification. During the initial stages of growth, this diversification in services was both a result of and the basis for broader exposure to domestic and foreign corporations and investors worldwide. JLW gained a global perspective and introduced more sophisticated and innovative services at a faster pace than its direct competitors, such as Cushman & Wakefield, because of its direct exposure to different national and local markets and its larger volume of diverse clients, projects and transactions. By having sixty offices in twenty countries and representing $13 billion to $16 billion of cross-border transactions annually,[52] JLW personnel gained a distinct advantage over direct competitors because of the firm's integrated international network of offices and client–adviser relationships. Initially, as Chandler and Williamson have argued, such client–adviser relationships were cultivated at a local level. Over time, with cross-border expansion, successful firms such as JLW exploited the strengths gained in one nation, or global financial market, to enhance the services they provided to clients in other foreign markets.[53] Moreover, JLW effectively and economically managed its global network of diversified services. The firm's position was strengthened during the second half of the 1980s by the heightened importance of international real estate finance.

In recognition of the increased importance of real estate finance, JLW's

Table 6. 5 Corporate profile of Jones Lang Wootton (1960–97)

Factors	1960	1970	1980	1997
Number of Employees				
Domestic	80	1,300	2,600	800
Foreign	0	50	100	2,935
Total	80	1,350	2,700	3,725
Number of Offices				
Domestic	1	3	5	6
Foreign	0	10	20	66
Total	1	13	25	72[a]
Alliances/Acquisitions				
Alliances	0	0	2	5
Mergers/Acquisitions	0	0	0	0
Total	0	0	2	5
Global Client Mix				
Manufacturing (%)	45	50	35	30
Services (%)	40	45	45	50
Government (%)	15	15	20	20
Sources of Revenue				
Manufacturing (%)	30	25	25	20
Services (%)	50	55	55	55
Government (%)	20	20	20	25

Sources: Corporate documents and publications; author's interviews with Jones Lang Wootton executives.

Note:
[a] Worldwide

Table 6.6 Competitive scope, service diversification and geographic expansion at Jones Lang Wootton (1960–97)

Competitive Scope	1960	1970	1980	1997
Services Scope	Commercial brokerage Appraisal Investment sales & purchases	Commercial brokerage Appraisal Investment sales & purchases Development consulting Property management	Commercial brokerage Appraisal Investment sales & purchases Development consulting Property management Research & consulting	Commercial brokerage Development consulting Property management Appraisal Financial services Investment sales & purchases Portfolio fund management Research & consulting
Geographic Scope	United Kingdom Australia	United Kingdom Australia New Zealand Ireland Belgium The Netherlands	United Kingdom Australia New Zealand Ireland Belgium The Netherlands France Hong Kong Singapore Malaysia Germany United States	United Kingdom Australia New Zealand Ireland Belgium The Netherlands France Hong Kong Singapore Malaysia Germany United States Japan Spain Canada Luxembourg Sweden Italy Thailand

Sources: Jones Lang Wootton, "The Story of Jones Lang Wootton" (1990), and author's interviews with and data confirmation from Jones Lang Wootton executives.

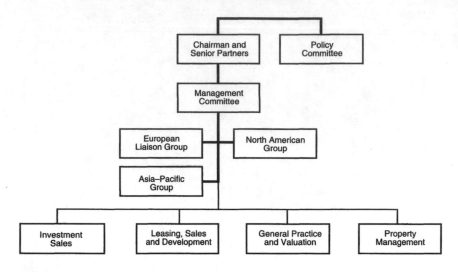

Figure 6.5 Jones Lang Wootton management structure (1975)

financial services led the firm's revenue growth and international expansion during the 1980s and early 1990s (Table 6.7). By 1990, in fact, 75 percent of the capital transactions JLW represented in Europe involved cross-border investments. To be sure, the firm's traditional core services in agency, surveying, appraisal and development management continued to be key products in retaining and attracting multinational clients, as well as providing important sources of sustained revenues. They were not, however, the services that aided JLW in expanding into new foreign markets and formulating innovative vehicles for cross-border investment.[54] Instead, the firm extended its global business and client roster by broadening the scope of financial services, portfolio fund management and investment sales and purchases.

Because JLW deliberately achieved a local presence and market-based knowledge in all the national markets in which it operated – such as a comprehensive understanding and presence in Frankfurt, Germany and in Washington, DC – the financial services group was equipped to advise domestic and foreign clients on investment and tax regulations, legal processes, exchange rates and accounting standards, for multiple cities and countries. The financial staff was also familiar with the return criteria and arbitrage alternatives acceptable to different types of clients in various countries.[55] For example, JLW completed eighteen transactions in the US in 1989, each having complex equity/debt structures. Because of this coverage in the world's most innovative financial market, the firm distinguished its capabilities among European and Asia–Pacific clients, diversifying their investments domestically and abroad.[56]

Table 6.7 Sources of revenue for Jones Lang Wootton (1960–97)

Services	1960	1970	1980	1997
Commercial Brokerage (%)	40	40	35	35
Land/Property Surveys (%)	30	25	15	15
Project (Development) Consulting (%)	–	5	10	10
Property Management (%)	–	5	5	5
Appraisal & Valuations[a] (%)	20	15	10	5
Investment Sales & Purchases (%)	10	10	10	10
Financial Services[b] (%)	–	–	5	10
Portfolio Fund Management (%)	–	–	5	5
Research and Consulting (%)	–	–	5	5
Total (%)	100	100	100	100

Sources: Private company records and reports; author's interviews with JLW executives.

Notes:
[a] General practice services include valuation, rent reviews, lease renewals and rating.
[b] Includes office, retail, hotel and residential investment services for corporate, institutional and individual clients.

During the 1990s, JLW continued to introduce new services. For example, in 1994 the firm launched two publications, *International Index* and *International Occupancy Cost Monitor*, to advise investors about the latest trends in international real estate. In 1996 it started an auction service.

Strategic alliances

Just as JLW's traditional core services were the foundation for international financial services, so too the firm's diversification of portfolio management services into foreign markets during the late 1980s was founded upon long-established core services: local market research, investment brokerage, tax evaluation and property management.[57] JLW's multinational coverage and market expertise were the principal reasons that Prudential Insurance Company of America, the largest US insurance company, entered into an exclusive affiliation with JLW in 1989 to manage jointly its global real estate investment fund (Figure 6.6). Even though Prudential had been active in billions of dollars of direct real estate investment in the US for several decades, the company's global investment group committed $2 billion in the late 1980s to acquire properties in Europe, North America and the Asia–Pacific regions. JLW's extensive ties with property owners were the deciding factor in Prudential's choice of JLW for its joint venture real estate adviser.[58] For the same selective factors that had influenced Prudential, in late 1990 the London Transport Pension Fund, a $260 million portfolio, also retained JLW to manage its global real estate assets and investments, located across the UK, Europe and North America.

The Prudential joint venture was a first for JLW in expanding internationally through an alliance with a second party. Perhaps an indication of the heightened competitiveness of real estate advisory services in the recessionary market of the early 1990s, the firm entered into three additional alliances during 1990–1, of which one was a formal merger. These alliances, together with the firm's international office network, established JLW as the largest property fund manager in the world.

Alliances

- Prudential Insurance Company of America (The Prudential Global Real Estate Investment Program), 1990
- Deutsche Grundbesitz Investment Gesellschaft mbH (DGI), Germany, 1990
- Arthur D. Little, Inc. with JLW USA, 1991

Mergers/Acquisitions/Joint Ventures

- Balay Prenot & Associés, France, 1991

Figure 6.6 Strategic alliances and acquisitions by Jones Lang Wootton

The first alliance was a five-year cooperative agreement with Deutsche Grundbesitz Investment Gesellschaft mbH (DGI), an open-ended institutional fund controlled by Frankfurt-based Deutsche Bank, with two-thirds of its $1.9 billion portfolio in real estate assets located throughout Germany. Regulatory changes in 1990 liberalized cross-border direct investment by German funds, freeing DGI to invest a portion of its capital abroad. It chose JLW to advise on strategy and to implement an investment program in newly opened EC countries, notably the UK, France, Spain and Belgium – markets in which DGI had no previous experience and in which JLW had extensive experience.[59]

The second alliance, with Arthur D. Little, was undertaken to diversify JLW's competitive scope, thus joining with the international management and technology consultants to provide financial advice and asset management services to hospitality and leisure property owners.[60] In response to the growing number of underperforming and insolvent assets in the hospitality sector, JLW's senior management entered this alliance to provide a comprehensive approach that was unavailable from any single competitor.[61]

Finally, in 1991, JLW acquired Lyon-based Balay Prenot & Associés to extend the firm's regional activities beyond Paris, where it had had an office since 1972. This merger departed from JLW's traditional expansion pattern of opening new offices led by experienced JLW personnel. Yet JLW's partners pursued the acquisition of the thirty-year-old, thirty-five-person firm because they believed they were handicapped in penetrating the Rhone–Alpes regional market beyond Paris without a formal alliance with the area's leading real estate advisory firm. JLW and Balay Prenot, moreover, had cooperated with one another on several engagements and enjoyed a solid working relationship. JLW chose vertical integration (acquisition) as the most economical way of diversifying into the Rhone–Alpes market.[62]

The firm continued to develop alliances in the mid-1990s. In 1995, for example, JLW and Prudential organized a close-ended fund to invest up to $300 million in the South East Asia property market, one of the fastest growing retail markets in the world. The following year, in 1996, JLW began merger talks – described as informal – with LaSalle Partners and other firms, as JLW looked for ways to expand its market share. At the time, JLW was managing assets totaling $4.5 billion.

By 1996, JLW was recovering from the downturn of the US and European property markets in the early 1990s. The firm boasted a worldwide network of more than 3,500 staff in twenty-six countries. As it looked to expand, the firm hoped to take advantage of the trend toward outsourcing corporate real estate business. In addition to looking at possible mergers, JLW also considered an expansion strategy based on acquiring smaller firms with strong regional businesses.

Ownership and management structure

For more than 200 years, Jones Lang Wootton has remained a privately-held partnership. Twenty-four partners, known as The London Partnership, hold centralized control of the name and the firm's ownership (Figure 6.7). By 1990, each JLW office throughout the world was directed by one of three regional groups which reported to the central management committee – the European Liaison Group, the North American Group, and the Asia–Pacific Group.[63]

Due to the nature of JLW's real estate advisory practice, which for any one engagement or client could extend across national boundaries and call on the firm's diversified services, centralized management was further delineated by core functional divisions, such as financial services, investment sales and purchases, and fund management. The "lead partners" of each service line constituted the Lead Partners Committee, which reported to the Management Committee. JLW established an integrated organizational structure to

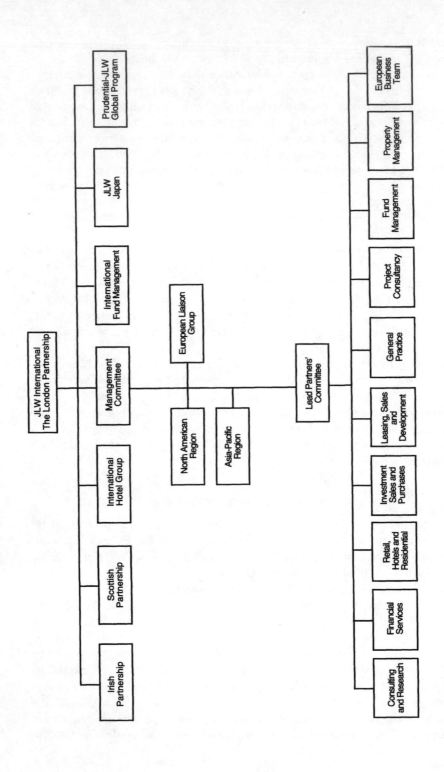

Figure 6.7 Jones Lang Wootton management structure (1997)

manage both geographic regions and core services throughout the worldwide
network of sixty offices. Each office, then, was ultimately accountable to both
an "entrepreneurial" regional partner as well as an "operational" lead (service)
partner.

Müller International Immobilien GmbH

Throughout the decade between 1975 and 1985, the Federal Republic of
Germany ranked as the world leader of outward direct real estate investment.
Since the late 1970s, the expansion of German foreign direct investment, from
$2.1 billion in 1975 to $17.4 billion by 1990, paralleled the incremental
growth over the same period of Müller International Immobilien GmbH, the
largest real estate advisory service firm in Germany.[64] Müller was founded in
1958 in Düsseldorf, West Germany, by Karl-Heinrich Müller. It was among
the first German estate agencies to focus its practice exclusively in commercial
real estate.

Corporate profile and clients

To a greater extent than the three other firms discussed in this chapter, Müller
continued to center its advisory practice around domestic clients and markets.
For example, 90 percent of the firm's clientele in 1990 was German-based; the
remaining 10 percent was made up of foreign investors and developers doing
business in Germany. And, in contrast to the international networks and
wide-ranging global strategies developed by Cushman & Wakefield and Jones
Lang Wootton, Müller specifically oriented the firm's service diversification
and geographic expansion to respond to the needs and potential market opportunities of investors residing or doing business in Germany.

The relative lack of sophistication of the German real estate market until
the mid-to-late 1970s played a central role in the evolution of Müller's organizational structure and expansion policies. Until about 1973, Germany's
commercial property markets were dominated by owner-occupiers, and
Müller's business centered around agency services for corporate and institutional clients (leasing, sales and acquisitions), and investment advice on
locational matters and new building development. Müller introduced consultancy that encompassed supply-and-demand analyses, property valuations and
financing strategies during the 1970s, and refined these services in the 1980s
as the speculative marketplace became more competitive. Until 1990–1 the
German real estate market was quite localized, stemming from the republic's
fragmented political and economic structure. Müller, like most real estate
advisory service firms in Germany, specialized in certain major domestic
markets – such as Düsseldorf – and not others – such as Frankfurt, the
republic's financial center and largest real estate market. Even though in 1990
Müller ranked as the largest German real estate service firm (or estate agency

business) based on number of personnel, its national presence was compart-mentalized within specific regions.

In contrast to JLW, Müller did not actively pursue new business opportunities abroad. Instead, it regarded its primary competitive strength as the firm's expertise in specific German markets and among German-based investors. Müller entered only foreign markets – Paris, London and Vienna – that matched the investment activities and prospects of long-standing clients, thereby dedicating corporate resources to broadening the firm's presence among German enterprises and deepening its knowledge of rapidly changing domestic markets. In light of this conservative strategy, Müller was the smallest of the four firms studied, growing from twenty-five employees in three domestic offices in 1970 to 250 professionals in eight German offices and four European offices in 1990 (Table 6.8).[65]

Competitive scope

As the largest and most prominent real estate services firm in the Düsseldorf region, Müller sustained a strong competitive position in its home nation by providing core real estate services to German-based institutional investors, including pension funds, commercial banks, insurance companies, and multi-national corporations that owned real estate for their own use – manufacturing and trade firms, service companies and commercial trading corporations (Table 6.9). Having been headquartered in Düsseldorf since the firm's founding in 1958, Müller opened branch offices in Frankfurt, Hamburg, Cologne, Munich and Stuttgart during the 1970s. The expansion represented the firm's intent to establish a presence in each of Germany's institutional investment markets and to capture a larger share of growing domestic and international property investment, even though these were secondary markets for Müller relative to its primary competitors outside of Düsseldorf.

To further diversify services and revenue sources, in 1982 Müller established two property management subsidiaries – Müller Management for office buildings and Center Management for retail properties. Similar to many German real estate service firms during this period, Müller was motivated by the steady increase in foreign real estate investment in Germany and high property management fees.[66] As a further extension of its core services, the firm established two additional subsidiaries in 1988 – Müller Financial Agency, to advise institutional investors and arrange debt and equity placements for properties in local markets, and Müller Consult, to counsel a diverse array of property owners: corporations, developers, investors and pension funds. Müller Consult took over the dominant share of the firm's consultancy and research activities.[67]

Müller's corporate expansion reinforced the firm's national reputation, with its international expansion founded principally on the foreign investment activities of domestic clients. Because of the growth of German investment in

Table 6.8 Corporate profile of Müller International Immobilien GmbH (1960–97)

Factors	1960	1970	1980	1997
Number of Employees				
Domestic	6	25	75	185
Foreign	0	0	5	5
	6	25	80	190
Number of Offices				
Domestic	1	3	5	8
Foreign	0	0	2	4
	1	3	7	12
Alliances/Acquisitions				
Cooperative Agreements	0	0	0	3
Mergers/Acquisitions	0	0	0	0
	0	0	0	3
Global Client Mix				
Manufacturing (%)	50	50	45	40
Services (%)	45	45	50	55
Government (%)	5	5	5	5
Sources of Revenue				
Manufacturing Clients (%)	45	45	40	35
Services Clients (%)	50	50	55	60
Government Clients (%)	5	5	5	5

Sources: Private company documents and reports, and industry publications; author interviews
with Müller executives.

real estate, domestically and abroad, Müller capitalized on a dynamic market, introducing new advisory services and expanding its operations abroad in response to the direction and growth of the market (Table 6.10). Moreover, foreign investment activity by Müller's multinational clients provided fertile ground for the German estate agency to open foreign offices in the major European markets of London, Paris, Amsterdam, Vienna and Brussels with

Table 6.9 Competitive scope, service diversification and geographic expansion at Müller (1960–97)

Competitive Scope	1960	1970	1980	1997
Services[a]	Commercial brokerage	Property management Research & consulting	Appraisal	Retail center management Development project management Financial services
Geographic Scope	Germany	Germany	Germany Holland The Netherlands Austria France	Germany Holland The Netherlands Austria France

Sources: Private company documents and reports, and industry publications; author interviews with Müller executives.

Note:
[a] Common terminology to define real estate advisory services is used for all four companies for purposes of consistency and comparative analysis; specific terms may depart from the company's specific terminology.

minimum capital exposure, a principal means of foreign diversification by service firms, according to Davis and Smales.[68]

During the early 1990s, Müller focused on expanding operations into Eastern Europe. That effort did not prove profitable, and the firm closed various offices in that region, including those in Erfurt and Potsdam.

Strategic alliances

By the mid-1980s, as cross-border real estate investment continued to rise, Müller (and several leading German estate agencies) recognized that a solid reputation in German markets and among German investors and corporations was both a competitive advantage and a disadvantage. At one level, the firm was the most experienced and knowledgeable full-service real estate adviser in the major markets of Düsseldorf and Munich, which were then among the most attractive locations in Europe for expanding foreign corporations and international property investors. At another level, however, the firm's national position was limited, and its international presence was handicapped by the domestically-focused, thirty-year practice. In an effort to exploit the firm's local expertise and broaden its exposure among international investors and

Table 6.10 Sources of revenue for Müller (1960–97)

Services	1960	1970	1980	1997
Commercial Brokerage (%)	100	85	55	40
Property Management (%)	0	5	10	10
Retail Center Management (%)	–	–	5	10
Development Project Management (%)	0	0	10	10
Appraisal (%)	0	0	5	5
Financial Services[a] (%)	0	0	0	5
Research and Consulting (%)	0	10	15	20
Total (%)	100	100	100	100

Sources: Private company documents and reports, and industry publications; author interviews with Müller executives.

Notes:
— Service line not formally established as a separate functional group.
[a] Includes investment sales and purchases.

property-intensive corporations, in 1985 Müller established an affiliation with The Office Network, an affiliation of real estate advisory firms worldwide, headquartered in Houston, Texas (Figure 6.8).[69]

Alliances

- Oncor International (The Office Network), US, 1985; terminated in 1997

Mergers/Acquisitions/Joint Ventures

- Comfort-Shopinvest (50 percent participation), Germany, 1989
- Commerzbank AG acquired 20 percent of Müller, Frankfurt, Germany, 1990

Figure 6.8 Strategic alliances and acquisitions by Müller

Sources: Company documents, publications and brochures, 1990–7 author's interviews with, and data confirmation from, Müller executives.

165

The Office Network, a for-profit association, was established in 1977 to provide realty advisers in one nation with a cross-reference network of their counterparts in another nation.[70] In the mid-1980s it formed a global cooperative of real estate advisory service firms – in such countries as Austria, Canada, Spain, the Netherlands, the UK and the US – and identified Müller as the best prospect in Germany. Müller became the only German operator among the Network's twenty-nine international affiliates, joining the cooperative with the expectation that the firm would gain greater exposure among foreign institutions and enterprises investing in Germany.[71] In truth, Müller derived minimum benefit from the alliance, with the first major joint engagement coming after five years, in 1990, to lease and manage an office building in downtown Frankfurt developed by US-based Tishman Speyer.[72]

While the Tishman Speyer match was profitable for both Müller and the US developer, which had sought to increase its links with foreign real estate businesses, the Network's board of directors recognized over time that the organization's mission was not being fulfilled, largely stemming from a loosely-held management and decision-making structure. For these reasons, the association was renamed Oncor International in 1991, and management was centralized to control the quality of services and the selection of real estate advisory firms for specific clients and engagements.[73] Oncor's primary purpose – and Müller's intent in establishing the affiliation – was to compete successfully against such global firms as Jones Lang Wootton. In keeping with Coase's observation that "it may be desired to make a long-term contract for the supply of some article or service"[74] rather than organizing the service within the firm, Oncor and Müller invested in the notion that managing international networks through multiple contracts was more economical than one firm dispersing its sole resources abroad. The twenty-nine worldwide affiliates ostensibly created a stronger office network, from one nation to the next, than did their direct competitors.[75]

In fact, Müller's own European network of wholly-owned offices – in London, Vienna, Paris, Amsterdam and Brussels – was more effective in securing new foreign clients than was the Oncor affiliation. As with many international alliances, prospective clients were not attracted to the combination of global advisory firms that would not have been attracted to one of the individual affiliates in its home market.[76] Over time, Müller executives recognized that equity participation in an international alliance would have greater prospects for gaining competitive advantage abroad than would a cooperative agreement. Müller's own capital resources were strained, however, and the firm required outside capital to expand throughout Germany and into the newly opened, former Eastern Bloc markets.

Beginning around 1985, German commercial and residential estate agency firms responded to the significant increase in real estate demand and property investment by merging with a commercial bank or an insurance company. These integrations were intended to offer a major injection of capital to finance growth, as well as access to international financial markets and investors. While many of its German competitors sold a majority interest to these new financial partners, Müller negotiated to sell 20 percent of its privately-held stock to Frankfurt-based Commerzbank AG, thereby retaining its administrative independence. Commerzbank, in turn, benefited by diversifying services and income sources. The partnership met the expansion strategies of both Müller and Commerzbank.

Alliances with other firms underwent changes during the 1990s. For example, in 1989 Müller acquired a 50 per cent stake in Comfort Gesellschaft für Geshäftslächen und Unternehmensvermittlung mbH, a firm specializing in buying and selling sites, an area in which Müller is not yet active. In 1993 Bernheim-Comofi, GBL's property subsidiary, ended its alliance with Müller. The alliance was composed of Müller International Property and Bernheim Müller Projekt Management. Müller then set up its own activities in Brussels. In 1994, Veba Immobilien AG, a property management firm based in Bochum with 135,000 homes and 500 commercial properties, acquired a one-third stake in Müller to improve its position in international property markets. Müller had eighteen offices across Europe at the time.

Management and ownership structure

Since Müller's founding in 1958, ownership and management were centralized in corporate headquarters in Düsseldorf. During the 1960s, as a localized real estate service firm of less than ten people, the company required no formal reporting structure. During the 1970s, with three branch offices, which grew to five throughout Germany within the decade, each operational subsidiary manager reported to the Board of Directors and the majority shareholder in Düsseldorf (Figure 6.9).[77] The most dramatic restructuring in management and the control of decision-making occurred during the late 1980s and early 1990s. Müller had grown to become a multidivisional real estate services firm with wholly- and partly-owned subsidiaries that were widely dispersed in domestic and foreign offices, such as Müller Comfort-ShopInvest (Figure 6.10). The Board created two holding companies: one to manage national and international commercial brokerage, property management, and consulting operations; and one to oversee development project management and financial services. Even though all shares of the Müller conglomerate were distributed among the directors and the employees, real estate advisory services were managed by individual branch offices and centrally controlled by one of the two holding companies.[78]

In 1996, Müller closed offices in Brussels, Luxembourg, Stuttgart, Erfurt, Potsdam, Prague and Hanover. The firm planned to concentrate on Berlin, Dresden, Düsseldorf, Essen, Frankfurt, Hamburg, Cologne, Leipzig, Munich, London and Paris. Müller reported renting 400,000 square meters

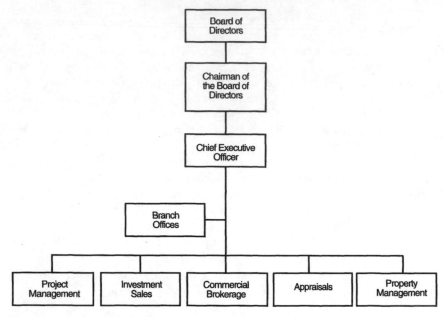

Figure 6.9 Müller management structure (1975)

of commercial space, brokering property worth about DM1.9 billion, and managing property worth DM6.5 billion annually over the last few years.

Orix Corporation

Orix Corporation was founded in 1964 in Osaka, Japan, and was capitalized by three trading companies and five major city banks – three of which in 1990 were among the world's twenty largest banks.[79] Characteristic of the concentration of economic control in Japan, the banks provided institutional financing and, together with the trading houses, created the subsidiary company of Orix to engage in international services and investment credit.[80]

Orix was originally established as an independent leasing enterprise for vessels and containers, office machines, aircraft, plant equipment and automobiles. Within the decade after its founding, however, the company had expanded its primary mission to include asset-based financial services to support the mainline leasing operations and to diversify the firm's credit operations. Several among Japan's largest companies initiated a similar type of expansion through financial services in the post-World War Two decades, especially those expanding throughout the global marketplace. The formation of Orix's financial subsidiaries enabled the company to procure capital by borrowing from its own banking shareholders and other financial institutions, as well as to issue commercial paper and corporate bonds, and to lend to

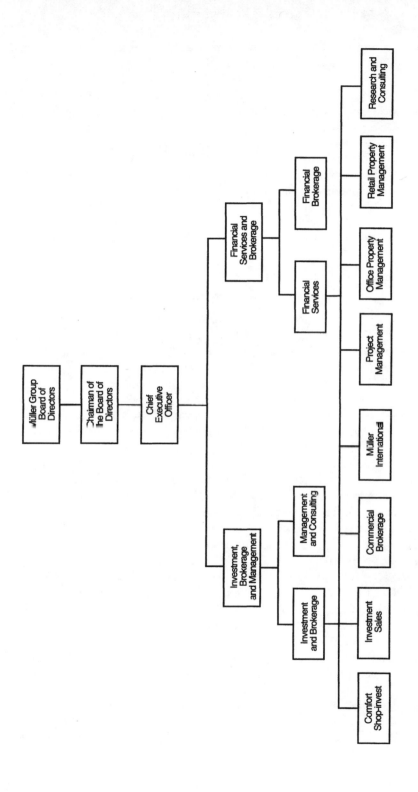

Figure 6.10 Müller management structure (1997)

trading customers.[81] During this same period, Orix also expanded its operations into Hong Kong, Singapore and Malaysia to engage in cross-border transactions, such as leases, installment sales and loan financings.[82] During the 1970s and early 1980s, Orix's management focused on expanding the leasing operations and financial services into new foreign markets, creating subsidiaries throughout the Pacific Rim, Western Europe and the US.

Orix's real estate services were introduced in the mid-1980s as an outgrowth of the mainline business – partly in response to client requests for diverse loan products, and primarily as a means for Orix and its shareholders to develop alternative investment vehicles in the face of deteriorating earnings from Japanese investment funds. Since the early 1990s, Orix has not engaged in any alliances, joint ventures or acquisitions. All of its efforts were focused on developing and creating value for its existing office, retail, residential and rental residential property portfolio.

Management and ownership structure

The firm's aggressive geographic expansion and product diversification during the 1970s were made possible by a restructuring of ownership. In 1970 Orix's shareholders reorganized from a privately-held to a publicly-traded company, and thereby increased the original capital base more than fourfold. By 1973, Orix was listed on the Tokyo, Osaka, and Nagoya stock exchanges, and the nominal value of its issued capital had increased to over one billion yen, from an initial base of 100 million yen in 1964. By 1990, Orix's paid-in capitalization had doubled to Y20.2 billion.[83]

Having been incorporated in Osaka with one branch office in Tokyo, Orix moved its headquarters in 1970 to Tokyo, where Sanwa Bank, the largest shareholder, was based. That same year, the company's senior managers and major shareholders also restructured central management, establishing a multiregional corporate structure designed to increase the flexibility of managing widely dispersed operations and to minimize the cost of international expansion and product diversification.

Throughout the 1970s and early 1980s, Orix established several foreign subsidiaries, entering very different cultures from those throughout Asia – such as, Brazil (1974), the UK (1974), the US (1974), the Philippines (1977), Chile (1980), China (1981), Pakistan (1986) and Australia (1986).[84] Because of its limited knowledge about these foreign regions, Orix's senior executives developed a centralized management structure that permitted localized decision-making within individual regions. Each foreign office, subsidiary or affiliate thus adopted tactical management strategies tailored to the requirements of its particular market, enabling Orix managers to act promptly. This localized orientation created the institutional structure for the real estate services division to tailor regional operations to regional conditions and clients. Orix partners and managers abroad had sufficient independence to respond to the particular market's clients and business environment, while overall corporate policy and finances were controlled by Tokyo. In addition, the consolidated company held to the expansion strategy of acquiring or affiliating with established local enterprises when entering new markets.[85]

Each foreign operation was accountable for the profitability of its individual operations, and thus to the holding company and Board of Directors. In conformance with Chandler's theory of vertical integration through combination and consolidation, central management maintained control of Orix's expansion strategy: it introduced and underwrote new services when local market conditions, profitability ratios and competitive performance measures warranted.[86] By 1989, this market-oriented central management was reflected in the company's organizational structure, which decisively separated domestic operations (in Tokyo, Osaka and Nagoya) and international operations (Figure 6.11).

The management structure, which remained in force in 1990, represented a classic example of a vertically integrated company, broadly organized by geographic scope, then by functional division of individual service operations. With more than 5,700 employees – 266 offices, subsidiaries, and affiliates in Japan, and 100 offices in twenty-one countries abroad – the structure of the overall holding company recognized distinctions between regional markets (Table 6.11). It did not, however, reflect wide-ranging differences between the holding company's diversified leasing and financial services divisions.[87]

The major exception to this overall management structure was the real estate division. The company unified the Japan real estate division, but separated it from the other headquarters in Tokyo, Osaka and Nagoya, creating a distinct rather than an integrated corporate entity in the domestic market. The division reported directly to the President and the Board, rather than to domestic regional managers. Within international headquarters, real estate services were also a separate operation, as were leasing and financial services. Orix's President and Chairman in Tokyo headquarters held ultimate control of real estate services and thereby created a quasi-independent (not fully integrated) business entity in the company's multinational scope.[88] Apart from the formal organizational structure, the real estate services division was effectively linked with financial services, which enabled the business (especially in the early years) to capitalize on the expertise and market presence of Orix's diversified financial products.

Product diversification and international real estate services

Since the 1970s, Orix's executives believed that financial services would constitute a major source of the company's global revenue growth. Access to low-priced investment capital through its major banking partners, particularly Sanwa Bank, accounted for this confidence. In advance of innovations by international investment banks and financial institutions, and prior to the

171

Table 6.11 Corporate profile of Orix Corporation (1960–97)

Factors	1960	1970	1980	1997
Number of Employees[a]				
Domestic	0	0	0	336
Foreign	0	0	0	66
	0	0	0	402
Number of Offices[a]				
Domestic	0	0	0	3
Foreign	0	0	0	7
	0	0	0	10
Alliances/Acquisitions[a]				
Cooperative Agreements	0	0	0	0
Mergers/Acquisitions	0	0	0	2
	0	0	0	2
Global Client Mix[a]				
Manufacturing (%)	0	0	0	37
Services (%)	0	0	0	63
Government (%)	0	0	0	0
Sources of Revenue				
Manufacturing Clients (%)	0	0	0	45
Services Clients (%)	0	0	0	55
Government Clients (%)	0	0	0	0

Sources: Public corporate statements and annual reports; author's interviews with Orix executives.

Note:
[a] Includes only real estate and financial services divisions and subsidiaries.

surge in 1985 of Japanese direct investment abroad, Orix invested substantial capital in developing more sophisticated financial products and services, such as mortgage-backed securities, and was committed to a long-term expansion

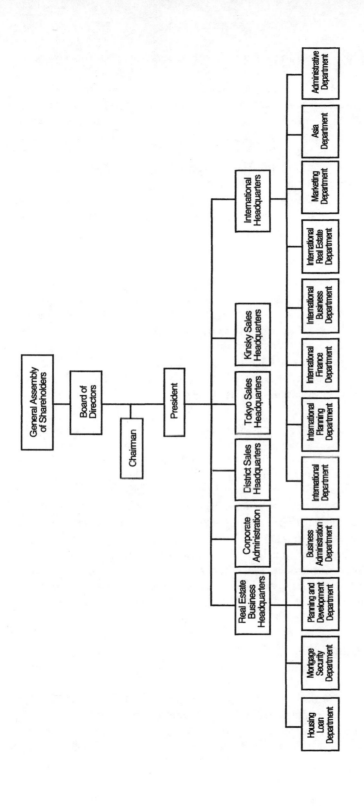

Figure 6.11 Orix management structure (1997)

strategy centered around innovative financial services, not the company's leasing operations.[89]

With twenty years of increasingly innovative experience in financing asset-backed equipment leases and operating leases, and an ongoing commitment to research and development, Orix was positioned by the mid-1980s to accelerate its global expansion. Orix competed against standard international real estate advisory services based on three factors: local responsiveness, cultivated expertise, and ready access to investment capital. As discussed in Chapter 2, the rapid increase in Japanese direct investment abroad beginning in 1985 stemmed from liberalization of monetary policy, strong yen appreciation, declining returns from interest-bearing funds domestically, and a rising stock market.[90] Moreover, while the barriers to capital investment in Japan real estate remained high, due to a scarcity of overvalued property, the markets in Western Europe and the US, in particular, were active and undervalued, especially in light of favorable yen–dollar exchange rates. In the UK and Germany, furthermore, the liberalized Euromarket permitted syndicated loan products and asset-backed investment banking by both brokerage houses and financial institutions. Orix perceived unlimited market opportunities in real estate services, capitalizing on the reputation and client base of the company's international financing and securities subsidiaries. Orix thus shifted its corporate strategy to focus on real estate finance, which deliberately advanced the globalization strategy of the controlling city banks.

Japanese real estate services

In 1985, Orix established a Japanese real estate services group and an international group. The latter focused principally on US and European markets. The Japan division engaged in real estate financial services – residential loans, mortgage-backed securities and international investment loan – and in housing and resort development for existing corporate clients such as computer service firms and insurance and securities brokerage houses.

Having no direct experience in resort development, yet perceiving a lucrative market, Orix acquired a 94 percent equity interest in Osaka-based Ichioka Corporation, a publicly traded property management and leisure facilities management company. By 1990 Orix had developed a mountain ski resort, Co-Members Resort Club RES Orix, for which the company sold and financed time-share memberships to Japanese corporations for their employee-benefits programs.[91] In addition, Orix built and leased more than fifty singles dormitories in the Tokyo metropolitan area near factories of expanding industries.

The real estate group's largest source of revenue, and the activity that experienced the greatest expansion in Orix's domestic financial services, was international lending, particularly syndicated financing for foreign construction projects. Real estate investment financings were completed for clients worldwide as well as the company's own account, which further enabled Orix to diversify revenue sources (Table 6.12). The largest project of this kind was a 30,700-acre joint venture development in Waikoloa, Hawaii, in partnership with the Bass Brothers of Houston, Texas. Orix invested 27 percent of the equity in the beachfront resort as well as securing debt and equity funding from Japanese investors for the project's long-term build-out.[92]

Orix's profitable expansion into real estate services in Japan stemmed directly from the parent company's competitive strength in innovative financial products and broad-based access to low-cost investment capital.[93] This access became particularly important to the Japan real estate group and the financial services division in 1990, when the Bank of Japan raised the nation's official discount rate. Orix, to sustain its competitive performance, readjusted its funding strategies to obtain lower-cost funds and increase its reserves against interest-rate fluctuations – in essence, managing market and corporate mechanisms in such a way as to maintain the efficiency of transaction costs, internally and with clients.[94]

US real estate services

The US real estate services group also grew out of Orix's asset-based financing activities, and first commenced in 1974 when Orix opened an office in New York City. By the mid-1980s, with Japanese direct investment in US real estate growing by up to 50 percent annually, Orix's president in Tokyo decided that local market knowledge and an established US presence were essential to expand the company's property investment services. He also sought to expand real estate services into development project management and institutional fund management, believing that the appreciation in US

Table 6.12 Sources of revenue for Orix (1960–97)[a]

Services	1960	1970	1980	1997
Financial Services (%)	–	–	–	45
Residential Loan Services (%)	–	–	–	20
Mortgage-backed Securities Brokerage (%)	–	–	–	15
Development Project Management (%)	–	–	–	15
Total (%)	0	0	0	100

Sources: Public corporate statements and reports; author's interviews with Orix executives.

Note:
[a] Includes only real estate and financial services divisions and subsidiaries.

property values would provide an additional source of revenue growth for the general company.[95]

Toward this end, Orix's Board and International Real Estate Department commissioned New York-based investment banking firm Kidder Peabody to identify potential acquisition or merger candidates – domestic real estate advisory service firms with consistent performance in development, acquisitions and asset management. Kidder Peabody identified one firm, Rubloff, Inc., founded in Chicago in 1930.[96] In 1987, Orix purchased 23.3 percent of Rubloff's holding company, which also included property management, commercial brokerage and consulting services (Figure 6.12). In 1990, because Orix was strategically committed to only long-term capital investments, the Tokyo-based company forced a split in Rubloff's holding company by acquiring a 70 percent equity interest in the acquisitions, development and asset management operations; the other operating groups were reorganized under separate management.[97]

Orix created Orix Real Estate Equities Fund to strengthen its global exposure (via Rubloff's US clients, experience and reputation) among private and institutional funding sources. For Rubloff, Orix provided direct access to Japanese capital seeking to invest in US real estate as well as financial expertise in asset-backed loan syndications. The Orix–Rubloff merger thus combined two companies of diverse, but complementary, services. Orix acquired Rubloff's expertise in US property markets and its existing client relationships and development projects. After four years, by 1991, Orix Real Estate Equities employed sixty-three professionals in New York, Chicago, Los Angeles, San Francisco, and Washington, DC.[98]

After the sale of Rubloff in the early 1990s, Orix kept its US assets and continued to create value by completing development of the US property portfolio it acquired in the 1980s, especially in Chicago, Washington, DC, Boston, Honolulu, Los Angeles, Miami, New York, Sacramento and San Francisco.

Alliances
- None

Mergers/Acquisitions/Joint Ventures[a]
- Ichioka Corporation (94 percent equity interest), Osaka, Japan, 1986
- Rubloff Real Estate and Capital, Inc. (70 percent equity interest), US, 1987; sale to Rubloff Management, 1990

Figure 6.12 Strategic alliances and acquisitions by Orix

Sources: Public corporate statements and annual reports; author's interviews with Orix executives.

Note:
[a] Includes only real estate and financial services divisions and subsidiaries.

European real estate services

The European real estate services group evolved in much the same way as Orix's US division, expanding directly out of asset-based lending, corporate finance and equipment leasing. Orix opened its first European office in London in 1974. Within the decade, the Board founded a London-based subsidiary, Orix Europe Ltd (1982) to coordinate operations across the continent. By the mid-1980s and continuing through 1990, the subsidiary acted as a principal for investor clients in Japan, arranging debt and equity fund placements in UK and German real estate markets. In 1989 the company broadened its presence in European financial markets by forming an investment banking subsidiary, Orix Corporate Finance Ltd, which moved into the deregulated Euromarket and arranged cross-border syndicates on behalf of European clients. In 1990–1, for example, the London group arranged syndicated financing through the sale of investment instruments to Japanese investors for the $132 million renovation of Romney House, a prestigious historic building in central London.[99] These two financial subsidiaries, similar to their counterparts in other Japanese corporations, also played an important role in securing financing and managing investment funds for the parent company.[100]

In summary, Orix advanced a strategy of global expansion throughout the 1970s and 1980s that followed in the path of expanding world financial markets and capital investors by consistently diversifying financial services and financial products for a growing range of real estate clients, institutional clients, corporate clients and its own account.[101]

Different cultures, different markets, different prospects

Each of these four firms grew out of different cultures and different market conditions; each approached internationalization independently of one another. How did these four real estate advisory service firms respond to rising cross-border investment activity between 1960 and 1997? What factors were most influential in defining each firm's prospects as they expanded into diversified, multiregional companies? From this discussion, several conclusions may be drawn regarding the effective and efficient internationalization of real estate advisory service firms between 1960 and 1997.

National factors: cross-border investment activity and skilled personnel

The rising volume of cross-border investment activity in the world's largest real estate markets appeared to be an important external macroeconomic factor in effective internationalization, affording each of these real estate advisory service firms a national client base to cultivate diversified and innovative services and to support expansion into foreign markets.

177

The availability of skilled labor was another important factor in the expansion of real estate services in each of these four firms. Even though an abundance of low-cost investment capital became a primary factor in the global competition among nations and firms during the finance-driven market of the 1980s, as S.B. Sagari documented for the financial services industry overall, an abundance of capital did not constitute a long-term factor advantage for international competitiveness.[102] As discussed in Chapter 3, over the long term, the UK's and JLW's sustained commitment to the education and professional standards of chartered surveyors, and Cushman & Wakefield's investment in and retention of trained professionals, are believed to have greater long-term value in the national and international competition among real estate advisory firms than did an abundance of investment capital.

Multinational clients

Another external market factor was each firm's ability to secure and retain multinational and foreign clients. None of the four companies agreed to reveal proprietary corporate records on specific clients and associated fee revenues, yet interviews with senior managers in each firm indicated the majority of clients that prompted or facilitated international expansion were either property-intensive enterprises (such as a manufacturing firm) or large, diversified investment funds (such as an institutional portfolio, pension fund or bank).[103] Guided by the cross-border investment activities of such clients, real estate advisory service firms entered property markets worldwide where real estate investment returns exceeded marginal profitability expectations in alternative markets.

Davis and Smales similarly observed from their research on the internationalization of accounting, law and public relations firms that service firms could internationalize expediently and economically by following multinational clients into foreign markets. Minimal differences between nations in the practice of certain professional services only facilitated internationalization.[104] The case studies indicate that those real estate advisory service firms that claimed sufficient business volume through multinational clients and access to foreign investment capital were able to sustain an extensive international network of offices and diversified services.[105] Differences in real estate service practices among the focal countries were indeed evident, yet acted as a real barrier to entry only in Japan.

Service diversification

The international expansion strategy formulated by each firm exploited the company's reputation in the domestic market to establish a position in foreign markets. Each firm sought multinational status through ongoing investment in diversified services and through engagements with clients and alliances with potential foreign competitors. The most significant innovations in real estate advisory services occurred in the 1970s and 1980s, as discussed in Chapters 4 and 6. While service diversification was an important factor in successful internationalization, the four case studies indicate that service diversification and geographic expansion are not always mutually dependent strategies, nor is one strategy the stimulus for the other. Service diversification became the basis for the geographic expansion of both Cushman & Wakefield and Müller, in their domestic markets and abroad, and geographic diversification inspired service innovations by Jones Lang Wootton and Orix – as each firm responded to the demands of a broadening array of clients worldwide.

Each of these real estate service firms initially grew by capitalizing on economies of scale that drew upon existing core services. The firms then achieved economies of scope by extending the range of core services and investing in new techniques and new professional capabilities. As Chandler argued, "the most common stimulus to diversification was the potential for economies of scope" in existing functional units.[106] For Cushman & Wakefield and Müller, brokerage and property management services spawned financial services, development management services and fund management services. For Jones Lang Wootton, investment brokerage and financial services grew into fund management services. And for Orix, real estate services grew out of asset-backed financing for equipment leases.

The three firms whose core real estate advisory practice was the foundation for growth were better positioned to diversify into new advisory services economically through internal expansion, rather than vertical consolidation. By extending their mainline businesses, they incurred lower capital costs to acquire new professional skills rather than having to diversify via marketplace mechanisms by acquiring or consolidating with an existing business. Only Orix, which operated primarily as an independent leasing enterprise, diversified through classic vertical integration by acquiring Ichioka and Rubloff.[107]

The fundamental weakness of the Rubloff partnership was not its intent. Instead, Rubloff had experienced a long period of contraction during the 1980s,[108] which gave Orix significant leverage in absorbing the Rubloff name and management control. Because Orix's administrative hierarchy had evolved out of the company's original focus on leasing, the previously fluid integration between equipment leasing and financial services became dysfunctional when the structure was extended to include a different service discipline and an outside firm in a foreign market. The shift into real estate services, moreover, was not reflected in a significantly revised structure. Neither the international real estate division nor the newly created Orix Real Estate Equities subsidiary (Rubloff) acquired economies of scale and scope from the international conglomerate. Real estate advisory services were compartmentalized, which was believed to inhibit innovation or diversification and respond to market shifts. Because real estate services grew out of financial services and depended on financially-driven investments, the real estate services group was apparently handicapped when Japanese capital markets contracted in 1990. The growth of Orix, as well as other real estate advisory firms founded principally on access to low-cost funds rather than expertise in local markets and clients, was restricted by a limited scope of specialized services and the higher costs of future service diversification.

Geographic expansion

These real estate advisory firms expanded into foreign markets to assure and broaden access to multinational investors, developers and corporations, and to low-cost investment funds for both domestic and foreign operations. Each firm elected a different strategy. Cushman & Wakefield chose a non-equity vertical alliance to enter the European market. Seeking to diversify the firm's business abroad without placing its own capital at risk, Cushman & Wakefield allied its practice and reputation with those of Healey & Baker in Europe. Yet Healey & Baker's retail services practice effectively compromised Cushman & Wakefield's international agenda and diffused the US firm's strong commercial reputation. Such a lower-cost foreign expansion was actually encumbered by diseconomies of scale. Neither firm's domestic reputation provided a competitive advantage for the foreign affiliate, and the alliance was largely unproductive.[109]

The obverse of this theory would be that "a firm with little reputation in a geographical market other than its own", such as Müller in Germany, would benefit from the established practice and reputation of a firm in a foreign market.[110] Müller lacked even a widespread national reputation, and understandably chose this lower-cost strategy. Müller had previously expanded into markets in Germany and Europe through business opportunities with existing clients. Yet it chose to enter an alliance with the international coalition of Oncor to gain a broader presence among global investors entering Germany. Müller's alliance with Oncor, however, combined two enterprises that lacked an established multinational clientele and a sound reputation in either national or international markets. Real estate advisory firms which had superior credentials and broader reputations superseded Oncor's position in the strong 1980s market. Oncor's scattered market presence was not improved in the 1990–1 restructuring, also concurrent with a declining economy and cross-border investment activity. Potential multinational clients appeared even less likely to be attracted to the Müller–Oncor alliance in a recessionary investment climate than in a strong market.

The international expansion of UK-based Jones Lang Wootton represented the most effective and resilient growth strategy, though one with the highest level of potential risk and capital costs. JLW's global expansion over a thirty-year period aligned with the capacities of management and corporate capital. The notable exception was its acquisition of Balay Prenot in the Rhone–Alpes region of France. Beyond this one merger, the London-based firm entered foreign markets by following clients and investing capital reserves. JLW's successful globalization provided evidence of "first mover" advantages for real estate advisory firms which pre-empted competitors in building a global office network to secure multinational clients and international funding sources.[111] By staffing each new office with internally trained personnel, JLW effectively standardized services and exploited economies of scale.[112]

During the period from 1960 and until the late 1980s, JLW's international expansion reinforced Penrose's theory that the rate of a firm's growth is limited by managerial capacity and the increasing costs of capital in moving into new markets and new services.[113] JLW's incremental globalization over a thirty-year period was too costly for competitors to match in a span of one or two years, once cross-border investment rose appreciably. Beyond sheer economic power, other factors such as administrative coordination, human resources and a complex multiregional and multifunctional management hierarchy, reflecting what Penrose called the "progressive subdivision of functions and decentralization of operations", could not be replicated in a short period.[114]

The question then arises: is the size and geographic dispersion of a real estate advisory service firm limited? In contrast to Penrose's theory, Stigler, in *The Organization of Industry*, argued that the theoretical assumption that a firm would not grow or diversify beyond a certain point generated a useless debate. If diseconomies of scale set in, Stigler observed, if the network of linkages became too complex and costly, the firm would contract.[115] Chandler's theory offered a bridge between the competing arguments set forth by Penrose and Stigler, concluding that the accretion of authority by managerial hierarchies was a key force of change. For a growing enterprise to continue to diversify and expand, Chandler argued, the corporate structure must economically internalize transaction costs, smooth the flow among and between service functions and widely dispersed regions, and consistently diversify products to meet the demands of the market.[116] JLW's evolutionary expansion and responsive management structure reaffirmed Chandler's thesis.

However, Chandler emphasized – as did Coase and Williamson – that the primary goal of a firm's growth is to economize transaction costs and increase profitability, internally and throughout the marketplace. Beyond 1990, declining growth rates for skilled labor, investment capital, cross-border investment activity and multinational businesses may well limit the ability of firms such as Jones Lang Wootton to risk its own capital in expanding into new markets by internal combination or acquisition. Instead, for these and other real estate advisory service firms, lower-cost strategies such as alliances and coalitions will likely prevail.[117]

Ownership and management structure

International expansion by the four firms prompted changes and adjustments in corporate structure. The central issue for these real estate advisory service firms was: what is the most effective multiregional and multidivisional structure to support efficient and economical management of the firm? A complementary issue was: what influence does a firm's ownership and capitalization structure have on the rate and scope of expansion into foreign markets?

The case studies indicate how executives of the different companies approached the problems of multiregional management. JLW and Müller provide examples of rational and systematic management, in which coordination, appraisal and planning were high priorities. Cushman & Wakefield viewed management and expansion in more intuitive terms, until 1976–7 when the firm was restructured, seeking systematic, market-based solutions to administration and growth. The organizational hierarchy of Orix took a rational approach, building an administrative structure rather than a functional one. But when Orix introduced real estate services into the holding company in 1985, the organization lacked an integrated, functional structure, which was essential to exploit economies of scale. Such differences in approach accounted for differences in the way the four real estate service firms fared in internationalizing into different property markets.

For Cushman & Wakefield and JLW, international expansion significantly altered the companies' structures; for Orix, expansion minimally affected the integrated corporate structure. Market-oriented expansion policies and localized management structures became hallmarks of the real estate advisory services of Cushman & Wakefield, Jones Lang Wootton and Müller.[118] Orix, while responsive to regional markets in the management of its international leasing operations and financial services, did not incorporate the real estate services groups in Japan and the US into a regionalized structure.

Cushman & Wakefield developed an internalized hierarchy that centralized entrepreneurial decision-making at the local level for its US office network. Throughout the 1960s and continuing to the early 1980s, this employee-owned company – similar to Jones Lang Wootton and Müller – was financially equipped to act promptly regarding entry into new markets because of deep reserves of retained earnings. The firm's domestic strategy and structure were internally capitalized and centered around combination, integration and corporate reputation. For its international expansion in the 1990s, Cushman & Wakefield instead chose a peer group coalition with Healey & Baker, to use Williamson's term.[119] In addition, it sold 41 percent of the company's privately-held stock to Mitsubishi (via The Rockefeller Group) in 1990 to finance both domestic and foreign operations and growth. Similarly, Müller elected a peer group coalition in 1985 with Oncor, a broadly dispersed and independently managed association. This stands in marked contrast to the firm's previous expansion into domestic and foreign markets through internal expansion. Moreover, Müller sold 20 percent of its stock to equity partner Commerzbank in 1990 to capitalize the firm's continued expansion into newly opened German markets – Berlin, Hanover, Leipzig and Essen.

Timing was an important element in the expansion strategies and resulting structures that both Cushman & Wakefield and Müller chose for broadening their national and international operations. During the 1970s and early 1980s, growing domestic real estate markets and cross-border direct investment activity in the US and Germany enabled these real estate advisory service firms to fund geographic expansion with excess earnings. By the late 1980s and early 1990s, however, when financial and real estate markets domestically and abroad were beginning to contract and becoming increasingly competitive, each firm chose an alliance to expand abroad rather than an acquisition that would require investing the firm's own capital. In 1990, each chose to sell a portion of the company's stock to a major financial partner, thereby diluting management control, yet infusing fresh capital for ongoing expansion and diversification – Cushman & Wakefield selling to Mitsubishi and Müller to Commerzbank.

Retained corporate earnings and external equity infusions – or public stock issuances in Orix's case – played a critical role in the rate and scope of international expansion by these real estate advisory firms. Real estate advisory firms, similar to professional service firms generally, were able only to gauge projected fees in foreign markets. In an expansive economic climate, these firms were willing and able to risk their own capital to enter foreign markets. During flat or declining periods, they instead required outside equity and/or a lower-cost alliance to pursue geographic expansion.

Jones Lang Wootton undertook incremental global expansion and developed a multiregional structure over a thirty-year period, which represented the most economical and effective approach for real estate advisory service firms. Because of unavoidable inefficiencies across borders, JLW's evolving corporate structure agreed with Chandler's bias that uniform administrative coordination within the international enterprise "permitted greater productivity, lower costs, and higher profits than coordination by market mechanisms."[120] Jones Lang Wootton demonstrated the greatest capability and foresight in planning and structuring an internationalized network of offices.[121]

Notes

1 A.D. Chandler, Jr., *Strategy and Structure: Chapters in the History of American Industrial Enterprise* (Cambridge, MA: MIT Press, 1962), pp. 30–3; and R.H. Coase, "The Nature of the Firm", *Economica* n.s. IV (1937), pp. 334–5, 337–8.

2 See P.A. Geroski, "The Interaction Between Domestic and Foreign – Based Entrants", Working Paper Series no. 44, Centre for Business Strategy (London School of Economics, 1987) for an analytical model of domestic-based and foreign entrants into new markets.

3 R.H. Coase, "The Nature of the Firm", *Economica* n.s. IV (1937), pp. 333–4, 338.

4 A.D. Chandler, Jr., *Strategy and Structure: Chapters in the History of American Industrial Enterprise* (Cambridge, MA: MIT Press, 1962), p. 15.

5 The size of the firm was measured by the total number of employees working in commercial real estate services, rather than by gross revenues, which are available on a very irregular basis and difficult to substantiate.

6 This assessment was based on critical evaluations published in trade journals and obtained by the author through interviews with corporate real estate executives.

7 T. Sarowitz, "Evolution of a Real Estate Firm", *Real Estate Forum* (April 1988), p. 116.

8 Public and private company reports; confirmed in interview with author, R. Hollander, Regional Director and Senior Vice President, Cushman & Wakefield (Washington, DC, 24 July 1991).

9 A.D. Chandler, Jr., *Scale and Scope: The Dynamics of Industrial Capitalism* (Cambridge, MA: Belknap Press of Harvard University Press, 1990), pp. 31–9.

10 T. Sarowitz, "Evolution of a Real Estate Firm", *Real Estate Forum* (April 1988), p. 118.

11 See Chapter 2, Table 2.2.

12 A firm which pre-empted competitors in diversifying into a new market, in A.D. Chandler, Jr., *Scale and Scope: The Dynamics of Industrial Capitalism* (Cambridge, MA: Belknap Press of Harvard University Press, 1990), p. 34.

13 Cushman & Wakefield, "Focus on Appraisal Services" and "Focus on Appraisal Services: Property Tax Consulting and Tax Management Services", unpublished corporate services brochures (1989); and interview with author, H.C. Carey, Senior Vice President, Cushman & Wakefield (1991).

14 Cushman & Wakefield, "Focus on Industrial/Technology Services", an unpublished corporate services brochure (1989); and interview with author, H. C. Carey, Senior Vice President, Cushman & Wakefield (1991).

15 R.H. Coase, "The Nature of the Firm", *Economica* n.s. IV (1937), pp. 21–5; O.E. Williamson, *Markets and Hierarchies: Analysis and Antitrust Implications* (New York: The Free Press, 1975), p. 82; M.E. Porter, *Competitive Advantage* (New York: The Free Press, 1985), pp. 41–4.

16 Cushman & Wakefield, "Focus on Financial Services", unpublished corporate services brochure (1990), p. 10; interview with author, H. C. Carey, Senior Vice President, Cushman & Wakefield (1991).

17 R.H. Coase, *Economica* n.s. IV (1937), pp. 21–5; A.D. Chandler, Jr., *Strategy and Structure: Chapters in the History of American Industrial Enterprise* (Cambridge, MA: MIT Press, 1962), pp. 30–6; A.D. Chandler, Jr., *Scale and Scope: The Dynamics of Industrial Capitalism* (Cambridge, MA: Belknap Press of Harvard University Press, 1990), pp. 37–41; M.E. Porter, *Competitive Advantage* (New York: The Free Press, 1985), pp. 57–66.

18 In 1988 Cushman & Wakefield managed over 78 million square feet of commercial space valued at $10 billion. Cushman & Wakefield, "Focus on Management Services", an unpublished corporate services brochure (1989); interview with author, H.C. Carey, Senior Vice President, Cushman & Wakefield (1991); and T. Sarowitz, "Evolution of a Real Estate Firm", *Real Estate Forum* (April 1988).

19 E. Davis and C. Smales, "The Internationalization of Professional Services", Working Paper Series No. 66, Centre for Business Strategy, London Business School, London (April 1989), pp. 11–14; and E. Davis, G. Hanlon and J. Kay, "Internationalization in Accounting and Other Professional Services", Working Paper series, no. 73. Centre for Business Strategy, London Business School (April 1990), pp. 11–12.

20 T. Sarowitz, "Evolution of a Real Estate Firm", *Real Estate Forum* (April 1988), p. 122.

21 *Ibid.*:, pp. 122, 124; interviews with author, H.C. Carey and R. McLean, Cushman & Wakefield (1991); Cushman & Wakefield/Healey & Baker, "A Global Real Estate Initiative", unpublished corporate service brochure (1990).

22 O.E. Williamson, *Markets and Hierarchies: Analysis and Antitrust Implications* (New York: The Free Press, 1975), p. 82.

23 Cushman & Wakefield executives recalled only that the restructuring was expensive relative to gross revenues, but reportedly did not have records in private company documents of actual costs.

24 T. Sarowitz, "Evolution of a Real Estate Firm", *Real Estate Forum* (April 1988), p. 124; interview with author, H. C. Carey, Cushman & Wakefield (1991).

25 O.E. Williamson, *Markets and Hierarchies: Analysis and Antitrust Implications* (New York: The Free Press, 1975), pp. xi, 55–6, 82. Also A.D. Chandler, Jr., *Strategy and Structure: Chapters in the History of American Industrial Enterprise* (Cambridge, MA: MIT Press, 1962), pp. 9–17, 30–3; and A.D. Chandler, Jr., *Scale and Scope: The Dynamics of Industrial Capitalism* (Cambridge, MA: Belknap Press of Harvard University Press, 1990), p. 43.

26 T. Sarowitz, "Evolution of a Real Estate Firm", *Real Estate Forum* (April 1988), p. 117.

27 A survey was commissioned by Cushman & Wakefield and Healey & Baker, and conducted by Louis Harris & Associates, which polled senior management from more than 900 American and European firms; "European Business Real Estate Monitor", brochure (1990). The poll showed that, of those American companies that already have facilities in Europe, 54 percent are in the manufacturing sector.

28 The strategies included: (1) opening branch offices in Berlin, Paris, London, Barcelona, Frankfurt, Brussels and other global real estate markets; (2) merging with a reputable firm that planned to enter the United States; (3) acquiring a European service firm; and (4) establishing a joint initiative, or an affiliation, with a foreign firm.

29 E. Davis and C. Smales, "The Internationalization of Professional Services", Working Paper Series No. 66, Centre for Business Strategy, London Business School, London (April 1989), pp. 13–14; and E. Davis, G. Hanlon and J. Kay, "Internationalization in Accounting and Other Professional Services", Working Paper series, no. 73. Centre for Business Strategy, London Business School (April 1990), pp. 11–12.

30 Confirmed in interviews with author, H.C. Carey and R. McLean, Cushman & Wakefield (1991).

31 E. Davis and C. Smales, "The Internationalization of Professional Services", Working Paper Series No. 66, Centre for Business Strategy, London Business School, London (April 1989), p. 4.

32 *Ibid.*, pp. 12–14.

33 Confirmed in interview with author, R. McLean, Cushman & Wakefield (1991).

34 Healey & Baker, "A Guide to our Services", unpublished corporate service brochure (1989). In addition, more recent information was obtained from *Chartered Surveyors 1991*, ed. L. Parkin (Oxford: Ivanhoe Press, 1990), p. 203.

35 Cushman & Wakefield/Healey & Baker, "A Global Real Estate Initiative", unpublished corporate service brochure (1990); and interview with H.C. Carey, Cushman & Wakefield (1991).

36 Cushman & Wakefield/Healey & Baker, "Background: The Joint Initiative Between Cushman & Wakefield and Healey & Baker", press release (1990). Also E. Davis and C. Smales, "The Internationalization of Professional Services",

Working Paper Series No. 66, Centre for Business Strategy, London Business School, London (April 1989), p. 12.

37 Confirmed in interview with author, H.C. Carey, Cushman & Wakefield (1991); also see A.D. Chandler, Jr., *Strategy and Structure: Chapters in the History of American Industrial Enterprise* (Cambridge, MA: MIT Press, 1962), pp. 31–3.

38 Jones Lang Wootton, "The Story of Jones Lang Wootton", unpublished brochure prepared for the firm's 200th anniversary (1990), pp. 1–3.

39 *Ibid.*

40 Confirmed in interviews with author, A. Burt, F. Charnock and M.J. Hodges, Jones Lang Wootton (29 July 1991).

41 Jones Lang Wootton, "International Property", unpublished corporate services brochure (1990).

42 Confirmed in interview with author, J. Lench, Jones Lang Wootton (1991).

43 *Real Estate Forum* vol. 46, no. 7 (July 1991), p. 11.

44 Jones Lang Wootton, "International Property", unpublished corporate services brochure (1991).

45 *Ibid.*

46 Confirmed in interviews with authors, A. Burt, F. Charnock, and M.J. Hodges, Jones Lang Wootton (29 July 1991).

47 R.M. March, "Foreign Firms in Japan", *California Management Review*, vol. 22, no. 3 (Spring 1980), pp. 42–50; M.Y. Yoshino, "Japan as Host to the International Corporation", *The International Corporation* (Cambridge, MA and London: The MIT Press, 1970), p. 350.

48 Jones Lang Wootton, "1989 in Review", unpublished brochure (1990).

49 Jones Lang Wootton, "International Property", unpublished corporate services brochure (1990).

50 Confirmed in interview with author, C. Nalen, Jones Lang Wootton, Washington, DC (1991).

51 Jones Lang Wootton, "The Story of Jones Lang Wootton" (1990), p. 5.

52 The value of transactions that Jones Lang Wootton represented annually, 1988–90.

53 A.D. Chandler, Jr., *Scale and Scope: The Dynamics of Industrial Capitalism* (Cambridge, MA: Belknap Press of Harvard University Press, 1990), pp. 38–9; O.E. Williamson, *Markets and Hierarchies: Analysis and Antitrust Implications* (New York: The Free Press, 1975), pp. 56, 82.

54 Jones Lang Wootton, "International Property", unpublished corporate services brochure (1990). Also Jones Lang Wootton, "Property Services in Europe", unpublished corporate brochure (1991).

55 *Ibid.*

56 Jones Lang Wootton, "1988 in Review", unpublished corporate brochure (1989).

57 Jones Lang Wootton, "International Property", unpublished corporate services brochure (1990).

58 *Ibid.*; and Prudential Real Estate Investors, "Global Watch Report", unpublished brochure (1990).

59 Jones Lang Wootton, *JLWorld*, unpublished corporate brochure (May 1991), p. 19; and "News Briefs", *National Real Estate Investor* (July 1991), p. 16.

60 "Jones Lang Wootton/Arthur D. Little Joint Effort", *Real Estate Forum* (July 1991), p. 22.

61 Laurence Geller, cited in *Ibid.*

62 Jones Lang Wootton, *JLWorld*, May 1991, p. 18. O.E. Williamson, *Markets and Hierarchies: Analysis and Antitrust Implications* (New York: The Free Press, 1975),

pp. 55–6, 82.

63 Each of the firm's continental European operations was established as a limited liability company, wholly owned by The London Partnership. In Germany, because of government regulations for corporations, JLW set up a Gesellschaft mit beschränkter Häftung (GmbH), or a private limited liability company. Among these three regional groups, the European partnership of eleven countries was functionally integrated to capitalize on potential opportunities that grew out of the consolidation of the Economic Community in 1992.

64 Chapter 2, Table 2.1. R. Gop, "The League Table of Estate Agents: The Leaders Stay Ahead of the Field", *Immobilien Manager* (February 1992), p. 16.

65 Since 1990, due to German unification and the privatization of property in newly democratized Eastern Bloc countries, Müller's operations have grown appreciably, standing as of April 1992 at 355 people and ten offices in Germany and five elsewhere in Western Europe. Personal interview, J. Pasch, Müller (12 June 1991); correspondence, B. Lohr, Müller (March 1992); and Müller company profile, unpublished memorandum (1991).

66 See J. Punter *et al.*, "Property in Europe", Working Papers in European Property, Centre for European Property Research, University of Reading (1991), pp. 62–5.

67 R. Gop, "The League Table of Estate Agents: The Leaders Stay Ahead of the Field", *Immobilien Manager* (February 1992), p. 17.

68 See E. Davis and C. Smales, "The Internationalization of Professional Services", Working Paper Series No. 66, Centre for Business Strategy, London Business School, London (April 1989), pp. 5, 7.

69 In 1991, The Office Network was renamed Oncor International.

70 Müller corporate brochure (1991), p. 3.

71 Oncor International, press release (3 May 1991); and Müller corporate brochure (1991), p. 3.

72 For a full description of this office building, see "MesseTurm: Facts and Figures", an unpublished corporate brochure (1990).

73 Oncor International, press release (3 May 1991).

74 R.H. Coase, "The Nature of the Firm", *Economica* n.s. IV (1937), p. 337.

75 M.A. Klionsky, "Driscoll Streamlines from Loose Network to Unified Organization", *Commercial Property News* (1 June 1991), p. 3.

76 E. Davis, G. Hanlon and J. Kay, "Internationalization in Accounting and Other Professional Services", Working Paper series, no. 73. Centre for Business Strategy, London Business School (April 1990), p. 12.

77 Correspondence, B. Lohr, Müller (March 1992). Also A.D. Chandler, Jr., *Strategy and Structure: Chapters in the History of American Industrial Enterprise* (Cambridge, MA: MIT Press, 1962), pp. 9–11.

78 Correspondence, B. Lohr, Müller (March 1992).

79 The original shareholders included Nichimen Company, Ltd, presently Nichimen Corporation; The Nissho Company, Ltd, Iwai & Company, Ltd, presently Nissho Iwai Corporation; The Sanwa Bank, Ltd; The Toyo Trust & Banking Company, Ltd; The Nippon Kangyo Bank, Ltd, presently The Dai-Ichi Kangyo Bank, Ltd; the Bank of Kobe, presently The Taiyo Kobe Mitsui Bank, Ltd; and The Industrial Bank of Japan, Ltd.

80 See M. Eli, *Japan, Inc.: Global Strategies of Japanese Trading Corporations* (Chicago: Probus, 1991), pp. 1–18.

81 *Ibid.*, pp. 76–9.

82 Orix Corporation, corporate history brochure (Tokyo, 1990), p. 40.

83 Orix Corporation, "History of Orix Corporations", memorandum (31 July 1990), unpaginated.

84 *Ibid.*

85 This paralleled the common strategy of the American industrial enterprises profiled by A.D. Chandler, Jr. in *Strategy and Structure: Chapters in the History of American Industrial Enterprise* (Cambridge, MA: MIT Press, 1962), pp. 16–17, 25.

86 *Ibid.*, pp. 28–33.

87 Personal communication, J.S. Nagashima, Orix Corporation (3 July 1991).

88 Orix Corporation, corporate history brochure (1990), pp. 15–16.

89 Orix annual report (1990), p. 3.

90 Chapter 2, pp. 51–3.

91 Orix Corporation, corporate history brochure (1990), p. 35.

92 *Ibid.*, pp. 34–5; and Orix annual report (1990), pp. 12–13.

93 Orix Corporation, corporate history brochure (1990), p. 35.

94 Orix annual report (1990), pp. 6–8.

95 *Ibid.*, pp. 10–12; and Orix Corporation, "The Period Under Review", *Orix Update* (Winter 1990), no. 2.

96 Confirmed in interview with author, W. Kullman, Orix Real Estate Equities, Chicago (July 1991).

97 C. Bloomfield, "Rubloff Property Gems Define Sinclair, Orix Mission", *Commercial Property News* (16 February 1991), p. 1; and interview with author, M. O'Kelly, Rubloff (21 June 1991).

98 Correspondence, J.S. Nagashima, Orix Corporation (3 July 1991); and James Nathan, "Ensuring More Bang For the Investment Buck", *Real Estate Forum* (April 1992), pp. 58–9.

99 Orix annual report (1991), pp. 18–20.

100 M. Eli, *Japan, Inc.: Global Strategies of Japanese Trading Corporations* (Chicago: Probus, 1991), p. 76.

101 Orix Corporation, *Orix Update* (Winter 1990), no. 2.

102 S.B. Sagari, "The Financial Services Industry: An International Perspective", (PhD dissertation, New York University, 1986), pp. 67–8.

103 Industry publications; confirmed by author in executive interviews, Cushman & Wakefield; Jones Lang Wootton; Müller; and Orix (1991).

104 E. Davis and C. Smales, "The Internationalization of Professional Services", Working Paper Series No. 66, Centre for Business Strategy, London Business School, London (April 1989), pp. 5–7.

105 A.D. Chandler, Jr. observed a similar condition among the American industrial enterprises he reviewed in *Strategy and Structure: Chapters in the History of American Industrial Enterprise* (Cambridge, MA: MIT Press, 1962), p. 32.

106 A.D. Chandler, Jr., *Scale and Scope: The Dynamics of Industrial Capitalism* (Cambridge, MA: Belknap Press of Harvard University Press, 1990), pp. 15, 41.

107 A.D. Chandler, Jr. observed that acquisition, or consolidation, was the most common approach to the formation of a vertically integrated enterprise among American industrial firms in *Strategy and Structure: Chapters in the History of American Industrial Enterprise* (Cambridge, MA: MIT Press, 1962), p. 29.

108 C. Bloomfield, "Rubloff Property Gems Define Sinclair, Orix Mission", *Commercial Property News* (16 February 1991), p. 34.

109 E. Davis, G. Hanlon and J. Kay, "Internationalization in Accounting and Other Professional Services", Working Paper series, no. 73. Centre for Business Strategy, London Business School (April 1990), pp. 9, 11.

110 *Ibid.*, p. 12.

111 A.D. Chandler, Jr., *Strategy and Structure: Chapters in the History of American Industrial Enterprise* (Cambridge, MA: MIT Press, 1962), p. 34.

112 *Ibid.*, p. 31.

113 E.T. Penrose, *The Theory of the Growth of the Firm* (White Plains, NY: M.E. Sharpe, Inc., 1959), pp. 88–103.

114 *Ibid.*, pp. 24–5, 55–8.

115 G.J. Stigler, *The Organization of Industry* (Chicago: University of Chicago Press, 1968), p. 99.

116 A.D. Chandler, Jr., *Strategy and Structure: Chapters in the History of American Industrial Enterprise* (Cambridge, MA: MIT Press, 1962); A.D. Chandler, Jr., *The Visible Hand: The Managerial Revolution in American Business* (Cambridge, MA: Belknap Press of Harvard University Press, 1977); A.D. Chandler, Jr., *Scale and Scope: The Dynamics of Industrial Capitalism* (Cambridge, MA: Belknap Press of Harvard University Press, 1990); B. Supple, "Scale and Scope: Alfred Chandler and the dynamics of industrial capitalism", *Economic History Review*, XLIV, no. 3 (August 1991), p. 504.

117 Collaborations between two firms involve increased administrative complexity and higher risk regarding coordination, personnel, corporate philosophies and expansion strategies. E. Davis, G. Hanlon and J. Kay, "Internationalization in Accounting and Other Professional Services", Working Paper series, no. 73. Centre for Business Strategy, London Business School (April 1990), p. 12.

118 A.D. Chandler, Jr. showed in his evaluation of industrial giants General Electric and Westinghouse that the firms developed departmental structures that reflected the types of markets in which certain products were sold, in *Scale and Scope: The Dynamics of Industrial Capitalism* (Cambridge, MA: Belknap Press of Harvard University Press, 1990), p. 28.

119 O.E. Williamson, *Markets and Hierarchies: Analysis and Antitrust Implications* (New York: The Free Press, 1975), pp. xi, 52–5.

120 A.D. Chandler, Jr., *The Visible Hand: The Managerial Revolution in American Business* (Cambridge, MA: Belknap Press of Harvard University Press, 1977), p. 6.

121 A.D. Chandler, Jr., *Scale and Scope: The Dynamics of Industrial Capitalism* (Cambridge, MA: Belknap Press of Harvard University Press, 1990), pp. 262–62.

7

CONCLUSIONS

Enhancing competitive advantage

This examination of the international growth and diversification of real estate advisory services in the United States, the United Kingdom, Germany and Japan between 1960 and 1997 highlighted, among other matters, the complexity of the subject – which encompassed four countries, several inter-disciplinary themes, and at least forty professional service companies. As shown by the corporate profiles and case studies, the internationalization of real estate advisory services was most efficiently and effectively achieved by firms that built solid reputations and multiregional organizations in their home nations.

Rising cross-border investment levels supported the growth of real estate advisory services through the foreign investment activities of existing and prospective clients. This enabled property advisory firms to enhance their competitive standing by diversifying into new services and by entering foreign markets; therefore they established relationships with foreign clients at the same time as they expanded services for existing domestic clients. In other words, real estate advisory firms achieved competitive advantages by developing an international service network and a diversified services practice while providing services to existing clients that were expanding globally. For example, CB Commercial failed in its initial international expansion in the late 1980s, but the firm successfully renewed its strategy for global expansion by entering into an alliance with DTZ Debenham in 1992. Although this alliance occurred several years after CB's flawed approach, it was one of many examples that proved a global orientation was required to thrive in the 1990s. By 1992 most of the focal firms were aligning with international firms and networks to survive locally by protecting established clients that were making international connections of their own.

Rising cross-border real estate investment and growth in real estate employment

The globalization of the real estate industry was driven by rising levels of inward and outward foreign real estate investment, particularly when it reached unprecedented levels in the late 1970s and 1980s. Until the mid-1970s cross-border property investment remained a small segment of each focal country's economy, with inward real estate investment stocks for all four focal countries, totaling only 0.8 percent of the world stock of inward direct investment in 1975.[1] As concluded in Chapters 2 and 3, the gradual liberalization of capital controls in the 1970s and early 1980s set the stage for an unprecedented increase in cross-border direct investment, including investment in real estate.[2] Among the most significant events was the abolition of the Bretton Woods standard, the advent of the floating exchange rate system in 1973, and the need to facilitate the recycling of dollar surpluses generated from OPEC oil price increases during the early 1970s.

During the 1960s and the first half of the 1970s, the UK and Germany stood as the largest investing countries. The US gained prominence in the international arena when, in 1980, it hosted the largest amount of inward direct investment in real estate, a position it sustained through the 1980s. The national government's open investment policy and diverse investment opportunities in several regional markets around the country contributed to this premier standing. German, British and other European investors accounted for the majority of US real estate investment during the early 1980s, while Japanese direct investment dominated after 1985. German outward real estate investment rose to unprecedented levels in 1986, 1987 and 1989, which prompted previously provincial German property advisers to expand to a national and international scope. UK outward investment in real estate increased much less in the 1980s than that of either Germany or Japan.

Japanese outward investment continued to dominate the international real estate industry in the first half of the 1990s, as it did during the second half of the 1980s. From 1990 through 1995, Japanese outward investment in real estate increased the fastest and by the largest amount of any focal country, and it remained at the highest proportion (15 percent) of any source country's outward direct investment. Japanese outward investment in real estate grew from $2.5 billion in 1985 to $46.4 billion in 1990, and to $78 billion by 1995. However, Japanese government data represents planned rather than completed investment, and thus does not reflect any write-downs of actual investment in response to the sharp decline in commercial real estate prices in the US and other countries during this period. In fact, the write-downs of US-held real estate from historical book values to current values occurred primarily between 1995 and 1997 among Japanese investors – and among the Japanese banks which financed those real estate ventures. During this time, the European markets, primarily London, Paris and

Frankfurt, also attracted Japanese investment in real estate, but to a much lesser extent than the US.

German outward direct investment in real estate also advanced, but at a much slower pace than Japanese direct investment. By 1994, the latest year for which German direct investment data are currently available, the stock of outward investment in real estate totaled about $25 billion, only about one-third as high as Japanese investment in real estate. The majority of property investment through the 1970s flowed to European countries, and a growing portion went to US markets in the 1980s. Outward investment data suggested that German real estate companies concentrated on domestic markets and, in 1989–90, immediate investment opportunities in East Germany.[3] German manufacturing and service companies, by contrast, implemented global strategies.

The UK had the second largest amount of inward real estate investment stock of any focal country in 1995, amounting to about $13 billion or one-half the size of the US stock. However, relative to the respective size of their economies – the US gross domestic product was about six-and-a-half times as large as the UK's in 1990 – inward investment in UK real estate is quite large due mostly to its location within Europe and the desire of foreign firms to locate in an English-speaking country. The UK hosted a significant increase in Japanese and other European property investment in the late 1980s, and the overall stock inward direct investment in UK real estate increased from $2.7 billion in 1985 to $14.5 billion in 1991, and then declined to $13.5 billion by 1995.

The four-nation historical profile in Chapter 4 suggested that the growth and maturation of real estate services was stimulated by the consistent growth of the domestic economy. Confirming Casson's theory that a nation's business culture and economic history were a source of long-term competitive advantage, the demand for real estate services in home markets influenced the competitive strength (or weakness) of each firm in the global market – by either providing or limiting opportunities to develop superior capabilities in diversified services and to gain exposure to a broad range of clients.[4] The real estate advisory services in the UK and US were superior to those of Japan and Germany because of the UK's long history of outward expansion, especially in Europe and the former British colonies of Australia, Canada and the Asian region, and because of significant inward investment in US real estate. Japan and Germany, by contrast, were characterized by a more fragmented history of domestic markets and foreign property investment.

In addition, the collective profile of forty real estate advisory firms presented in Chapter 4 revealed that 92.5 percent of firms surveyed increased in size over the 37-year period (measured by the number of personnel employed), and 85 percent expanded the operating business into foreign countries. The experience of these forty firms indicated that foreign expansion and absolute growth defined the evolution of firms within this professional services sector from 1960 to 1997. Firms principally internationalized to respond to the demands of multinational clients, confirming Davis and Smales's basic premise that professional service firms internationalized largely through multinational clients and enabled by minimal differences in service practices across national borders.[5] Reinforcing the findings of the recent study of London's City Research Project, a real estate advisory firm's reputation and home-base location in an international market capital such as London, New York or Tokyo, made an important contribution to the firm's international growth. Competitive advantage stemmed most of all from knowledge and reputation in local markets and a firm's reputation and technical capabilities among major national and international clients. Firms were retained for objective counsel – avoiding conflicts of interest by independent advice and providing sometimes disagreeable conclusions – and secured their good reputations by providing clients with critical guidance.

Because the growth of international property services was closely related to the growth of cross-border direct investment and international finance, the firms having solid reputations in international financial centers had a competitive advantage in attracting international business in their home "international" market, or abroad in foreign markets.[6] It is no coincidence that the premier real estate advisory service firms with strong reputations in cross-border investment were headquartered in the international market centers of New York City or Los Angeles in the US, London in the UK, Tokyo in Japan and Frankfurt or Munich in Germany.

During the 1990s, the US Real Estate Investment Trusts (REITs) increased in number from almost zero to nearly 200 publicly traded trusts with a total market capitalization of more than $140 billion. REITs represent a "total return" investment offering shareholders current income from cash dividends and the strong potential of long-term share price appreciation. They have outperformed both the stock and bond markets in the US in the six years up to 1996. In addition, they have produced a greater annual total return than the Standard & Poor 500, while offering investors the benefits of a diversified real estate portfolio with professional management and stock liquidity. REITs currently own only 8 percent of the $1.28 trillion institutionally owned commercial real estate market in the US, and they should continue to grow aggressively over the next ten years.

Pension funds have always had difficulty in both managing and selling their directly owned real estate; this was especially true in the late 1980s. The REIT share ownership has solved both of these management-intensive problems.[7] As pension funds invest large sums of capital into REITs for ownership of stock rather than real estate, this development will assist REITs in their continued growth and make it easier to monitor investments. REITs in the US have been competing with "opportunity funds" created by Starwood, Goldman Sachs/Whitehall, Apollo, AEW's Partners I & II, and other firms. Opportunity funds (which fall into the alternative investment class for investors) and REITs allow domestic and foreign pension funds to invest in securities instead of directly holding properties. Over the next ten years, most pension funds will hold their entire core real estate portfolios as real estate securities. This will allow pension funds to discontinue their relationships with investment fund managers and directly hold board seats on the various REITs and opportunity funds in which they invest.

This restructuring of the pension fund holdings of real estate has and will continue to greatly change real estate advisory services in the US and globally. Advisory firms will be forced to consolidate further worldwide, establishing new strategies to compete in the real estate securities arena. The evolution of commercial real estate investment techniques will be a driving force behind a more globally oriented real estate advisor. Because of this development and other factors, in his PhD thesis at the London School of Economics the author predicted that advisory firms would consolidate, and this has proven to be the case during the period between 1990 and 1997. With the emerging global real estate securities market, the marketplace will become even more financially sophisticated and innovative, therefore increasing the professional skills and geographic scope required by each advisory firm. Recognition of the importance of these subjects will even lead to more rigorous educational standards and advanced technical training, though regrettably the author has observed little evidence of this to date.[8]

Skilled personnel and market knowledge

The availability of skilled labor within each focal country constituted a primary factor in the growth of real estate services in those countries. The case studies in Chapters 4 and 6 confirmed Sagari's argument that an educated workforce appears to be an important long-term advantage in the financial services profession.[9] This was particularly evident among UK firms: the British system was unmatched in its commitment to high educational standards for property professionals and the regulation of professional competence through the Royal Institute of Chartered Surveyors. US firms had no centralized regulatory body to monitor professional standards and educational guidelines, yet the leading firms (defined by reputation and size) consistently invested corporate capital in recruiting and retaining well-educated professionals from quality colleges and universities.

Firm allegiance by senior managers, moreover, played an influential role in effective international expansion. Most leading real estate advisory firms from the UK, US, Germany and Japan transferred senior staff abroad to sustain corporate loyalty and internal coordination across widely dispersed regions. The key strengths of real estate advisory firms were, first, local market knowledge, and, second, the firm's singular and collective presence in any given market, or their reputation. Both of these attributes depended on the quality of the firm's professionals. Thus, while the author believes that Davis, Hanlon

194

& Kay overrated the value of reputation in the competition among service firms, he agrees with Kay's later work in *The Foundation of Corporate Success* (1993), in which Kay states that "reputation is the most important commercial mechanism for conveying information to consumers. But reputation is not equally important in all markets."[10]

Reputation was often the key to a real estate advisory firm establishing its value with clients, at home and abroad: investors sought to retain property advisers with strong credentials and known expertise in a particular market or technical service. Kay argued that reputation was such a powerful source of competitive advantage that it directly affected the market pricing of a firm's services as well as the firm's market dominance.[11] The forty-firm profile and four case studies confirmed that the perceived and actual "value creation" for clients' property investments was crucial to each firm's growth and profitability. Moreover, the size of a firm's staff and annual revenues was a less meaningful measure of the firm's reputation than was the quality of its senior professionals and major clients – a direct result of the firm's service breadth and knowledge of diverse local markets. The case of Jones Lang Wootton reinforced the notion that the pricing of real estate services was directly correlated with reputation: JLW remained the premier international real estate advisory firm, and commanded the highest billing rates of all firms surveyed.

During the early 1990s, JLW continued to focus on high-fee markets. From 1989 to 1993, the US real estate market was in deep recession, and JLW's partners were not realizing acceptable fee income. Therefore many of the partners in the US left the firm, due to the shrinking fee potential as well as to their desire to avoid risk. During that time, JLW's focus shifted from the US to Asia and Eastern Europe, where growth in the real estate market was tremendous. The only problem with this global strategy was the long-term results on the firm's US market position. For example, JLW's US reputation has not been helped by the lack of commitment over the last five to seven years. This is why the ongoing merger talks in 1997 with LaSalle Partners have been so important to JLW's position in the marketplace. These developments underline the cyclical nature of the business and draw an important lesson: large global firms must remain focused on higher yielding markets without affecting the firm's position in other substantial markets that will mature in the long term.

National trade policies and practices and international real estate services

Each country's tax structure and cross-border trade regulations influenced domestic real estate practices and market standards; they defined the competitive environment for international real estate advisory services. In addition, national foreign trade policies and domestic investors' orientation to foreign markets influenced the internationalization of that country's real estate advisers.[12] The US established a favorable tax and market system, as well as a liberal trade and investment environment. Since the mid-1970s, foreign advisers representing foreign investors were unhindered in the openly competitive US environment, with US policies and business practices remaining the most liberal among the focal countries.[13] By comparison, UK real estate advisers prevailed in the UK and European markets, having decades before set the standards and unofficial conditions by which all advisers operated. While liberal regulatory standards prevailed in the UK, the small domestic market ultimately limited competitive opportunities for foreign real estate advisory firms.

Japan's and Germany's restrictive domestic regulations bolstered the economic interdependency of domestic investors and domestic advisers, which virtually closed service networks to foreign property advisers. In Germany, after the government lifted regulatory restrictions on foreign investment by large German open-end funds in 1990, foreign property and financial advisers began to gain prominence with German investors in both domestic and foreign markets. Japan's Ministry of Finance remained the omnipresent government agency that controlled the incremental liberalization of Japan's outward real estate investment, and gradually opened the highly restrictive domestic market to foreign investors and service firms in the second half of the 1970s. When, in 1983, the MOF lifted capital export controls and the foreign exchange value of the yen soared, the global expansion of Japanese real estate investment and advisory services followed, particularly between 1985 and 1989. As of 1990, foreign investment in Japan still remained hindered by explicit and tacit regulations. These restrictions assist and pressure firms in service economies – such as those in the UK and the US – to create competitive advantages in the Japanese marketplace. Therefore, due to these historical, cultural and investment differences, the government restrictions have held back Japanese firms from relating to and participating in the service industry.

Competition and innovation

Competitive pressures prompted real estate advisory firms in all of the focal countries to introduce innovative services and diversify into new practice areas. Innovations typically emerged when firms perceived intensified competition from new entrants or lower profitability from existing service divisions. The major multinational accounting and investment banking firms, which operated a network of offices worldwide and which engaged in allied real estate disciplines, constituted the most formidable competition to real estate advisory firms.

An important factor affecting the innovation process and service diversification was the unstructured and ever-changing client market, ranging from individual investors to multinational corporations: commercial and merchant banks, building societies in the UK, savings and loan associations in the US, insurance and pension funds, universities and local governments, securitized investment and unit trusts, and international developers and construction firms. Service diversification enabled real estate advisers to broaden the range of potential client types, and supplemented periodic weaknesses in specific market segments. The degree to which cross-border real estate investment influenced the innovation process and service diversification can be inferred from the growth of foreign (versus domestic) personnel and fee revenues, based on a simple analysis of the forty firms in Chapter 4. Revenues derived from foreign sources constituted a disproportionate amount of revenue growth over the period, increasing from negligible levels in 1960 to an average of 27 percent of total revenues among US firms in 1990, 44 percent for UK firms, 17 percent for German firms, and 5 percent among Japanese firms.

The experience of these forty firms, and the case studies in Chapter 6, indicate that functional service innovations and technical innovations became essential factors in attracting and retaining domestic and foreign investors through volatile investment cycles,[14] and appeared to advance the internationalization of real estate advisory services. During periods of significant changes in inward/outward stocks and flows and/or volatility in the national economy, real estate service firms had more incentive to introduce innovative services and techniques.[15] Exceptionally active cross-border markets – the UK in the 1960s (outward investment), Germany in the 1970s (outward investment), and the US and Japan in the 1980s (inward and outward investment, respectively) – stimulated a higher degree of innovative technologies during these periods. In the 1990s, the US continued to take the lead in innovative tools for financing property portfolios and expanding aggressively into foreign markets.

Client demand and foreign expansion

Geographic expansion, rather than service diversification, appeared to have a greater impact on employment growth in real estate services and the number of offices operated by property service firms. International expansion was supported by domestic clients moving into foreign markets, as well as by the increase in foreign property investment and by the maturation of commercial real estate markets in the focal countries. Competition also became an important factor in the internationalization of real estate advisory firms, especially after 1985 when international investment banks expanded and strengthened their real estate and property finance services in foreign markets.

The Chapter 6 case studies indicate that only those real estate service firms that claimed sufficient business volume through multinational clients and access to cross-border capital were able to sustain an extensive international network of offices.[16] The majority of clients that prompted international expansion were either property-intensive enterprises (such as manufacturing, trading and warehousing companies) or large, diversified investment funds (such as pension and insurance funds). A firm's experience in foreign markets and with the logistics of international expansion appeared to play an important role in real estate services. This confirmed Davis and Smales's argument that service firms which successfully imported "creative services" into new markets acquired competitive advantage in international expansion.[17]

Japanese advisory firms were born into international enterprises, and foreign expansion typically occurred within a decade of the firm's founding between the mid-1920s and mid-1950s. These firms were vertically integrated within multinational group companies, and international expansion did not necessarily require a foreign establishment. Japanese real estate advisers accelerated their overseas expansions in the late 1980s – by counseling Japanese investors in landmark acquisitions and by acquiring partnership interests in US investment banks and real estate service firms.

UK firms, by contrast, internationalized into a greater number of foreign markets than did firms in any other focal country. They established offices abroad between 1958 and 1968, concurrent with a significant rise in outward direct real estate investment by UK sponsors. Foreign expansion exceeded domestic growth during the 1960–97 period, and UK estate agents secured a competitive advantage early on by cultivating local expertise and client relationships in diverse foreign markets. They were well-positioned in Europe to assist US multinationals entering European markets, the exception being Germany, where they (as other foreign advisers) had limited opportunities to penetrate German markets until 1988–9.

Germany's fragmented property markets until the early 1980s hindered the service capabilities and the professional sophistication of domestic property firms. German property advisers began to internationalize in the late 1970s by affiliating with foreign firms or joining global network associations. Even while Germany led the other focal countries in outward direct investment during the 1980–7 period, most German real estate advisory firms lacked international practices and, on average, entered only two foreign markets over the 1960–97 period.

US firms internationalized between 1975 and 1997 in response to increased multinational activity by domestic clients and the liberalization of globalized financial markets. Competition from US investment banks active in Euromarket activities and the London market may have been the principal factor in prompting US real estate advisory firms to move abroad in the late 1980s. Having advised and invested substantially in US markets, they were less adept at shaping multinational deal structures and adapting to foreign cultural and business practices.

After 1985, several real estate advisory firms in the four focal countries entered foreign financial markets (by opening new offices and/or through correspondent relationships) to counteract direct competition from investment and merchant banks in corporate real estate services. Most major property service firms concurrently diversified into innovative financial services. UK chartered surveyors faced new competition from investment banks and the Big Six accounting firms. While UK property advisers gained prominence among financial institutions during the 1973–5 property crash, in the 1980s clients demanded access to international capital sources. UK and German chartered surveyors alike were challenged in the 1986–90 period to redefine financial services generally to encompass transactional representation. Japanese real estate advisory firms, too, expanded their presence in foreign property and financial markets to capitalize on their affiliations with Japanese financial institutions.

Expansion strategy and organizational structure

The complexity and cost of managing several offices across different regions and cultures constituted the greatest challenge for internationalizing real estate advisory service firms. In addition, cumulative service diversification necessitated an increasingly more complex structure of multiple divisions, regardless of whether new services were added or developed through staff recruitment, innovation and technical training, merger and acquisition, or affiliation. Yet few firms could operate on a large enough scale to support a fully integrated operation in every domestic and foreign market. The research findings confirmed Coase's theory that the main activity of a firm was coordinating business relationships, arguing that the most successful expansions were tied to the management of a firm's move into a new market and the amount of capital placed at risk.[18] The strongest competitors among foreign clients were companies that developed an effective network to bring locally cultivated services into the international marketplace. Moreover, a real estate service firm's business philosophy and organizational structure determined its ability over the long term to capitalize on economic growth and to defend a diversified, international practice in the face of periodic economic decline, as well as to function in various cultures and government settings while maintaining the loyalty of staff. While Coase emphasized superior management over markets and the economy,[19] this book presents evidence that growth by real estate advisory firms depended equally on the capacity of both management and markets.

Recognizing the limits of organic growth, most firms in the four focal countries determined it was more efficient to affiliate, contract with or merge with a third party for certain services in certain regions.[20] UK property advisers tended to enter the majority of foreign markets through "organic" expansion. Most US, German and Japanese firms, by contrast, chose to affiliate or merge with potential competitors in foreign markets. Japanese firms acquired ownership interests in US firms in the 1980s to gain access to pools of investors and to participate directly in operating property assets. US and German firms affiliated or merged with other firms to reduce the firm's perceived risk in entering alien markets. Particularly in markets where the "right of establishment" was costly, relative to projected fee revenues, incoming property advisers chose to operate through an established affiliate or limited partner rather than invest corporate capital in a satellite office.

The collective profile of firms also indicated that, regardless of native country, a firm's earliest or previous organizational structure influenced the manner and pace in which the firm grew. Firms that diversified or expanded early in the 1960s or before – Jones Lang Wootton, Weatherall Green & Smith, Cushman & Wakefield, Mitsubishi – were structurally organized to disperse more efficiently into multiple markets in the 1970s and 1980s and incorporate new skills and functions into the mainline business.[21] For real estate advisory firms, first mover status appeared to be an important factor in achieving competitive advantage.

Because property service firms initially grew by capitalizing on economies of scale that drew upon established core services and invested in new professional capabilities, a semi-decentralized, multidivisional structure appeared to be most effective in foreign expansion. Such an organization recognized the critical importance of in-depth market knowledge at the local level, and of entrepreneurial initiative and innovation within specific divisions. These firms were sensitive to market and technical trends and were able to exploit new services globally in a prompt and efficient manner. In addition, an organizational structure that evolved over a longer time period enjoyed greater opportunities to centralize standards of quality and decentralize authority to divisions and regions.[22] Japanese firms, which remained highly centralized, had the least structural flexibility to respond to market and client shifts.

The company profiles and case studies also revealed that privately owned service enterprises, which were governed by conservative financial stewardship, gained competitive advantage by having greater flexibility to capitalize service diversification and geographic expansion. The firm's retained capital was at risk, yet those firms that did invest corporate capital – either in vertical integration or by a merger/acquisition – typically received a greater proportion of fee revenues from foreign sources than did those firms that internationalized through a nonequity (and less controllable) affiliation. Higher investment costs tended to produce higher long-term benefits. Moreover, in privately held firms directly owned by partners, principals and/or employees, corporate managers enjoyed a greater degree of control and freedom to implement long-term structural changes than did, for example, public companies answerable to shareholders.[23]

The international expansion of UK-based Jones Lang Wootton represented the most effective and resilient growth strategy, though one with the highest level of potential risk and capital costs. JLW expanded worldwide in incremental stages over the period studied, keeping pace with the capacities of management and available corporate capital. JLW began to internationalize in 1958 and thereby pre-empted competitors in building a global office network and securing the business of multinational clients. Moreover, JLW staffed each new office with internally trained personnel to standardize service quality and exploit economies of scale. Because JLW's incremental globalization was too costly for competitors to match in a one- or two-year timeframe, when cross-border investment rose appreciably in the 1980s, the company's success and global reputation provided evidence that there were real first mover advantages for internationalizing real estate advisory firms. Beyond sheer economic power, such other factors as administrative coordination, human resources and an established multiregional and multifunctional management hierarchy, could not be replicated by competitors in a short period. These were important (and sound) findings relative to the standard business literature, particularly Chandler's controversial theory about first mover advantages and Stigler's argument about an efficient enterprise.[24]

Real estate advisory services in the twenty-first century: an outlook

The global economic restructuring that evolved in the US in the early 1990s, and that subsequently moved through Japan and Europe, had a fundamental impact on real estate markets and related investors worldwide. Declining cross-border direct investment growth, government regulations and recessionary markets severely devalued property investments during this period and prompted investors to disinvest or creatively restructure their real estate assets. Real estate advisory service firms were challenged to respond to changing client demands as well as significantly reduced demands for services: staff reductions and office closings replaced the international expansion of the 1980s. The importance of real estate investments and investment advisory services was further highlighted by these significant events. In particular, the creativity of real estate advisory services was showcased worldwide, while the impact of real estate investments on the national economic structures of the US and Japan primarily, and the UK and Germany to a lesser extent, became obvious.

The profile of investors in the late 1990s will continue to be different from that which dominated through the 1980s, a change already noticeable as insurance and pension funds and corporations invest in real estate by using REITs and other creative investment vehicles of the opportunity fund type. The question then arises: what impact will the growth of cross-border direct investment in real estate have on strategies for and the structure of international real estate advisory services? The negative real estate investment climate of the late 1980s and the early 1990s provided some indications, in that the early 1990s challenged real estate advisers to redirect the focus of advisory services and their types of private institutional and corporate clients. In all focal countries, the focus of property services for investors shifted from growing direct investment portfolios, through acquisitions and new development, to maximizing returns (or minimizing losses) on existing assets through investment vehicles such as REITs and opportunity funds, which were used by developers and investment owners to de-leverage their portfolios during the severe recession.

The emphasis for advisors also shifted away from staff growth to reducing overhead and operating costs. The firms that had the greatest structural flexibility to respond to changing markets and the shifting of clients tended to be centralized organizations in which standards of quality and overall management were well defined; they also made effective use of decentralized authority established by individual managers in regional, national and international offices.

By the mid-1990s, the focus further shifted to consolidating and expanding by acquiring or merging advisory firms, as profit margins decreased due to the competitive environment. For example, the LaSalle acquisition of Galbreath greatly improved the asset utilization and management efficiencies of these two fierce US competitors. This acquisition, coupled with LaSalle's alliance with Savills and its ongoing merger discussions with Jones Lang Wootton, typify the strategic "model" for the future success of global firms. The service company model could evolve into a similar worldwide structure as an Arthur Andersen, where it is a globaly owned organization.

How can firms best adapt and thrive in this constantly changing global marketplace? To rephrase the question, and to return to the central question raised at the beginning of this book: what are the fundamental strategies that will help real estate advisory services grow in coming years? The author believes that further consolidation of advisory firms and the future development of international REITs and opportunity funds will grow exponentially during the coming years. The key for advisory firms is to lead the process by acquiring assets and developing existing personnel to allow for corporate growth and innovation – and thereby to avoid being acquired. The best strategy is to remain focused, utilizing the firm's core competencies to grow globally.

Notes

1 US Department of Commerce, International Trade Administration, *International Direct Investment: Global Trends and the U.S. Role*, 1988 edition, p. 91. The world stock of inward direct investment was estimated at $208 billion in 1973.

2 There is virtually no research on the relationship between the growth in total foreign direct investment between 1960 and 1990 and the liberalization of capital controls by the focal countries.

3 Beginning with data for 1991, investment in the former German Democratic Republic (East Germany) is considered as domestic rather than foreign direct investment.

4 M. Casson, *Enterprise and Competitiveness: A Systems View of International Business* (Oxford: Clarendon Press, 1990), p. 88; Casson also addresses this argument in his

introduction to M. Casson, ed., *Global Research Strategy and International Competitiveness* (London: Basil Blackwell, 1991), p. 11.

5 A.D. Chandler, Jr., *Scale and Scope: The Dynamics of Industrial Capitalism* (Cambridge, MA: Belknap Press of Harvard University Press, 1990), p. 41; E. Davis and C. Smales, "The Internationalization of Professional Services", Working Paper Series No. 66, Centre for Business Strategy, London Business School, London (April 1989), p. 5.

6 In this way, real estate advisory service firms were similar, in part, to London law firms (which had national and foreign financial clients with international business) and accountancy firms (which followed corporate multinational into foreign markets). See R. Cohen *et al.*, "The Competitive Advantage of Law and Accountancy in the City of London", The City Research Project (London: London Business School, 1994).

7 Association documents from the National Association of Real Estate Investment Trusts (Washington, DC: 1997).

8 H.F. Kelly, "Can Universities Teach Real Estate Decision Making? ", *Real Estate Review,* vol. 20, no. 2 (Summer 1990), p. 81.

9 S.B. Sagari, "The Financial Services Industry: An International Perspective", (PhD dissertation, New York University, 1986), pp. 67–8.

10 Author's italics added. E. Davis, G. Hanlon and J. Kay, "Internationalization in Accounting and Other Professional Services", Working Paper Series No. 78, Centre for Business Strategy, London Business School, London (April 1990), pp. 9–10; J. Kay, *Foundations of Corporate Success* (Oxford: Oxford University Press, 1993), pp. 87 and 88–93.

11 *Ibid.*, pp. 87–9.

12 Again, this confirms M. Casson's thesis that a nation's business culture and economic history are "a source of long–term competitive advantage", in M. Casson, *Enterprise and Competitiveness: A Systems View of International Business* (Oxford: Clarendon Press, 1990), p. 88.

13 The caveat to this statement is that foreign real estate advisory firms partially diminished the competitive advantage of US firms by hiring skilled professionals away from many domestic firms.

14 A. Baum and A. Schofield, "Property as a Global Asset", Working Papers in European Property, Centre for European Property Research, University of Reading (March 1991), p. 67.

15 This agrees with A.D. Chandler, Jr.'s findings that manufacturing firms were highly sensitive to limitations of the nation's economy; for example, UK firms expanded abroad due to the country's small land area and limited investment potential, in A.D. Chandler, Jr., *Scale and Scope: The Dynamics of Industrial Capitalism* (Cambridge, MA: Belknap Press of Harvard University Press, 1990), pp. 249–50.

16 Chandler observed a similar condition among the American industrial enterprises he reviewed in A.D. Chandler, Jr., *Strategy and Structure: Chapters in the History of American Industrial Enterprise* (Cambridge, MA: MIT Press, 1962), p. 32.

17 E. Davis and C. Smales, "The Internationalization of Professional Services", Working Paper Series No. 66, Centre for Business Strategy, London Business School, London (April 1989), p. 10. Jones Lang Wootton was the best example among international real estate advisors: the firm had unmatched experience in acquiring and transporting innovative services into a diverse and multiple array of foreign markets.

18 R.H. Coase, "The Nature of the Firm", *Economica*, n.s., vol. 4 (November 1937), p. 65.

19 *Ibid.*

20 O.E. Williamson, *Markets and Hierarchies: Analysis and Antitrust Implications* (New York and London: Free Press, 1975), pp. 56, 82ff; see also L.S. Bacow, "Foreign Investment, Vertical Integration, and the Structure of the U.S. Real Estate Industry", Working Paper No. 25, Massachusetts Institute of Technology Center for Real Estate Development (January 1990), pp. 16–17. Counter to the varied experience of these real estate service firms, E. Davis and C. Smales found that US accounting firms internationalized largely by merging with local firms world-wide, in "The Internationalization of Professional Services", Working Paper Series No. 66, Centre for Business Strategy, London Business School, London (April 1989), p. 5.

21 The experience of real estate advisory service firms reinforced G.B. Richardson's argument that "a firm has to settle down and 'digest' large expansions before it can successfully carry out others", otherwise "managerial diseconomies" would result from rapid expansion in widely dispersed markets, in G.B. Richardson, *Information and Investment: A Study in the Working of the Competitive Economy* (Oxford: Clarendon Press, 1990), p. 59.

22 This finding concurs with important theories set forth by A.D. Chandler, Jr. and E.T. Penrose. A decentralized operation was most economical, argued Penrose in *The Theory of the Growth of the Firm* (1959; reprint, White Plains, NY: M.E. Sharpe Inc., 1991), p. 55; and in *Scale and Scope: The Dynamics of Industrial Capitalism* (Cambridge, MA: Belknap Press of Harvard University Press, 1990), p. 41, Chandler concluded that innovation occurred through multiple tiers of vertical integration and geographic diversification.

23 This argument would be tested by a few UK firms (Chesterton, Savills, and DTZ Debenham Thorpe) that went to the public stock markets in the late 1980s and early 1990s to capitalize future operations and growth, a step which portended future financial management of real estate services.

24 A.D. Chandler, Jr., *Scale and Scope: The Dynamics of Industrial Capitalism* (Cambridge, MA: Belknap Press of Harvard University Press, 1990), p. 34; G.J. Stigler defined an "efficient enterprise" as that which "meets any and all problems the entrepreneur actually faces" in *The Organization of Industry* (Chicago: University of Chicago Press, 1968), pp. 73 and 88.

APPENDIX A

Analytical framework

Analytical framework

A critical issue in an examination of international real estate advisory service firms is that real estate, in all its manifestations, is ultimately a localized industry that requires expert knowledge and understanding of local property and investment markets. Whether regional, national, or international in their scope, real estate advisory firms reviewed in the course of this study succeeded or failed due to their collective local expertise, reputation and professional relationships.

The twin, and often competing, requirements for local responsiveness and a multinational organizational structure define the broad outlines for evaluating the relevant factors that have prompted and sustained the growth of international real estate services since 1960. Unlike the capital and securities markets, real estate lacked a centralized market mechanism; each market, large or small, was discrete and fiercely independent. Thus, to a greater extent than other financial services, real estate advisory services depended on both market mechanisms and the firm as a coordinating element.

International trade in real estate advisory services stemmed not just from the transfer of investment capital by a client, but ideally from open markets to permit cross-border mobility of service factors (investors and professional advisors) and service products (real estate advisory services). In this way, real estate advisory firms introduced innovations to capitalize on growing volumes of cross-border investment by and among certain investors and financial markets – pension and insurance funds, corporations, financial institutions, and securities and investment banks.

As discussed in Chapters 2 and 3, different investor groups tended to prevail in different national markets at different times. An increasingly globalized financial environment was facilitated by the emergence of the Eurobond market after 1963, and by deregulated capital restraints in the 1980s. Thus, the internationalization of real estate advisory services constituted one major sector in the evolution of globalizing financial services after 1960. Property advisory firms sought to advance their competitive standing by moving into new products (services) and new functions (foreign markets and foreign investor clients).[1] Competitive advantage in innovative services, by both firms and nations, appeared to depend on a constantly growing volume of cross-border investment activity, which then attracted the best advisors and investors. This, in turn, expanded the national market's ability to attract new investors and professional skills, and to support ongoing innovation.[2]

"Failure" in foreign markets is an important dimension to this evaluation of the "successful" expansion and diversification of real estate advisory services. In an enterprise where people and organizational management are believed to be central to the allocation of capital and professional resources, the definition of failure and the causes of firm failure provide valuable references for evaluating successful competitive advantage in international growth and diversification.

One of the distinctive features of commercial real estate investment is the localized nature of property markets. Each unit of real estate is an illiquid and unique asset, whose value largely depended on the local economy and local property markets. Until the late 1980s, real estate assets lacked a centralized or unified global market, such as that of corporate stocks and government securities. Moreover, historical documentation of this subject was limited by the lack of uniform government and industry data, both within domestic markets and among the four countries. In the absence of consistent primary sources, the author has relied on case studies of leading firms based in each of the focal countries, cross-border direct investment statistics, general economic statistics, numerous personal interviews with academic and industry leaders, industry publications, professional journals, and press and consultancy reports from each country. While the lack of uniform and comprehensive information on property markets and real estate services limited previous research, it provided an ideal subject for examining international services trade theories and factors influencing the foreign expansion of certain service organizations.

During the early 1990s, the ten largest source countries of total cross-border direct investment were the US, UK, Japan and Germany, followed by several other European countries and Canada (Table A.1). The four largest source countries, i.e. the focal countries, accounted for over three-fifths of the total world stock of direct investment. The US and UK have been the two largest sources of direct investment capital since at least 1960. But it was not until 1980 that Germany overtook the Netherlands as the third largest source of foreign investment capital, and not until 1986 that Japan superseded the Netherlands as the fourth largest source country. Japan went on to overshadow Germany in 1988 as the third largest source of direct investment abroad.

Table A.2 presents the rank order of countries by the stock of outward direct investment in real estate specifically, with Japan the largest investing country worldwide, followed by Germany, Canada, Switzerland, the UK and the US. Few other countries provided separate data on cross-border direct property investment. Other major nations, such as France, the Netherlands and Sweden, did not identify real estate investment separately from investment in the financial and service sectors.[3]

Even though Canada and Switzerland recorded larger amounts of foreign direct investment in real estate than the UK or US, neither country was examined extensively due to special circumstances: the great majority of Canada's overseas real estate investment is located in the US, with only a nominal amount in the UK and other countries;[4] Switzerland serves as a politically neutral and low-tax conduit for residents of third-party countries investing in both real estate and other assets in Europe and the US, and is not an ultimate source of direct investment capital. Moreover, the economic interdependencies among US, UK, German and Japanese markets prompted the greatest advances in real estate advisory services.

By reviewing national fluctuations in cross-border direct investment in real estate, and periodic changes and major episodes in the foreign expansion of real estate advisory services in the focal countries, this book seeks to identify and evaluate specific national factors that influenced effective internationalization in domestic property services.

Scope, sources, and methodology

The study that is the basis for this book focused on real estate advisory firms that internationalized their business practice and their client services. This explicit focus enabled the most directly relevant economic and organizational factors to be identified as advancing international trade in this one important sector of national economies.

Real estate advisory services represented a highly unregulated profession that encompassed a number of professional disciplines: brokerage and agency, property management, development and construction management, appraisal and portfolio valuation, real estate investment banking, market research, and portfolio investment management. As examined in the collective profile of leading firms in Chapter 4, different firms combined various disciplines, ranging from the fully diversified firm of Jones Lang Wootton of the UK to the single-purpose core business of an individual firm, such as Goldman Sachs and Co., and to other globalized brokerage houses and estate managers, appraisers and cost consultants, investment banks and securities houses, accountants and attorneys, mortgage lenders and financial counselors.[5]

The growing cross-border real estate investment market attracted affiliated professions, which were previously inexperienced in domestic and international real estate transactions. Financial intermediaries, especially those with a long history in real estate debt and equity instruments, represented the most formidable competition – merchant and commercial banks as well as investment banks and brokers. In addition, allied firms in management consulting, accounting, law and construction also diversified into property services as a defensive move to protect and increase client revenues. Each brought

Table A.1 World stock of outward direct investment by the ten largest source countries in 1990 rank order (1960, 1973, 1980, 1990)

Ten Largest Source Countries	(Billions US $)				Percent Distribution				Rank			
	1960	1973	1980	1990	1960	1973	1980	1990	1960	1973	1980	1990
United States[a]	31.9	101.3	220.2	426.5	47.1	48.0	42.6	25.9	1	1	1	1
United Kingdom	12.4	27.5	79.2	244.8	18.3	13.0	15.3	14.9	2	2	2	2
Japan[b]	0.5	10.3	19.6	201.4	0.7	4.9	3.8	12.2	9	5	8	3
Germany	0.8	11.9	43.1	155.1	1.2	5.6	8.3	9.4	8	4	3	4
France[b]	4.1	8.8	20.8	114.8	6.1	4.2	4.0	7.0	4	6	7	5
Netherlands	7.0	15.8	42.4	99.2	10.3	7.5	8.2	6.0	3	3	4	6
Canada	2.5	7.8	21.6	74.7	3.7	3.7	4.2	4.5	5	7	5	7
Switzerland	2.3	7.1	22.4	64.9	3.4	3.4	4.3	3.9	6	8	6	8
Italy	1.1	3.2	7.0	60.0	1.6	1.5	1.4	3.6	8	9	10	9
Sweden	0.4	3.0	7.2	50.7	0.6	1.4	1.4	3.1	10	10	9	10
Subtotals												
Ten Largest Source Countries	63.0	196.7	483.5	1492.1	93.0	93.2	93.5	90.5				
Other Countries	4.7	14.4	33.4	152.1	6.9	6.8	6.5	9.3				
All Countries	67.7	211.1	516.9	1644.2	99.9	100.0	100.0	99.8				

Source: US Department of Commerce, International Trade Administration, Recent Trends in International Direct Investment, August 1992.

Notes:
[a] Data for the United States exclude the negative US direct investment position in the Dutch Antilles finance industry
[b] Of the countries shown separately in this table, reinvested earnings data are not collected by Japan or France. If reinvested earnings data were included, Japan's estimate stock of direct investment abroad would have been about $218 billion at year end 1990. The outward stock for France would probably also have been slightly higher, but not enough to change its rank order.

Table A.2 Stock of outward direct investment in real estate by the major source countries in 1990 rank order (1966–90, in millions of US dollars)

	1966	1975	1980	1985	1990
Japan	35	251	595	3,128	46,444
Germany	377	2,136	4,696	8,546	17,382
Switzerland	–	573	964	1,300	8,000
Canada	–	–	2,195	3,385	3,385
United Kingdom	–	2,795[a]	3,320[c]	4,141	4,560
United States	163	227[b]	251	384	1,860

Sources:
For Japan, Ministry of Finance, *Reported Outward and Inward Direct Investment*, May/June issues; for Germany, *Monthly Report of the Deutsche Bundesbank*; for Canada, Statistics Canada, Balance of Payments Division, unpublished data based on *Canada's International Investment Position*; for Switzerland, Union Bank of Switzerland, *Switzerland in Figures*, and unpublished estimates from Union Bank; for the United Kingdom, *Census of Overseas Assets*; for the United States, US Department of Commerce, Bureau of Economic Analysis, *Survey of Current Business*.

Notes:
Data on outward direct investment in real estate are generally not available before 1966. Only the United States has published data before 1966 (see Chapter 2, Table 2.1).
— Not available.
[a] Data are for 1974 and include insurance.
[b] Data are for 1977.
[c] Data are for 1981.

specialized expertise to the field, thus further intensifying competition and prompting service innovations in the industry.

The book examines the impact of these related, and competitive, service sectors, primarily investment banks and accounting firms, by way of evaluating international expansion strategies and pioneering innovations that were subsequently adopted by real estate advisory firms. However, it omits detailed analyses of the organizational structures and expansion strategies of particular investment banking and accounting firms, in contrast to the detailed case histories of leading real estate service firms in each of the four focal countries. Also omitted are detailed analyses of advisory services related to residential property, agricultural land, natural resources and manufacturing and retailing facilities. The economic and market factors that impacted these other property markets were quite different from those that shaped commercial real estate investment markets. Moreover, residential property historically constituted only a small portion of cross-border investment, and the stock directly invested in the latter three categories was combined (not itemized) in general industry statistics on international trade.

Finally, each sector of the real estate industry was not independently examined. Real estate development and construction services, for example, encompassed a number of economic and governmental processes which differed from those involved in cross-border direct investment. However, as they related to competition and innovation in international investment-grade property services, specific facets of real estate development, portfolio management and financial services are discussed throughout the book, particularly in Chapters 3 through 5.

The modest amount of secondary source material available on the "history" of real estate advisory services in each of the focal countries, and their relationship to the growth and rising influence of cross-border property investment, required the consultation of various sources to document emerging trends. Secondary sources chronicling international real estate advisory services included publications from the United States, the United Kingdom, Germany and Japan. In addition, the working paper series published by the Centre for Business Strategy at the London Business School, the Centre for European Property Research at the University of Reading, the Real Estate Center of The Wharton School, the London School of Economics, and the Center for Real Estate at the Massachusetts Institute of Technology, provided findings of recent research on specific sectors of real estate investment, property markets and professional services.

Because so little comprehensive secondary source material was previously published, research required compilation of two types of published and unpublished "primary" source material: direct investment stock data recorded (and sometimes published) by official government agencies, which remained the single most consistent source of time-series statistics on cross-border direct investment among the four countries, and detailed historical case studies of forty real estate advisory service firms that moved into foreign markets and diversified services. The latter drew on annual reports, trade reports, internal corporate documents, press reports, surveys, industry publications and interviews with executive managers.

Defining cross-border direct investment and other types of investment

Cross-border direct investment involves the international transfer of capital for the purpose of purchasing and controlling foreign assets, going beyond the international sale of products or services generated from the use of domestic assets. The International Monetary Fund defines "cross-border direct investment" as "an incorporated or unincorporated enterprise in which a direct investor, who is resident in another economy, owns 10 percent or more of the ordinary shares or voting power (for an incorporated enterprise) or the equivalent (for an unincorporated enterprise)."[6]

A "direct investment enterprise" (affiliate) is defined as an incorporated or unincorporated enterprise in which a single person (an individual, company, government, or group of related individuals) owns a significant share of the voting securities, or an equivalent interest, either directly or indirectly through another affiliate.[7] Ownership and/or control of land or structures in a foreign country is also considered to be cross-border direct investment. Any other type of cross-border private investment that is made without the intention to achieve some degree of control over the investment is referred to as portfolio investment.

"Portfolio investment", by contrast, is defined as any other cross-border investment made that does not secure control over the investment.[8] The broad definition of portfolio investment encompasses many other different types of international investment, including the purchase and sale of equity securities (usually less than 10 percent of total outstanding voting securities), long-term debt securities (bonds, debentures, etc.), short-term (money market) debt instruments, trade financing, bank lending or borrowing, and financial derivatives (options, futures, etc.) when they generate financial claims on or liabilities to nonresidents.[9] Some of these types of portfolio investment can ultimately be used to finance the purchase of land or structures. However, balance of payments data record only the type of cross-border portfolio investment that has occurred, not its ultimate use or the industry or occupation of the owner of the capital. (The banking industry is the only exception, but even with investment reported by that industry there is still no distinction made as to the ultimate use of the funds.) Accordingly, portfolio investment that flows into real estate is not identified separately in the data and thus is not available for use in this study.

Because there is no universal system or method for data collection on cross-border direct investment, the specific definitions and data collection methodologies for the focal countries are reasonably but not strictly comparable. Specific definitions of cross-border direct investment differ. For instance, the definition of what constitutes "an effective voice in the management of the enterprise" varies. Japan and the United States use a 10 percent minimum level of ownership of the voting securities of a foreign business enterprise held directly, or indirectly through another affiliate, as the threshold for identifying foreign investors. (Japan has no specific published minimum percentage ownership for inward investment, but it is believed to be defined for administrative purposes generally at the 10 percent level.) The United Kingdom uses a 20 percent minimum ownership threshold for all directly and indirectly held affiliates. Germany defines a direct investor as anyone who holds directly or indirectly 25 percent or more of the shares or voting rights of an enterprise which must have a balance sheet total equivalent to more than DM500,000 or maintains branches or permanent business establishments having gross operating assets totaling more than DM500,000 each.[10]

A few countries, including Germany, have collected data on cross-border private real estate investment intended for non-commercial use, such as vacation homes, but none of the other focal countries collected non-commercial real estate investment data. Real estate investment made through open-end property funds or by means of limited partnerships are also not identified separately in portfolio data. Direct purchases of land or structures by pension funds or property companies are reported directly to the national governments by those companies, or reported by the managing general partner of the enterprise, and are included in cross-border direct investment data.

Cross-border direct investment is categorized in government data by industry. The real estate industry also includes activities typically found in the construction and service industries, such as designing structures and building commercial or residential projects, providing leasing services, or performing advisory services related to real estate markets. Data are collected only for the total business enterprise, and not for each business establishment and/or division – for the legal entity rather than for each physical location. Real estate activities are not identified separately from non-real estate activities of the overall enterprise.

In Chapter 2, direct investment stock data from official sources are used for purposes of analysis because they are the single most consistent and comprehensive source of data available on cross-border direct investment of the focal countries. Stock data measure the cumulative outstanding value of direct investment made up until any given point in time, including valuation adjustments for changes in market value, foreign exchange rate gains or losses, and valuation of intangible assets. By comparison, direct investment flow data record only the annual flow of foreign investors' capital invested in a foreign enterprise. However, since there is no universally applied system or method for the collection of data on cross-border direct investment, the specific definitions of the four focal countries are generally, but not strictly, comparable.

Other indicators of the global expansion of commercial real estate, not explored in Chapter 2 because of data inadequacies, include the total asset value of commercial real estate held by foreign-owned affiliates (which, by accounting definition, is much higher than the value of foreign investors' equity ownership in real estate); real estate investment included indistinguishably with the investment made by non-real estate companies; property held by non-real estate companies used for non-commercial purposes; or cross-border real estate activities that either are not defined as direct investment, are not identified separately by statistics on portfolio investment, or are not identified separately in statistics measuring cross-border trade in services.

Composition of direct investment stocks

In developing direct investment data, both the IMF and the Organization for Economic Cooperation and Development (OECD) have recommended that the composition of direct investment stocks and flows include:

1   *Equity investment:* any contribution of capital to a foreign affiliate in which the owner (parent firm) holds or acquires at least a 10 percent share of the voting stock or equivalent interest in the affiliate. (An interest of less than 10 percent is defined as portfolio investment.)

2   *Intercompany debt:* intercompany loans between parent and affiliate, including the cash or other liquid assets, charges for shipments of products or equipment, or charges for the transfer of intangible assets.

3   *Reinvested earnings:* the parent company share of foreign affiliate earnings not repatriated, but reinvested by the parent, is included as part of the direct investment stock and flow.[11]

Each of the focal countries, except Japan, include these three elements in their direct investment stock and flow estimates. Japan does not collect reinvested earnings data, nor are stock estimates by the Bank of Japan available by country or by industry. Therefore "notifications data" from Japan's Ministry of Finance are used instead for both total Japanese outward and inward direct investment, and for Japanese direct investment in real estate. Stocks include more than just the cumulative value of flows, taking into account changes in the value of the investment due to valuation adjustments (e.g. accounting write-ups or write-downs of assets due to inflation, deflation, fire loss, write-offs of equity including goodwill, or foreign exchange translation gains and losses).

Foreign exchange translation gains or losses are typically not included in affiliate earnings (and thus not included in direct investment flows) but taken directly to the balance sheet of the affiliate. Large exchange rate fluctuations can result in major changes in stock values due to the translation of foreign-currency-denominated assets and liabilities of foreign affiliates into the home country currency for purposes of inclusion in the global consolidated net worth of the parent company.[12]

Comparability of definitions

Both the UK and the German definitions are basically comparable to the US definition, but less inclusive, chiefly because their reporting thresholds are higher. Most important, all three definitions rely on the use of a fully consolidated accounting system in which the income statements and balance sheets of foreign affiliates are consolidated into those of the parent company. For outward direct investment, the financial statements of foreign affiliates are prepared in accordance with the generally accepted accounting principles of the parent company's home country for eventual consolidation into one combined set of financial statements for the entire company worldwide.

This does not mean, however, that the stock and flow data compiled by these three countries are fully comparable. There are differences between countries in accounting principles used to compile and consolidate financial data, and in the timing and coverage of government surveys used to collect data, as well as in the level of industry and country disaggregation of published data. Some of these differences are discussed below.

Differences in data collection and measurement[13]

Besides differences in specific definitions, there are differences among the focal countries in the scope and coverage of the various national data collection systems. Also, the methods of classifying direct investment by industry and by country often differ.

Scope and coverage of data collection

The quality of data collection may vary because different thresholds exist for reporting information to national governments. For example, to minimize the burden on reporting companies, surveys may require reports only from those affiliates with certain levels of assets, sales or net income. For example, Germany requires reports only from direct investors whose affiliates have total assets of DM500,000 or more. Because relatively few large MNCs typically account for most direct investment, the total direct investment stock is seldom materially affected by reporting thresholds. However, stock estimates for smaller industries such as real estate could be affected, especially if a number of relatively small real estate investments below the reporting threshold were made in any given year.

The level of disaggregation of industry and country data collected and published also varies by focal country. Industry classification methodology among the focal countries is discussed separately below.

Stock data collected by company survey are available mostly on an annual basis, and sometimes quarterly. A notable exception is the UK, which compiles stock data from company surveys only on a triennial basis with no estimates for intervening years. Stock and flow data collected through the UK's banking system are available annually. However, no country or industry detail is available.

Industry classification

Direct investment data collection systems gather data at the enterprise level rather than at the establishment level. (An "enterprise", or company, represents a distinct, legally defined business operation which may have one or more establishments with operations in one or more industries. An "establishment" is defined as an economic unit owned by an enterprise, generally at a single physical location, where only one type of economic activity is conducted.) In cases where an enterprise has a number of establishments engaged in different kinds of business operations, the question in which industry the enterprise should be classified arises.

214

The US industry classification system assigns the enterprise to the major industry group in which the majority of its sales are made.[14] For example, an enterprise in which sales are 50 percent in finance, 40 percent in insurance and 10 percent in real estate would be classified in finance, and the entire direct investment stock and other financial data associated with that enterprise would be classified in finance even though activities are conducted in other industries. Thus, direct investment data for real estate may be understated because real estate investment is included indistinguishably in other industries such as finance or insurance. However, the degree of understatement cannot be determined.

In the US data system, however, *sales* data are classified both by the industry of the affiliate (according to the method described above) and the industry of the actual product(s) sold by the affiliate. These cross-classifications are available for both inward and outward direct investment. Presumably, any major differences in industry classification found by comparing the results of the cross-classification of *sales* would also apply to stocks, flows, assets and other financial data.

Because of the cross-classification system, only a relatively small proportion of real estate activity in the US is conducted outside the real estate industry for either inward or outward direct investment. However, the gross book value of commercial property held by foreign-owned US affiliates in non-real estate industries is substantial. In 1990, for example, foreign-owned real estate affiliates held $80 billion of commercial property, while affiliates in all other industries held $66 billion of commercial property.[15] Much of this commercial property is probably owner-occupied by non-real estate companies and not leased or held solely for capital opportunities. Unfortunately, comparable analyses cannot be conducted for the other focal countries because the statistics are unavailable.

Other measures of cross-border direct investment

Other than direct investment stocks or flows, there is a limited number of alternative types of financial data – total assets; stockholders' equity; and gross book value of property, plant, and equipment – that deal with various aspects of foreign direct investment. Some of the more important data and their uses as they relate to cross-border direct investment in real estate are described below. Only the US collects and publishes these other types of data.

Total assets

"Total assets" are defined as the historical book value of all current and fixed assets carried on the balance sheets of affiliates. Total assets measure the total gross financial value of foreign direct investment in real estate, regardless of the foreign ownership share in the enterprise. Total assets values are always much larger than direct investment stock values because (1) affiliate liabilities – whether owed to the parent company or to unaffiliated third parties – have not been deducted from assets; and (2) assets obtained through local borrowing instead of from funds furnished by the foreign parent are not included in stock values. In 1990, total assets of foreign-owned US affiliates in real estate amounted to $112 billion, compared with an inward stock in US real estate of $35 billion.[16]

Equity

"Equity", or stockholders' equity, represents the book value of an investor's share of the capital stock, reinvested earnings and other capital reserves of an affiliate. Equity is distinct from direct investment stocks in that it does not include the net value of loans by the parent company to the affiliate. Stockholders' equity can also be useful as a measuring device of the level of foreign ownership of total equity in private domestic business. Stockholders' equity in foreign-owned US affiliates in real estate amounted to $18 billion in 1990.[17]

Property, plant and equipment

"Property plant, and equipment" (PP&E) is the single largest and most important balance sheet asset of most companies. It is these assets (as well as managerial talent and technical knowledge) that are the ultimate foundation of the profit potential of a company. The gross book value of PP&E of real estate companies totaled $87 billion in 1990, of which $23 billion was land.

Data limitations

A few data limitations must be mentioned: national statistics were compiled for only the sectoral business enterprise (i.e. real estate), and not for each type of investment (property) by each type of business establishment (i.e. the real estate division of a multinational corporation). Real estate activities were therefore not identified separately from the major non-real estate activities of multinational enterprises.

"Cross-border direct investment in real estate" was defined in national government statistics as the purchase or sale in a host country of land or structures for commercial use, or changes in existing investments in land or structures. In terms of economic motivation or global market strategy, investment in land or structures was more akin to the purchase of natural resources than to the acquisition of manufacturing or services facilities. However, the real estate industry includes activities typically found in the construction and services industries, such as designing and building commercial or residential projects, providing leasing services, or giving advice about, or performing services related to, real estate markets and investments.

Notes

1 A.D. Chandler, Jr., *Strategy and Structure: Chapters in the History of American Industrial Enterprise* (Cambridge, MA: MIT Press, 1962), p. 14; and R.W. Jones and F. Ruane, "Appraising the Options for International Trade in Services", *Oxford Economic Papers*, vol. 42 no. 4 (October 1990), pp. 672–87.

2 M. Casson, *Global Research Strategy and International Competitiveness* (London: Basil Blackwell, 1991), pp. 77–9.

3 Inconsistent with International Monetary Fund standards, many countries, including the US, the UK and Japan, do not collect data on direct investment in non-commercial real estate, such as foreign investment by individuals in "vacation homes" intended for private use. Because of the private nature of many property transactions, especially by individuals, official country estimates of cross-border real estate investment likely are understated.

4 In addition, very little cross-border direct property investment is located in Canada. Thus, Canada's real estate industry lacks a global orientation, even though Olympia & York recently developed one major project in the London area, Canary Wharf, which was reacquired by the international bank consortium in summer 1992.

5 M.A. Hines, *Marketing Real Estate Internationally* (New York: Quorum Books, 1988), pp. 16–17, 77, 81, 142.

6 International Monetary Fund, *Balance of Payments Manual*, 5th edition, (Washington, DC: 1993), p. 86.

7 *Ibid.*

8 In practice, if there is no unambiguous 10 percent minimum ownership criterion applied in an individual case, a qualitative judgment is typically made by the government statistical agency as to whether there is sufficient influence over the management of the enterprise or property to be classified as direct investment.

9 *Ibid.*, p. 91.

10 Organization for Economic Cooperation and Development, Committee on International Investment and Multinational Enterprises, *Recent Trends in International Direct Investment* (1987), p. 113.

11 International Monetary Fund, *Balance of Payments Manual*, 5th edition, (Washington, DC: 1993), p. 86; Organization for Economic Cooperation and Development, *The Revised Detailed Benchmark Definition of Foreign Direct Investment* (3 February 1992), pp. 14, 18.

12 United Kingdom Central Statistical Office, *Business Monitor, Census of Overseas Assets* (1987), pp. 3, 10.

13 Much of the research for this section is taken from US Department of Commerce, International Trade Administration, *International Direct Investment: Global Trends and the U.S. Role* (1988), pp. 174–7.

14 U.S. Department of Commerce, Bureau of Economic Analysis, *U.S. Direct Investment Abroad: 1982 Benchmark Survey Data*, p. 9.

15 U.S. Department of Commerce, Bureau of Economic Analysis, *Foreign Direct Investment in the United States, Operations of the U.S. Affiliates of Foreign Companies, Revised 1990 Estimates*, Table D-20.

16 *Ibid.*, Table B-6.

17 *Ibid.*, Table B-2.

APPENDIX B

A brief history of restrictions on international
investment by the focal countries

This appendix reviews the chronology of the gradual liberalization of capital
controls and other restrictions on both outward and inward investment,
including cross-border direct investment. Historically among the focal countries, relatively few restrictions limited outward direct investment. Except for
Japan, the focal countries had no formal statutory restrictions on outward
direct investment. Inward direct investment, in contrast, was subject to more
restrictions. Among the focal countries, these restrictions generally related to
national security concerns or regulated industries. By 1990, some specific
statutory restrictions on foreign direct investment in real estate remained, yet
the individual governments typically did not enforce them. With perhaps the
exception of Japan before 1980, the focal countries were, and remain, among
the world's most open economies, with relatively few restrictions on cross-
border direct investment.

In addition to formal restrictions, unrelated regulations and private practices directly and indirectly acted as obstacles to foreign investment, such as
those that remain in Japan.

Restrictions on outward investment

After World War Two and until the 1980s, the focal countries were among
several nations that periodically imposed controls on investment abroad,
including outward direct investment, usually as a means to manage balance of
payments, as well as to ensure that financial sectors remained solvent and in
response to specific and temporary industry, currency or monetary policy
concerns. These controls were implemented primarily through foreign
exchange convertibility restrictions, as well as through restrictions on
domestic banks and finance companies seeking to conduct specific types of
overseas investment with associated capital outflows.[1]

In 1955, the US introduced a voluntary program to help reduce private
capital outflows and improve the country's balance of payments. In 1968,
mandatory controls replaced voluntary constraints on outward capital flows
for direct investment and the government introduced taxes on interest

receipts arising from outward investment. The other focal countries maintained oversight by requiring specific government approval of proposed individual investments, and controlling foreign exchange transactions necessary to conduct outward investment. Partly in response to these restrictions on outward investment, newly established international monetary and capital markets surged in the late 1960s, such as the Eurodollar (short-term) and Eurobond (long-term) financial markets. These international financial markets facilitated through circumvention outward investment in general, including cross-border direct investment.

In 1974, the US abolished taxes and capital outflow restrictions on outward investment, in conjunction with transforming the dollar floating exchange rate system. In the late 1970s and 1980, other countries began to remove restrictions on outward investment: the UK removed foreign exchange controls, and Japan abolished the Foreign Investment Law, which required government approval of both outward and inward investment.

Since World War Two, limitations on certain kinds of portfolio investment remained the strictest (albeit modest) and most continuous form of restriction affecting outward direct investment from Germany, the UK and the US. Subsequent liberalizations of capital controls on outward investment by Japan and many other non-focal countries occurred during the 1980s, following the leads of the UK and the US. These liberalized government policies represented an awareness to permit and facilitate access to new technologies and financial resources possessed by foreign firms. Importantly, Eurodollar markets encouraged the growth of cross-border trade and investment. And so, with the gradual liberalization of international financial controls in the 1980s, the globalization of investment markets, heightened competition and favorable macroeconomic conditions in the focal countries, outward direct investment in real estate expanded rapidly.

Restrictions on inward investment

Post-World War Two reconstruction demands in the 1950s created a favorable policy climate for cross-border direct investment. This was a period in Europe and Japan when capital was in great demand and foreign direct investment was generally welcomed. However, foreign exchange controls were used to prevent the outflow of scarce capital which, in turn, limited inward investment in these countries.

But as prosperity and economic growth returned in the 1960s, many host countries became more skeptical about the benefits of foreign direct investment, and some countries strengthened barriers by setting maximum levels of foreign ownership and/or control of domestic companies, as well as by opposing takeovers of domestic firms in certain industries and limiting or taxing at higher rates income remittances from existing foreign-owned companies. Except for Japan, the focal countries did not have formal new barriers, and remained generally open to cross-border direct investment. Japan required advance approval for new foreign investments, which typically meant that foreign investors held minority ownership positions or licensed technology to Japanese companies as a means of gaining market access. Extensive cross-shareholdings among Japanese companies within *keiretsu* groups made hostile foreign takeovers virtually impossible. Also, Germany had no formal restrictions, but extensive cross-shareholdings between German companies and German banks impeded foreign takeovers.

As a consequence of slower growth and higher inflation in the late 1970s, some countries sought to encourage foreign direct investment, and in the 1980s began to grant tax, financial and other incentives to foreign investors. However, until the late 1980s a wide range of restrictions was imposed on inward direct investment. Among the focal countries these restrictions encompassed limitations on foreign investment in banking, insurance, transportation, communications and natural resources (Table A.3). Access to some of these sectors hinged on reciprocity conditions or involved public monopoly constraints. In real estate, Japan's Alien Land Law of 1926 allowed foreigners to acquire land in Japan only if reciprocal conditions were available in source countries. Nineteenth-century laws in many US states required reciprocity or prohibited foreign ownership of agricultural or natural resource lands. However, neither country was known to have enforced these laws during the 1988–90 period. Again, restraints typically were designed to address concerns related to national security, economics and public welfare.

Foreign direct investment was encouraged by nearly all countries during the 1980s, including the focal countries. Since there were relatively few formal restrictions on inward direct investment in the focal countries, the surge in inward direct investment in the UK and the US stemmed principally from extraordinarily strong macroeconomic conditions and a shift to a global outlook by multinational corporations. In addition, deregulation and privatization of certain services sectors in these countries presented new opportunities for foreign investors. Japan was continuously liberalizing its inward direct investment regulations since the late 1960s, and by 1988 it maintained official restrictions in only a few sectors. In April 1991, Japan amended its Foreign Exchange and Foreign Trade Control Law by, among other items, permitting post-notification of new foreign investments, making Japan (technically) consistent with the foreign investment regulations of the other focal countries. Japan's Ministry of International Trade and Industry (MITI) actually began to assist and offer subsidies to foreign investors in the late 1980s. Nevertheless, because of a legacy of impediments to foreign investment, inward direct investment in Japan remained relatively low due to a domestic cultural aversion to takeovers, higher costs and lower anticipated returns on new investments, and cross-shareholdings of voting securities among Japanese firms.

In the US, in response to the phenomenal surge in inward direct investment in 1980, the US Congress enacted the Exon–Florio provision of the Omnibus Trade and Competitiveness Act in 1988. This legislation granted the President authority to veto proposed or reverse completed individual foreign direct investment transactions which might threaten national security. Between 1988 and 1991, one transaction was rejected, several were modified, and it is likely that others were never proposed on account of the new legislation. Another section of the law granted authority to the Federal Reserve to refuse to designate as a primary dealer a foreign-owned US bank if reciprocal conditions were not present in the foreign investor's home country. In addition, numerous laws were proposed but not enacted that sought reciprocal treatment for US investors abroad in certain services sectors, or sought to protect certain US high-technology sectors from foreign dominance. These proposals might also have discouraged certain new foreign investments.

Table A.3 Foreign investment restrictions in main sectors in the focal countries (1997)

	Germany	Japan	UK	US
Banking	LR	LR	R	R
Insurance	–	L	R	R*
Radio & Television	L	L	L	L
Telecommunications	L	L	L	L
Road Transport	C	–	–	–
Rail Transport	C	L	C	C*
Air Transport	LR	L	L	L
Water Transport	L*	L	L	L
Mining	–	C	L	L
Oil & Gas	–	C	–	–
Fishing	–	L	L	L
Real Estate	–	R	–	R*
Tourism	–	–	L	–
Public Utilities	-	L	C	L*

Sources: Organization for Economic Cooperation and Development, *Code of Liberalization of Capital Movements*, 1992 Edition, May 1992, and revised editions.

Notes:
L = Limited
R = Reciprocity
C = Closed
* = Measures at a subnational level

NOTE

1 Although there were, and in a few cases still are, outright restrictions by the focal countries related to national security or external policy, these generally address trade with former Communist and certain Middle Eastern countries.

APPENDIX C

Historical yields and rates of return on real estate investment in the focal countries

The comparative, multinational data arrayed in Table A.4 represented the most thorough presentation of cross-border investment yields which the author knew to exist (confirmed by economists and property professionals). Such a comprehensive report of multinational yield data could not be found to exist in any one data source, and was never previously compiled in a published or unpublished report. The author, therefore, sought to compile and refine systematically operating and capital yield data from different data sources for each focal country to achieve relative annual parity. While imperfect due to the lack of unity of data sources and exact comparability of national statistics, the table presents an unprecedented comparative illustration of national investment yield data. In addition, the rates of return have been provided for the period for the UK. These rates of return highlight the differences between yields and rates of return. The data also capture the relevant trends and movements of yields in the focal countries.

The table illustrates national averages, rather than published yield data for the major international financial centers in which investors actually acquired/developed properties and real estate portfolios. Such data is not directly relevant to the topic of cross-border investment in the focal countries. The intent was to provide a gross measure across countries (and the only statistical yield measure available) which portrayed even to a moderate degree the investment diversification that attracted international investors to specific major markets in London, Los Angeles, New York, Washington, DC, Honolulu, Dallas, Frankfurt and Munich.

The purpose of professional real estate advisory services, as argued in this book, is to enhance (or create) value, one important measure of a firm's reputation and the reason one investor would retain one firm rather than another. Real estate advisory services gained value and reputation by exceeding national and local market averages by identifying the highest yielding market location, property (or investment trust/portfolio) and financial structure.

The internationalization of the commercial real estate advisory industry was a result of the industry's goal to maximize its clients' expected profits at a minimum risk. Given relative tax treatments and capital controls, the decisions on portfolio investment flows respond to the differences in yields across countries accounting for expectations about foreign exchange rate movements. Covered interest arbitrage theory argues that higher foreign returns can be offset if the foreign currency is expected to depreciate. For example, during the early 1980s, the US received large capital inflows. Returns relative to other countries were high and the international exchange value of the dollar was rising. In contrast, after this period foreign investors, particularly Japanese, have taken losses on investments in the US because of the 50–60 percent decline in the dollar relative to the yen.

Given that the different data sources would be required to illustrate the most credible historical data, only the most respected data sources for property investment yields were consulted. In the US, the Russell–NCREIF Property Index was and remains the nation's leading and most highly regarded measure of stock data, often compared by investors to such comparable indices as the New York Stock Exchange and American Stock Exchange for equities. For the UK, Hillier Parker May & Rowden had the best data for yields and rates of return. The rates of return were only available in the UK, and are shown to provide an example of the yields and rates of return differentials during this period.

Table A.4 Historical yields and rates of return on real estate investment in the focal
countries (1960–90)

	United States (%)	United Kingdom[a] (%)	United Kingdom[b] (%)	Germany (%)	Japan[c] (%)
1960	–	–	–	–	–
1961	–	–	–	–	–
1962	–	–	–	–	–
1963	–	–	–	–	–
1964	–	–	–	–	–
1965	–	–	–	–	26.1
1966	–	–	–	–	4.0
1967	–	–	–	–	3.6
1968	–	–	–	–	29.0
1969	–	–	–	–	61.7
1970	–	–	–	–	(4.9)
1971	–	–	–	–	8.6
1972	–	6.3	–	–	9.3
1973	–	5.9	54.7	–	9.2
1974	–	8.6	(12.3)	–	(6.5)
1975	–	8.5	14.1	7.0	0.3
1976	–	7.1	32.7	7.4	(0.7)
1977	–	7.0	14.4	7.4	(0.3)
1978	16.1	6.1	36.2	7.3	3.6
1979	20.8	5.5	39.3	7.2	4.1
1980	18.0	5.5	22.8	6.7	6.2
1981	16.9	5.5	16.1	6.3	5.6
1982	9.5	5.7	9.0	6.3	8.1
1983	13.3	6.3	0.2	6.3	4.3
1984	13.0	6.6	8.7	6.3	5.8
1985	10.1	7.0	9.7	6.3	5.5
1986	6.6	7.5	9.4	6.4	22.8
1987	5.7	7.7	17.8	6.4	9.2
1988	7.0	7.3	47.3	6.4	10.8
1989	6.2	7.2	29.5	5.9	14.1
1990	1.5	8.4	1.0	5.9	15.6

Sources:

For the United States, Russell–NCREIF Property Index rate of return property level index in the US; set at 100 for 4ᵗʰQ77, and returns represent an aggregation of individual property returns before deduction of management fee; each property's return is weighted by its market value, and income and capital changes are calculated individually. For the United Kingdom, Hillier Parker May & Rowden property annual average yields and rates of return 1972–90; in *Investors Chronicle*, Rates of Return, June 1987, July 1990, and 1994. For Germany, Weatherall, Green & Smith property yields, published in *Property Reports* 1992. For Japan, the average annual yield for net earnings (sales and operating income) reported by publicly traded commercial real estate companies; in *Japan Company Directory*, 1960–73 and *Japan Company Handbook*, 1974–91.

Notes:

The purpose of the comparative data is simply to illustrate differences in real estate investment performance among the focal countries during the study period. The data have been compiled, by necessity, from different types of sources for each country. There is no uniform global market mechanism which might document real estate investment return data for national markets. The data for the US, UK and Germany are most comparable, arraying annual yields (operating income and appraised capital value) of investment property surveyed by private firms, as shown above. In the absence of such information for Japan, the author has relied instead on published annual yield data (corporate return performance on present capital) for publicly traded property companies. (Japan's data would be most comparable with the UK *Financial Times* Actuarial Series for British Property Companies, but the UK data presented in this table are more accurate in the context of this book and better reflect actual market performance.)

— Not available.

a   Defined by C. Gordon and G. Arnott as the ratio of net income to total capital costs, and the overall yield upon sale (or another capital event) relative to total development/capital costs, in "Some Observations on Property Financing", *Investors Chronicle*, Property Supplement (23 February 1962), p. xvii.

b   Rates of return are defined by Hillier Parker and calculated as the sum of the income received in that period plus the change in value of the investment expressed as a percentage of the initial value of the investment; in *Investors Chronicle* (June 1987).

c   According to an expert on Asia at The Frank Russell Company, the leading US portfolio indexer, "Time-series real estate returns that are comparable to those recorded for U.S., U.K. and German commercial properties are not readily available in Japan. Japanese land prices, by contrast, have been more systematically tracked. As such, property companies that trade on the Tokyo stock exchange provide a good proxy for real estate values in Japan: Long-run returns on stock should reasonably reflect the underlying value of properties held in a company's portfolio. Moreover, stock share prices are derived by a more objective supply/demand market trading mechanism than the more subjective appraisal system of return indices in the U.S., U.K. and Germany."

BIBLIOGRAPHY

Books

Allen, D. *A Handbook of International Company Structures*. London, Foulsham, 1990.

Alletzhauser, A.J. *The House of Nomura*. New York: Arcade Publishing, 1990.

Arthur Andersen and Nabarro Nathanson. *Building a Stake in Europe – Guidelines for Investors in Real Estate*. Chicago, IL: Arthur Andersen & Co. and Nabarro Nathanson, June 1991.

Barrere, A., ed. *The Foundations of Keynesian Analysis*. London: Macillan Press Ltd, 1988.

Barter, S.L., ed. *Real Estate Finance*. London: Butterworth, 1988.

Bartlett, C.A. and S. Ghoshal. *Managing Across the Ocean*. Boston: Harvard Business School Press, 1989.

Barty-King, H. *Scratch a Surveyor*. London: William Heinemann, Ltd, 1975.

Baumol, W.J. *Economic Theory and Operations Analysis*. 4th edn. Englewood Cliffs, NJ: Prentice-Hall, 1977.

Baumol, W.J., S.A.B. Blackman and E.N. Wolff. *Productivity and American Leadership: The Long View*. Cambridge, MA: MIT Press, 1989.

Berghahn, V.R. *The Americanisation of West German Industry 1945–1973*. Warwickshire, UK: Berg Publishers Ltd, 1986.

Bergsten, C.F. *America in the World Economy: A Strategy for the 1990s*. Washington, DC: Institute for International Economics, 1988.

Biggadike, E.R. *Corporate Diversification: Entry, Strategy, and Performance*. Reprint, Cambridge, MA: Harvard University Press, 1981 [1979].

Bloomfield, A. *Patterns of Fluctuation in International Investment Before 1914*. International Finance Section, Department of Economics, Princeton Studies in International Finance, no. 20. Princeton, NJ: Princeton University Press, 1968.

Borchardt, K. *Perspectives on Modern German Economic History and Policy*. Translated from German by P. Lambert. Cambridge: Cambridge University Press, 1991.

Braun, H.J. *The German Economy in the Twentieth Century*. London: Routledge, 1990.

Brock, W.E. and R.D. Hormats. *The Global Economy: America's Role in the Decade Ahead*. New York: W.W. Norton & Company, 1990.

Buckley, P., Z. Berkova and G. Newbould. *Direct Investment in the United Kingdom by Smaller European Firms*. London: MacMillan Press Ltd, 1983.

Burk, K. *Morgan Grenfell 1938–1988: The Biography of a Merchant Bank*. Oxford: Oxford University Press, 1989.

Cadman, D. and L. Austin-Crowe. *Property Development*. 2nd cdn. New York: E & FN Spon, 1989.

Cameron, R. *A Concise Economic History of the World: From Paleolithic Times to the Present*. New York: Oxford University Press, 1989.

Carosso, V.P. *The Morgans: Private International Bankers 1854–1913*. Cambridge, MA: Harvard University Press, 1987.

Casson, M. *The Economics of Business Culture: Game Theory, Transaction Costs, and Economic Performance*. Oxford: Clarendon Press, 1991.

—— *Enterprise and Competitiveness: A Systems View of International Business*. Oxford: Clarendon Press, 1990.

—— *The Firm and the Market*. Cambridge, MA: MIT Press, 1987.

—— ed. *Global Research Strategy and International Competitiveness*. London: Basil Blackwell, 1991.

—— ed. *The Growth of International Business*. London: George Allen & Unwin, 1983.

Chandler, A.D., Jr. *Scale and Scope: The Dynamics of Industrial Capitalism*. Cambridge, MA: Belknap Press of Harvard University Press, 1990.

—— *Strategy and Structure: Chapters in the History of American Industrial Enterprise*. Cambridge, MA: MIT Press, 1962.

—— *The Visible Hand: The Managerial Revolution in American Business*. Cambridge, MA: Belknap Press of Harvard University Press, 1977.

Chartered Institute of Building, with UK Department of Enterprise. *The Single Market*. London, n.d.

The Chartered Surveyors Survey. London: Tann vom Hove, 1987–1991.

Chernow, R. *The House of Morgan: An American Banking Dynasty and the Rise of Modern Finance*. New York: Atlantic Monthly Press, 1990.

Christens and A. Hansen. *Teaching and the Case Method*. Boston: Harvard Business School, 1987.

Claassen, E.M. *International and European Monetary Systems*. New York: Praeger, 1990.

Coase, R.H. *The Firm, the Market, and the Law*. Chicago: University of Chicago Press, 1988.

Cooke, T.E. *International Mergers and Acquisitions*. Oxford: Basil Blackwell, 1989.

—— *Mergers and Acquisitions*. Oxford: Basil Blackwell, 1988.

Cowan, S. *The Guide to European Property Investment*. Vol. 1. London: Waterlow Publishers, 1989.

Cushman, R.F. and R.L. Soares, eds. *Business Opportunities in the United States: A Complete Reference Guide to Practices and Procedures* (New York: Price Waterhouse, 1992): 306–42, 821–52.

Davis, S.I. *Managing Change in the Excellent Banks*. New York: St. Martin's Press, 1989.

Dell, S. *The United Nations and International Business*. Durham, NC: Duke University Press, 1990.

DeMond, C.W. *Price, Waterhouse & Co. in America*. New York: Arno Press, 1980.

Dermine, J., ed. *European Banking in the 1990s*. Oxford: Basil Blackwell, 1990.

Dertouzos, M.L., R.K. Lester, R.M. Solow and the MIT Commission on Industrial Productivity. *Made in America: Regaining the Productive Edge*. Cambridge, MA: MIT Press, 1989.

Dudley, J.W. *1992: Strategies for the Single Market*. London: Kogan Page Ltd, 1989.

Dueser, J.T. *International Strategies of Japanese Banks: The European Perspective*. London and New York: Macmillan Academic and Professional Ltd, 1990.

Eatwell, J., M. Milgate and P. Newman. *The New Palgrave: A Dictionary of Economics*. Vols 1–4. London: MacMillan Press Ltd, 1987.

Eccles, R.G. and D.B. Crane. *Doing Deals: Investment Banks at Work*. Boston: Harvard Business School Press, 1988.

The Economist Guide: Japan. Reprint, London: Hutchinson, 1990 [1987].

Eli, M. *Japan Inc.: Global Strategies of Japanese Trading Corporations*. Chicago: Probus Publishing, 1991.

Erdman, E.L. *People & Property*. 1967. Reprint, London: B.T. Batsford Ltd, 1982.

Gaikoku Shihon no Tainichi Toshi: Gaikukuhen. Tokyo: Kaizai Chosa Kyoka, 1969, 1970, 1980, 1990.

Gleed, R., A. Baker and A. Blacknell. *Deloitte's 1992 Guide*. London: Butterworths, 1989.

Global Info-Net, Inc., comps. *Pension Funds and Their Advisors 1990/91: The Blue Book of the Global Pension Fund Industry*. Tiburon, CA: Global Info-Net Inc., 1990.

Goldenberg, S. *Hands Across the Ocean: Managing Joint Ventures with a Spotlight on China and Japan*. Boston: Harvard Business School Press, 1988.

Goodhart, C.A.E. and G. Sutija, eds. *Japanese Financial Growth*. London: MacMillan Academic and Professional Ltd, 1990.

Hall, P.A., ed. *The Political Power of Economic Ideas: Keynesianism across Nations*. Princeton: Princeton University Press, 1989.

Hannah, L., ed. *Pension Asset Management: An International Perspective*. Homewood, IL: Richard D. Irwin, 1988.

Hart, A., ed. *International Directory of Company Histories*, Vol. IV. London: St. James Press, 1991.

Hay, M. and P. Williamson. *The Strategy Handbook*. Oxford: Basil Blackwell, 1991.

Hayes, S.L. III and P.M. Hubbard. *Investment Banking: A Tale of Three Cities*. Boston: Harvard Business School Press, 1990.

Hayes, S.L. III, A. M. Spence and D.V.P. Marks. *Competition in the Investment Banking Industry*. Cambridge, MA: Harvard University Press, 1983.

Heckscher, E.F. and B. Ohlin. *Heckscher-Ohlin Trade Theory*. Translated and edited by H. Flam and M.J. Flanders. Cambridge, MA: MIT Press, 1991.

Hines, M.A. *Global Corporate Real Estate Management: A Handbook for Multinational Businesses and Organizations*. New York: Quorum Books, 1990.

—— *Guide to International Real Estate Investment*. New York: Quorum Books, 1988.

—— *Investing in Japanese Real Estate*. New York: Quorum Books, 1987.

—— *Marketing Real Estate Internationally*. New York: Quorum Books, 1988.

Hobson, C.K. *The Export of Capital*. London: Constable and Company, 1914.

Hobson, D. *The Pride of Lucifer – Morgan Grenfell 1938–1988: The Unauthorised Biography of a Merchant Bank*. London: Hamish Hamilton, 1990.

Hogan, J. *The European Marketplace*. London: MacMillan Press Ltd, 1991.

Ishihara, S. *The Japan That Can Say No*. Translated from Japanese by F. Baldwin. London: Simon & Schuster, 1991.

Ishikawa, K. *Japan and the Challenge of Europe 1992*. London: Pinter Publishers, 1990.

Johnson, C. *MITI and the Japanese Miracle: The Growth of Industrial Policy, 1925–1975*. Stanford, CA: Stanford University Press, 1982.

Jones, G. *British Multinational Banking, 1830–1990*. Oxford: Oxford University Press, 1993.

Julius, D. *Global Companies & Public Policy: The Growing Challenge of Foreign Direct Investment*. New York: Council on Foreign Relations Press, 1990.

Kay, J. *Foundations of Corporate Success*. Oxford: Oxford University Press, 1993.

Kay, J., C. Mayer and D. Thompson, eds. *Privatisation and Regulation: The UK Experience*. Oxford: Clarendon Press, 1989.

Kay, W., ed. *Clay and Wheble's Modern Merchant Banking*. 3rd edn. Cambridge: Woodhead-Faulkner Ltd, 1990.

Kester, W.C. *Japanese Takeovers: The Global Contest for Corporate Control*. Boston: Harvard Business School Press, 1991.

Kindleberger, C.P. *Economic Response: Comparative Studies in Trade, Finance, and Growth*. Cambridge, MA: Harvard University Press, 1978.

Kirzner, I.M. *Discovery and the Capitalist Process*. Chicago: University of Chicago Press, 1985.

Kohls, S., ed. *Dictionary of International Economics*. Berlin: A.W. Sijthoff Intl. Publishing, 1978.

Levitt, T. *Thinking about Management*. New York: Free Press, 1991.

Lincoln, E.J. *Japan's Unequal Trade*. Washington, DC: The Brookings Institute, 1990.

Liston D. and N. Reeves. *The Invisible Economy: A Profile of Britain's Invisible Exports*. London: Pitman Publishing, 1988.

Locke, R.R. *Management and Higher Education Since 1940: The Influence of America and Japan on West Germany, Great Britain, and France*. Cambridge: Cambridge University Press, 1989.

Lodge, G.C. *Perestroika for America: Restructuring U.S. Business-Government Relations for Competitiveness in the World Economy*. Boston: Harvard Business School Press, 1990.

Lodge, G.C. and E.F. Vogel. *Ideology and National Competitiveness*. Boston: Harvard Business School Press, 1987.

Lomax, D.F. and P.T.G. Gutmann. *The Euromarkets & International Financial Policies*. London: MacMillan Press Ltd, 1981.

Marriott, O. *The Property Boom*. 1967. Reprint, London: Abingdon Publishing, 1989.

Mason, M. and D. Encarnation, eds. *Does Ownership Matter? Japanese Multinationals in Europe*. Oxford: Clarendon Press, 1994.

Mason, M. *American Multinationals and Japan: The Political Economy of Japanese Capital Controls, 1899–1980*. Cambridge, MA: Council on East Asian Studies, Harvard University, 1992.

McCraw, T.K. *Prophets of Regulation: Charles Francis Adams, Louis D. Brandeis, James M. Landis, and Alfred E. Kahn*. Cambridge, MA: Belknap Press, 1984.

—— ed. *America vs. Japan*. Boston: Harvard Business School Press, 1986.

Mergers, Acquisitions, and Alternative Corporate Strategies. London: Mercury Books with Confederation of British Industry, 1989.

Morishima, M. *Ricardo's Economics: A General Equilibrium Theory of Distribution and Growth*. Cambridge: Cambridge University Press, 1989.

Newland, K., ed. *The International Relations of Japan*. Houndmills, England: MacMillan Academic and Professional Ltd, 1990.

Nikkei Annual Corporation Reports (Kaisha nenkan). Tokyo: Nihon Keizai Shinbunsha, 1960, 1970, 1980, 1990.

Ohmae, K. *The Borderless World: Power and Strategy in the Interlinked Economy*. New York: Harper Business, 1990.

—— *Triad Power: The Coming Shape of Global Competition*. New York: Free Press, 1985.

Okimoto, D.I. *Between MITI and the Market*. Stanford, CA: Stanford University Press, 1989.

Parkin, L., ed. *Chartered Surveyors 1991: The Ivanhoe Guide*. Oxford, Ivanhoe Press, 1990.

Penrose, E.T. *The Theory of the Growth of the Firm*. Reprint, White Plains, NY: M.E. Sharpe Inc., 1991 [1959].

Perry, K. *Business in Europe: Opportunities for British Companies in the EEC*. Philadelphia: Heinemann, 1987.

Peters, T.J. and R.H. Waterman, Jr. *In Search of Excellence*. New York: Harper & Row, 1982.

Piore, M.J. and C.F. Sabel. *The Second Industrial Divide: Possibilities for Prosperity*. New York: Basic Books, 1984.

Porter, M.E. *Competitive Advantage*. New York: The Free Press, 1985.

—— *Competitive Advantage: Creating and Sustaining Superior Performance*. New York and London: Free Press, 1985.

—— *The Competitive Advantage of Nations*. New York and London: Free Press, 1990.

—— ed. *Competition in Global Industries*. Boston: Harvard Business School Press, 1986.

Powell, C.G. *An Economic History of the British Building Industry, 1815–1979*. London: Methuen, 1982.

Prahalad, C.K. and Y.L. Doz. *The Multinational Mission: Balancing Local Demands and Global Vision*. New York and London: Free Press, 1987.

Pratten, C. *The Competitiveness of Small Firms*. Cambridge: Cambridge University Press, 1991.

Rassam, C. and D. Oates. *Management Consultancy: The Inside Story*. London: Mercury Business Books, 1991.

Reich, C. *Financier: The Biography of Andre Meyer, A Story of Money, Power, and the Reshaping of American Business*. New York: William Morrow and Company, 1983.

Reich, R.B. *The Work of Nations: Preparing Ourselves for 21st-Century Capitalism*. New York: Alfred A. Knopf, 1991.

Richardson, G.B. *Information and Investment: A Study in the Working of the Competitive Economy*. Oxford: Clarendon Press, 1990.

Roberts, P.C. *The Supply-Side Revolution: An Insider's Account of Policymaking in Washington*. Cambridge, MA: Harvard University Press, 1984.

Robock, S.H. and K. Simmonds. *International Business and Multinational Enterprises*. 3rd edn. Homewood, IL: Richard D. Irwin, 1983.

Rosenbloom, R.S., ed. *Research on Technological Innovation, Management and Policy*. London: JAI Press, 1989.

Rosovsky, H. *The University: An Owner's Manual*. New York: W.W. Norton, 1990.

Royal Institution of Chartered Surveyors. *Finance in Property*. London: October 1977.

Rugman, A.M. *Global Corporate Strategy and Trade Policy*. London: Routledge, 1990.

—— *Inside the Multinationals: The Economics of Internal Markets*. New York: Columbia University Press, 1981.

Rugman, A.M. and A.D.M. Anderson. *Administered Protection in America*. London: Croom Helm, 1987.

Schwartz, T.A. *America's Germany: John J. McCloy and the Federal Republic of Germany*. Cambridge, MA: Harvard University Press, 1991.

Scott, B.R. and G.C. Lodge, eds. *U.S. Competitiveness in the World Economy*. Boston: Harvard Business School Press, 1985.

Seidman, L.W. and S.L. Skancke. *Productivity: The American Advantage: How 50 U.S. Companies Are Regaining The Competitive Edge*. New York: Simon & Schuster, 1990.

Silva, M. and B. Sjoegren. *Europe 1992 and the New World Power Game*. New York: John Wiley & Sons, 1990.

de Smidt, M. and E. Wever. *The Corporate Firm in a Changing World Economy*. London: Routledge, 1990.

Smith, R.C. and I. Walter. *Global Financial Services: Strategies for Building Competitive Strengths in International Commercial and Investment Banking*. New York: Harper Business, 1990.

Sobel, R. *Trammell Crow, Master Builder: The Story of America's Largest Real Estate Empire*. New York: John Wiley & Sons, 1989.

Spencer, P.D. *Financial Innovation, Efficiency and Disequilibrium: Problems of Monetary Management in the UK, 1971–1981*. Oxford: Clarendon Press, 1986.

Spicers Centre for Europe and P. Quantock. *Opportunities in European Financial Services: 1992 and Beyond*. New York: John Wiley & Sons, 1990.

Stevens, M. *The Big Six: The Selling Out of America's Top Accounting Firms*. New York: Simon & Schuster, 1991.

Stigler, G.J. *The Organization of Industry*. Chicago: University of Chicago Press, 1968.

Strange, R. *Japanese Manufacturing Investment in Europe: Its Impact on the UK Economy*. London and New York: Routledge, 1993.

Suzuki, Y. *Japan's Economic Performance and International Role*. Tokyo: University of Tokyo Press, 1989.

——*Japanese Management Structures, 1920–80*. New York: St. Martin's Press, 1991.

Thomsen, S. and P. Nicolaides. *The Evolution of Japanese Direct Investment in Europe*. London: Simon & Schuster, 1991.

Treays, M. *1992: A General Practice Guide to the Single European Market*. London: Royal Institution of Chartered Surveyors, 1989.

Turner, J.A. and L.M. Dailey, eds. *Pension Policy: An International Perspective*. Washington, DC: U.S. Government Printing Office, 1991.

Vernon, R. *Storm over the Multinationals: The Real Issues*. Cambridge, MA: Harvard University Press, 1977.

Vernon, R. and L.T. Wells. *The Manager in the International Economy*. 6th edn. Englewood Cliffs, NJ: Prentice-Hall, 1991.

Volhard, R., D. Weber and W. Usinger, eds. *Real Property In Germany: Legal and Tax Impacts of Development and Investment*. Frankfurt: Fritz Knapp Verlag, 1975, 1991.

Walter, I. and R.C. Smith. *Investment Banking in Europe: Restructuring for the 1990s*. Oxford: Basil Blackwell, 1990.

Whitehouse, B.P. *Partners in Property*. London: Birn, Shaw and Company, 1964.

Wiener, M.J. *English Culture and the Decline of the Industrial Spirit 1850–1980*. New York and London: Penguin Books, 1985.

Wilkins, M. *The Emergence of Multinational Enterprise: American Business Abroad from the Colonial Era to 1914*. Cambridge, MA: Belknap Press of Harvard College, 1970.

—— *The Maturing Multinational Enterprise: American Business Abroad from 1914 to 1970*. Cambridge, MA: Harvard University Press, 1974.

Wilks, S. and M. Wright. *Comparative Government–Industry Relations: Western Europe, the United States, and Japan*. Oxford: Clarendon Press, 1987.

Williamson, J.P., ed. *The Investment Banking Handbook*. New York: John Wiley & Sons, 1988.

Williamson, O.E. *The Economic Institutions of Capitalism*. New York and London: Free Press, 1987.

—— *Markets and Hierarchies: Analysis and Antitrust Implications*. New York and London: Free Press, 1975.

Williamson, O.E. and S. G. Winter, eds. *The Nature of the Firm: Origins, Evolution, and Development*. New York: Oxford University Press, 1991.

Winters, L.A. and A. J. Venables, eds. *European Integration: Trade and Industry*. Cambridge: Cambridge University Press, 1991.

H. Yoshihara and S. Khan, *Strategy and Performance of Foreign Companies in Japan*. Westport, CT: Quorum Books, 1994.

Journal articles, published essays and chapters in books

Armour, H.O. and D.J. Teece. "Vertical Integration and Technological Innovation", *The Review of Economics and Statistics* 62, no. 3 (August 1980): 470.

Bailey, A. "Property People". *The Estates Gazette* 219 (July 31, 1971): 597–601.

—— "Putting the Professional Under One Roof", *Director* (April 1988): 37–8.

Baker, J.C. and T. Kondo. "Joint Ventures in Japan and How to Obtain Managerial Control". *MSU Business Topics* 19, no. 1, (Winter 1971): 49.

"Bankers Trust Co., On the Move in Tokyo". *Euromoney* (February 1988): 40–3.

Barsky, N. "Olympia & York, New York City Set Restructuring of Firm's Property Taxes". *Wall Street Journal*, 22 May 1992: A3.

Bergsman, S. "Extravagant '80s Produce Grim '90s". *National Real Estate Investor* (February 1991): 31.

Berman, A., R.J. Jinnett and R.A.N. Cudd. "Strategic Use of Real Estate Against a Hostile Takeover Bid". *The Real Estate Finance Journal* (Winter 1989): 1–15.

Bingham, B.B. "Managing Corporate Real Estate in a Takeover". *Site Selection* (February 1989).

Blanton, K. "Dispute Over Control Leads to Richard Ellis Departures". *Pensions & Investment Age* 17 October 1983: 2, 44.

Bloomfield, C. "Rubloff Property Gems Define Sinclair, Orix Mission", *Commercial Property News* 16 February 1991: 1.

Blundell, G.F. and C.W.R. Ward. "Property Portfolio Allocation: A Multi-Factor Model". *Land Development Studies* (May 1987): 147–56.

Blysh, J.L. "Baukostenplanung (Quantity Surveying in Germany)". *The Quantity Surveyor* (July/August 1972): 3–5.

Bramson, D. "The Mechanics of Joint Ventures", *Real Estate Finance* ed. S.L. Barter. London: Butterworth, 1988: 139–49.

Brett-Jones, A.T. "Development, The Economy and the Chartered Quantity Surveyor". *Chartered Surveyor* 5 November 1965: 243–6; and May 1966: 595–7.

—— "The Future Role of the Quantity Surveyor". *Chartered Surveyor* (July 1969): 13–15.

"British Bank is Hit for $352 million Loss in America". *The European* (1–3 February 1991).

Brock, W.E. "A Simple Plan for Negotiating on Trade in Services". *The World Economy* 5, no. 3 (1982): 235.

Brown, R.K. "Competitiveness, the CEO and Real Estate Decisions". *National Real Estate Investor* (October 1987): 54.

Brown, S. "Real Estate Networks". *National Real Estate Investor* (July 1989).

Buck, R. "New Japanese and U.S. Investments in Europe". *Site Selection Europe* (November/December 1990): 14 and (March 1992): 12–13.

Claiborne, W. and K. Day. "Bank Experts Differ on Impact of Surprise Bankruptcy Filings". *The Washington Post* 16 May 1992: C1.

—— "A Dynasty of Control". *The Washington Post* 26 April 1992: H1.

Coase, R.H. "The Nature of the Firm", in *The Firm, the Market, and the Law*, pp. 33–55, ed. R.H. Coase. Chicago: University of Chicago Press, 1988 [first published in *Economica* n.s., 4 (November 1937)].

Cohen, P. "New Face of Finance". *Chartered Surveyor Weekly* 32, no. 5 (August 1990): 33.

Cohen, R., J. Kay, C. Murroni, A. Pototsching and S. Trussler. "The Competitive Advantage of Law and Accountancy in the City of London", The City Research Project. London Business School, London (1994).

"Comparative Advantage and Trade in Services". *The World Economy* 7, no. 4 (December 1984).

Cooper, R.N. "Towards an International Capital Market?", in *North American and Western European Economic Policies*, compiled by International Economic Association. London: Macmillan, St. Martin's Press, 1971.

"Corporate Boon: Real Estate". *The New York Times* 20 August 1987: D-1.

Dean, A.O. "European Forecast". *Architecture* (January 1989).

Delamaide, D. "The Long Wait for Rich Pickings". *Euromoney* (August 1990).

Derven, R. "Goldman Sachs Credits Innovative Financing for Success in a Changing Mortgage Market". *National Real Estate Investor* (June 1986): 131.

"Development, The Economy and the Chartered Quantity Surveyor". *Chartered Surveyor* 5 November 1965: 243–6.

DiSciullo, A.M. and J.B. Wood. "Financing Real Estate Development Through Participation Leases". *Real Estate Review* 20, no. 4 (Winter 1991): 30.

Dufey, G. "The Role of Japanese Financial Institutions Abroad", in *Japanese Financial Growth*, pp. 132–55, eds C.A.E. Goodhart and G. Sutija, London: Macmillan Academic and Professional Press, 1990.

Dunning, J.H. "Changes in the Level and Structure of International Production: The Last One Hundred Years", in *The Growth of International Business*, ed. M. Casson. London: George Allen & Unwin, 1983: 84–139.

Dunning, J.H. and G. Norman. "The Theory of the Multinational Enterprise: An Application to Multinational Office Location. *Environment and Planning* 15, 1983: 675–92.

The Economist 16 January 1963: 348; 28 January 1967: 356; 20 January 1973: 90–2; 30 March 1963: 1–91 and 1291; 2 March 1968: 61; 18 March 1972: 8; 3 April 1976: 117–18; 28 May 1988: 609; 10 June 1961: 152; 10 June 1978: 3–11, 152; 381; 22 July 1961: 381; 6 July 1968: 69; 25 July 1970: 81; 1 July 1972: 22; 14 July 1973: 77; 6 July 1974; 13 July 1985: 480; 14 July 1993: 77; 10 August 1968: 12–13; 1 August 1970: 60; 2 August 1980: 67; 14 September 1963: 946; 28 September 1968: 77–8; 12 September 1970: 91; 19 September 1970: 104; 11 September 1971: 93; 25 September 1971: 106–7; 23 September 1972: 100–1; 8 September 1973: 70–1; 11 September 1976: 99–100; 24 September 1988: 565; 30 September 1989: 1138; 5 November 1966: 610; 11 November 1967: 638–9; 25 November 1972: 124; and 3 November 1984: 334.

"European Firm Buys First U.S. Golf Resort, Wants More". *Golf Business & Real Estate News* 8 April 1991: 3.

Evans, P. "Property Research – Into the 1990s". *Estates Gazette* 21 April 1990: 2.

Frankel, G. "Futuristic London Project Threatened". *The Washington Post* 24 May 1992: A39.

Fredrick, S.E. "Unleashing Property Values to Finance M&A Deals". *Mergers and Acquisitions* (January/February 1990).

French, M. "M & A? – We Just Didn't Think of It". *Euromoney* (November 1988).

"The French are Coming – International Investors in Germany". *European Real Estate Insider* 2, no. 3 (Fall 1992): 3–5.

Froggat, A. and T. Oliver. "Japanese Investment in European Property". *World Property* 27, no. 3 (May 1990).

Geller, L., cited in "Jones Lang Wootton/Arthur D. Little Joint Effort", *Real Estate Forum* (July 1991): 22.

Gladstone, J. and N. Nohria, comp. *Colliers International Property Consultants*. Boston: Harvard Business School Press, 1990.

Golf Business & Real Estate News 15 July 1991: 2.

Goodman, G.A. "Pacific Basin Investment in U.S. Real Estate". *The Real Estate Finance Journal* 5, no. 3 (1988).

Gop, R. "The League Table of Estate Agents: The Leaders Stay Ahead of the Field". *Immobilien Manager* (February 1992): 16–18.

—— "Player £plus; Profile". *Immobilien Manager* (February 1992): 11.

—— "Player £plus; Profile: New Game Rules". *Immobilien Manager* (December 1993): 9–20.

Gordon, J.N. "Property Performance Indexes in the United Kingdom and the United States". *Real Estate Review* (Summer 1991): 34.

Green, J.S. "Development and Investment Opportunities in U.K. Properties". *The Real Estate Finance Journal* (Spring 1991).

Greer, N.R. "Americans Abroad: Some Coming Attractions". *Architecture* (January 1989).

—— "Foreign Exchange". *Architecture* (September 1990).

Grubel, H.G. "All Traded Services Are Embodied in Materials or People". *The World Economy* 10, no. 3 (September 1987): 319.

Hannah, L. "International Perspectives on Competition and Regulatory Change in Pension Fund Asset Management", in *Pension Asset Management: An International Perspective*, ed. L. Hannah. Homewood, IL: Richard D. Irwin, 1988.

Harpham, J. "Mitsui Real Estate Development Co., LTD". *International Directory of Company Histories*, ed. A. Hast. Vol. 4. London: St. James Press, 1991: 715.

Hawkins, R.G. "Intra-EEC Capital Movements and Domestic Financial Markets", in *International Mobility and Movement of Capital*, eds F. Machlup, W.S. Salant and L. Tarshis. National Bureau of Economic Research. New York: Columbia University Press, 1972.

"Head Start", *Forbes* 1 October 1970: 46.

Healey, T.J., R.N. Papert and S.P. Shepherd. "Real Estate Finance Alternatives in Corporate Restructuring". *The Real Estate Finance Journal* (Spring 1990).

Heisey, S.L. "Financing Real Estate-Related Corporate Expansion". *The Real Estate Finance Journal* 4, no. 3 (1987).

Hindley, B. and A. Smith. "Comparative Advantage and Trade in Services". *The World Economy* 7, no. 4 (December 1984): 375.

Hines, M.A. "The Emergence of Real Estate Investment Banking with Global Dimensions". *The Real Estate Finance Journal* 6 (1989).

—— "Global Real Estate Services". *The Appraisal Journal* (April 1992): 206–13.

—— "Impact of Real Estate Investment Banking on the Global Capital Markets". *The Real Estate Finance Journal* (Spring 1989).

—— "Investing in Japanese Real Estate". *Real Estate Review* (1989).

Holmes, K. and R. Butler. "1992: Joint Ventures in the EC". *Single Market Monitor* 2, no. 7 (April 1990): 56.

Houlder, V. "How Under-Used Assets Can Be Exploited". *Financial Times* 17 May 1991.

Hughes, D. "Necessity is the Mother of Invention". *Accountancy* (April 1987): 118.

"Identifying the Issues in Trade in Services". *The World Economy* 8, no. 2 (June 1985).

"International Property Players". *International Real Estate Journal* (July/August 1991): 24.

Jackson, J.H. "Constructing a Constitution for Trade in Services". *The World Economy* 11, no. 2 (June 1988): 187–202.

"Japanese Purchases of U.S. Real Estate Fall on Hard Times". *The Wall Street Journal*. 21 February 1992.

Jenkinson, T.J. "Initial Public Offerings in the United Kingdom, the United States, and Japan". *Journal of the Japanese International Economies* 3, no.4 (December 1990): 428–49.

Jinnett, R.J. "Strategic Use of Real Estate in Defending Against Hostile Takeovers". *Industrial Development Section* (February 1990): 119–24.

Johnson, W.D. "Designing Corporate Real Estate Policy from the Ground Up". *Site Selection* (December 1988).

"Jones Lang Wootton/Arthur D. Little Joint Effort", *Real Estate Forum* (July 1991): 22.

Jones, R.W. and F. Ruane. "Appraising the Options for International Trade in Services". *Oxford Economic Papers* 42, no. 4 (October 1990): 672–87.

Kalanik, L.M. "Mitsubishi Estate Company". *International Directory of Company Histories*, Vol. IV, pp. 713–14, ed. A. Hast. London: St. James Press, 1991.

—— "Sumitomo Realty & Development Co.". *International Directory of Company Histories*, Vol. IV, p. 726, ed. A. Hast. London: St. James Press, 1991.

Kavanaugh, P. "Levy, Younce, Roth Ease U.S. Firms' Entree Into Europe". *Commercial Property News* 16 April 1991: 14.

Kay, W. "Bringing Security to Hearth and Home". *Euromoney* (December 1987): 159–60.

Kazilionis, P.D. "Real Estate Finance", in *The Investment Banking Handbook*, ed. J.P. Williamson. New York: John Wiley & Sons. 1988: 176–8.

Kelly, H.F. "Can Universities Teach Real Estate Decision Making?" *Real Estate Review* 20, no. 2 (Summer 1990): 81.

Kelman, H. "Most Experts See Steady Growth for Cross-Border Deal-Making". *Real Estate Forum* (January 1991).

Klionsky, M.A. "Driscoll Streamlines from Loose Network to Unified Organization", *Commercial Property News* 1 June 1991: 3.

Knutsen, K.C. "The Impact of Real Estate on Operations and Financial Statements: Sale-Leaseback Transactions". *Site Selection* (November 1990): 27, 1409.

Kotch, R.A. "Benchmarking Corporate Real Estate Performance at AT&T". *Industrial Development Section* (August 1989): 1311–13.

Lake, D. "Japan and Mortgage-Backed Securities". *World Property* (March 1990).

Lawrence, P.R. and J.W. Lorsch. "Organizing for Product Innovation". *Harvard Business Review* (January–February 1965): 109–22.

Lehmann, J.P. "Corporate Global Strategies in the 1990s". *Site Selection* (April 1990).

Lee, P. "Commercial Banks Move In". *Euromoney* (February 1990).

Leslie, I.A. "Service to the Industry". *Building* (2 May 1969): 91.

Lewis, J. "MPT Comes To Real Estate". *Institutional Investor* (February 1990): 153–60.

Levy, A.H., E.M. Marks and J.B. Weller. "Convertible Mortgages Lure Creative Investors and Owners". *Real Estate Review* 18, no. 4 (Winter 1989): 30.

Light, L. "Even the Reichmanns are Feeling the Pinch". *Business Week* 8 October 1990: 128–9.

Liston, P. "Peter Ball of Philips: Advocate for Asset Management". *Site Selection Europe* (March 1992).

Lorsch, J.W. and P.R. Lawrence, "Organizing for Product Innovation", *Harvard Business Review* (January/February 1965): 109–22.

Love, D.A. "U.S. Pension Fund Asset Management". *Pension Asset Management: An International Perspective*, ed. L. Hannah. Homewood, IL: Richard D. Irwin, 1988.

Lyne, J. "LaSalle Partners' Mike Bell: Sharp-Eyed Insights from the Service-Provider Side". *Site Selection* (December 1990).

—— "The Out-Sourcing of Real Estate: Entrenched, Growing and Controversial". *Site Selection* (February 1991): 50–8.

Macchia, A.F. "The Securitization of Real Estate: Strategies for Investment Banking". *The Real Estate Finance Journal* (Fall 1987).

Maier, B.K. and S. G. Kucera. "Property Securitization in the United Kingdom". *The Real Estate Finance Journal* (Summer 1987).

Mallinson, M. "Equity Finance", in *Real Estate Finance*, ed. S. Barter. London: Butterworth, 1988.

Manning, C.A. "Getting Things Done: The Economics of Real Estate Decisions". *Harvard Business Review* 6 (November/December 1986): 12–23.

March, R.M. "Foreign Firms in Japan". *California Management Review* 22, no. 3 (Spring 1980): 42–6.

Marshall, R. "The QS in Europe". *Building* 24 September 1976.

Martin, J. "JMB Realty Corporation", in *International Directory of Company Histories*, Vol. IV, pp. 702–3, ed. A. Hast. London: St. James Press, 1991.

Mayer, C. and I. Alexander. "Banks and Securities Markets: Corporate Financing in Germany and the United Kingdom". *Journal of the Japanese and International Economies* 3, no. 4 (December 1990): 450–75.

McBee, S. "Japanese Development Deals in the United States". *Urban Land* (August 1990).

McCraw, L.G. "Developing Global Strategies at Fluor Corp". *Site Selection* (October 1988).

McGrath, W.T. "Unwrapping Leasehold Equity: An Introduction to the 'Wraparound Lease'". *Real Estate Review* 19, no. 4 (Winter 1990).

McLean, R., III. "Real Estate Markets and Innovative Services". *Focus* 24 June 1987.

Metcalfe, J.S. and M. Gibbons. "Technology, Variety and Organization: A Systematic Perspective on the Competitive Process", in *Research on Technological Innovation, Management and Policy*, ed. R.S. Rosenbloom. London: JAI Press, 1989, pp. 154–8, 190.

Mitani, H. "Capital from Japan: Japanese Investment in U.S. Real Estate". *The Real Estate Finance Journal* 4, no. 1 (1987).

Mitani, H. "Capital from Japan, Part II: Gaining Access to Japanese Investors". *The Real Estate Finance Journal* 4, no. 4 (1988): 19–25.

Morris, N. "Competition, Regulation, and Deregulation in Pension Fund Portfolio Management: The Case of the United Kingdom", in *Pension Asset Management: An International Perspective*, ed. L. Hannah. Homewood, IL: Richard D. Irwin, 1988.

Nakao, H. "Implementing a Corporate Global Strategy at NEC Corp". *Site Selection* (April 1990).

Neidich, D. and T.M. Steinberg. "Corporate Real Estate: Source of New Equity". *Harvard Business Review* 4 (July/August 1984): 76–83.

"News Briefs". *National Real Estate Investors* (July 1991).

Nisbet, J. "The Future Private Practice". *Chartered Surveyor* (July 1969): 33–6.

Nobuyuki, K. "Getting Serious About Land Prices". *Japan Quarterly* 37, no. 4 (October/December 1990): 392–401.

Orix Corporation. "The Period Under Review". *Orix Update*, no. 2 (Winter 1990).

Ozanne, J. "Teaming Up to Trade on the Continent". *Estate Times European Supplement* 2 March 1990: 7–8.

"Pension Fund Advisor Funds Golf Resort". *Golf Business & Real Estate News* 8 July 1991.

"Pension Funds Off Target". *World Property* (March 1990).

Petersen, H. "International Real Estate and the American Express Experience". *Site Selection* (April 1990).

Plender, J. "The Bankers' House of Cards". *Financial Times* 12 November 1991.

Porter, M.E. and V.E. Millar. "How Information Gives You Competitive Advantage". *Harvard Business Review* (July/August 1985): 151.

Raney, D. "Managing International Real Estate at Hewlett-Packard". *Site Selection* (April 1990).

Real Estate Forum 46, no. 7 (July 1991): 11.

Rees, T.L. "Site Selection in Europe: A Case Study". *Site Selection* (October 1988).

Reich, R.B. "Who is Them?". *Harvard Business Review* (March/April 1991): 77–88.

Reinbach, A. "Ellis Principals Do Buy-Out". *Pensions & Investment Age* 12 June 1989: 37, 39.

—— "Use of Property Gains Popularity as Financial Tool". *Pensions & Investment Age* 8 January 1989.

"Richard Ellis and County Bank Join Forces", *Accountancy* (July 1986): 34.

"Richard Ellis Inc. Sold to Executives in All-Cash Deal". *National Real Estate Investor* (July 1989): 28–30.

Rooney, J.M. "Benchmarking Corporate Real Estate Performance at Xerox Corp.". *Site Selection* (August 1989).

Rosenberg, H. "Will U.S. Pension Funds Go Global?". *Institutional Investor* (March 1989).

Ross, S. and S. Duffy. "Capital Alliances in the 1990s". *Real Estate Review* 20, no. 3 (Fall 1990): 26.

Roulac, S.E. "The Globalization of Real Estate Finance". *The Real Estate Finance Journal* 4, no. 2 (Spring 1987): 40.

Royal Institute of Chartered Surveyors, *Finance in Property*. London: Royal Institute of Chartered Surveyors, October 1977: 23, 24.

Sampson, G.P. and R.H. Snape. "Identifying the Issues in Trade in Services". *The World Economy* 8, no. 2 (June 1985): 171–82.

Sarowitz, T. "Evolution of a Real Estate Firm", *Real Estate Forum* (April 1988): 116.

Schubert, T.S. "Publicly Traded Real Estate and the Myth of Inherent Appreciation". *The Real Estate Finance Journal* 7, no. 3 (Fall 1990): 58.

Scott, P. "The Hammerson Investment & Development Corp., PLC", in *International Directory of Company Histories*, Vol. IV, pp. 696–97, ed. A. Hast. London: St. James Press, 1991.

—— "Learning to Multiply: The Property Market and Growth of Multiple Retailing in Britain, 1919–39", *Business History* 36, no. 3 (1994): 23, n. 51, n. 63.

—— "MEPC PLC", in *International Directory of Company Histories*, Vol. IV, pp. 710–12, ed. A. Hast. London: St. James Press, 1991.

—— "Slough Estates PLC", in *International Directory of Company Histories*, Vol. IV, p. 722, ed. A. Hast. London: St. James Press, 1991.

Selvin, B.W. "Networks Help Firms Branch Out". *Real Estate* 17 July 1990.

Sermon, J.B. "In the Contracting Camp". *Building* 2 May 1969: 91.

Shale, T. "Clipping the Wings Of Japan's High Flyers". *Euromoney* (June 1990): 70, 72.

Stanislas, P. "British Investors in the U.S. Real Estate Market". *The Real Estate Finance Journal* 4, no. 2 (Spring 1987).

Star, M.G. "Financing Arranged for Office". *Pensions & Investments* 17 September 1990.

"Strategic Planning Perspectives". *Business International* 7 (1989).

Supple, B. "Scale and Scope: Alfred Chandler and the Dynamics of Industrial Capitalism". *Economic History Review* 44, no. 3 (August 1991): 500–14.

"Surveying New Partnerships". *Chartered Surveyor Weekly* 12 March 1992.

Taylor, W. "The Logic of Global Business: An Interview with ABB's Percy Barnevik". *Harvard Business Review* (March/April 1991).

Terada, N. "Pension Fund Portfolio Management in Japan". *Pension Asset Managomont: An International Perspective* (1988): 167.

Tolliday, S. "Business History of Real Estate". *Business History Review* (Summer 1989).

Tucker, T.H. "Tokyu Land Corporation". *International Directory of Company Histories*, Vol. IV, p. 728, ed. A. Hast. London: St. James Press, 1991.

"U.K. Funds Still Shunning Real Estate, Fixed Income". *Pensions & Investments* 1 October 1990.

Van den Bos, J. "JLW Signs up to Manage Germany Buying Spree". *Chartered Surveyor Weekly* 31 January 1991: 7.

The Wall Street Journal 19 January 1970: 1, 19; 6 March 1970: 3; 30 July 1970: 10; 20 March 1980: 1; 15 October 1980: 31; 8 October 1984: 37; 25 January 1990: C6; 9 February 1990: B11C; 3 April 1990: 46; and 13 September 1990: C1, C9.

Walter, I., and R.C. Smith. "European Investment Banking: Structure, Transaction Flow and Regulation", in *European Banking in the 1990s*, ed. J. Dermine. London: Basil Blackwell, 1990.

Waters, R. "Goldman Sachs Heads Towards a Half-Way House". *Financial Times* 12 June 1991.

Weiss, M.A. "The Politics of Real Estate Cycles". *Business and Economic History*, 2nd ser., 20 (1991).

—— "Real Estate History: An Overview and Research Agenda". *Business History Review* 63, no. 2 (Summer 1989).

Wells, L.T., Jr. Review of *International Trade in Services*. *Business History Review* (Spring 1991): 224–6.

Wilkins, M. "Japanese Multinationals in the United States: Continuity and Change, 1879–1990". *Business History Review* 64 (Winter 1990): 620.

Wolfe, R.J. "Debt Finance", in *Real Estate Finance*, ed. S.L. Barter. London: Butterworth, 1988: 83, 96.

Wood, C. "Considerations for Going Global". *Site Selection* (April 1990).

Wyplosz, C. "Macro-economic Implications of 1992", in *European Banking in the 1990s*, ed. J. Dermine. London: Basil Blackwell, 1990.

Yoshino, M.Y. "Japan as Host to the International Corporation", in *The International Corporation*. Cambridge, MA: The MIT Press, 1970.

—— "Japan as Host to the International Corporation", in *The Japanese Economy in International Perspective*, ed. I. Frank. Baltimore, MD: The Johns Hopkins University Press, 1975.

Zeckhauser, S. and R. Silverman. "Rediscover Your Company's Real Estate". *Harvard Business Review* (January/February 1983): 111–17.

Unpublished papers and proceedings

Bacow, L.S. "Foreign Investment, Vertical Integration, and the Structure of the U.S. Real Estate Industry". Working Paper No. 25. Massachusetts Institute of Technology, Center for Real Estate Development, Cambridge, MA (January 1990).

—— "The Internationalization of the U.S. Real Estate Industry". Working Paper No. 16. Massachusetts Institute of Technology, Center for Real Estate Development, Cambridge, MA (November 1988).

—— "The Tokyo Land Market: An Essay". Working Paper No. 26. Massachusetts Institute of Technology, Center for Real Estate Development, Cambridge, MA (October 1990).

—— "Understanding Foreign Investment in U.S. Real Estate". Working Paper No. 12. Massachusetts Institute of Technology, Center for Real Estate Development, Cambridge, MA (November 1987).

Baum, A. and A. Schofield. "Property as a Global Asset". Working Papers in European Property. Centre for European Property Research, University of Reading (March 1991).

Bennett, J., R. Flanagan and G. Norman. "Capital & Counties Report: Japanese Construction Industry". Centre for Strategic Studies in Construction, University of Reading (May 1987).

Currie, S. and A. Scott. "The Place of Commercial Property in the U.K. Economy". Paper presented to the London Business School, London (January 1991).

Davis, E., G. Hanlon and J. Kay. "Internationalization in Accounting and Other Professional Services". Working Paper Series No. 78. Centre for Business Strategy, London Business School, London (April 1990).

Davis, E. and C. Smales. "The Internationalization of Professional Services". Working Paper Series No. 66. Centre for Business Strategy, London Business School, London (April 1989).

DeAnne, J. "Foreign Direct Investment: The Neglected Twin of Trade". Occasional Papers No. 33. Group of Thirty, Washington, DC (1991).

Dohner, R.S. "Japanese Financial Deregulation and the Growth of Japanese International Bank Activity". Occasional Paper 89–05. The Program on U.S.–Japan Relations, Center for International Affairs, Reischauere Institute of Japanese Studies. Harvard University, Cambridge (1989).

Flanagan, I. [of Landauer Associates.] Interview by author. London, 30 July 1991.

"Future Opportunities for Pension Fund Investment in Real Estate". Proceeds of papers presented at a seminar. Massachusetts Institute of Technology, Center for Real Estate Development. Cambridge, MA (3 December 1984).

Geroski, P.A. "Entry, Innovation and Productivity Growth". Working Paper Series No. 53. Centre for Business Strategy, London Business School, London (August 1988).

—— "The Interaction Between Domestic and Foreign-Based Entrants". Working Paper Series No. 44. Centre for Business Strategy, London Business School, London (1987).

Geroski, P.A. and S. Toker. "Picking Profitable Markets". Working Paper Series No. 59. Centre for Business Strategy, London Business School, London (November 1988).

Gosling, J.A. and A.J. Thornley. "The Role of the European Property Professional: France, Spain, The United Kingdom and Germany". Working Papers in European Property, Centre for European Property Research, University of Reading (March 1991).

Hannah, L. [of Barclays Bank]. Untitled ms. (January 1994): 277–87.

Hsia, M. "Corporate Location in Europe: The Implications of a Single Market". Working Papers in European Property, Centre for European Property Research, University of Reading (March 1991).

241

Joroff, M.J. "Corporate Real Estate 2000: Management Strategies for the Next Decade", Industrial Development Research Foundation, Washington, DC (1992).

Julius, D. "Inward Investment and Foreign-owned Firms in the G-5". The Royal Institute of International Affairs Discussion. Paper 12, London (1989).

Julius, D., and S.E. Thomsen. "Foreign Direct Investment Among the G-5". The Royal Institute of International Affairs Discussion. Paper 8, London (1988).

Kimbler, L. "Corporate Real Estate Outside Services Survey". Paper presented at the Industrial Development Research Council Conference, Atlanta, GA (Fall 1991).

Louargand, M.A. "Foreign Bank Participation in United States Mortgage Markets". Working Paper No. 24. Massachusetts Institute of Technology, Center for Real Estate Development (December 1989).

Müller. Corporate brochure (1991): 3.

Oncor International. Press release (May 1991).

Orix. Annual Report (1990): 6–8.

Orix Corporation. "History of Orix Corporations", memorandum (31 July 1990).

—— corporate history brochure, Tokyo (1990): 12–13, 34–5, 40.

Ostrom, D. "Japanese Insurance Companies". Japan Economic Institute Report, No. 31A, Washington, DC (12 August 1988).

Parkin, L., ed. *Chartered Surveyors 1991* Oxford: Ivanhoe Press, 1990: 203.

Punter, J., G. Keogh, M. Hsia and J. Gosling. "Property in Europe". Working Papers in European Property, Centre for European Property Research, University of Reading (1991).

Rutter, J. "Recent Trends in International Direct Investment: The Boom Years Fade", Office of Trade and Economic Analysis, U.S. Department of Commerce (August 1993): 13.

—— "Trends in International Direct Investment". Trade Information and Analysis Staff Paper No. 91–5. U.S. Department of Commerce, International Trade Administration. Washington, DC (July 1991).

Sagari, S.B. "The Financial Services Industry: An International Perspective". PhD dissertation, Graduate School of Business Administration, New York University, 1986.

Schuck, G. "Outsourcing in the 1990s: Managing Corporate Real Estate Consultants". Working Paper No. 33. Massachusetts Institute of Technology, Center for Real Estate Development, Cambridge, MA (June 1991).

Scott, P. "Financial Institutions and the British Property Investment Market, 1960–1980". Unpublished D.Phil Thesis, Oxford University, 1992.

Dr. Seebauer & Partner, Statistisches Bundesamt (1991).

Tietmeyer, H. and W. Guth. "Two Views of German Reunification". Occasional Papers No. 31. Group of Thirty, Washington, DC (1990).

White, B. Richard Ellis untitled paper presented at the Melbourne Investment Group meeting, 8 November 1990.

"Working with Foreign Partners at Home and Abroad". Proceedings of the Members Meeting, Massachusetts Institute of Technology, Center for Real Estate Development, Cambridge (December 1989).

Public documents and government reports

Bank of Japan. *Economic Statistics Annual*. Tokyo, 1976.

Central Statistical Office of the UK Government. *Business Monitor, Census of Overseas Assets*, 1974, 1981, 1984, 1987.

—— *United Kingdom Balance of Payments, CSO Pink Book*, 1960–1990.

Deutsche Bundesbank. *Monthly Report of the Deutsche Bundesbank*. Series 3, Balance of Payments Statistics, Statistical Supplements. Deutsche Bundesbank. ["Statistische Beihefte zu den Monatsberichten der Deutschen Bundesbank", Reihe 3, Zahlungsbilanzstatistik.] Frankfurt, March and April issues, 1976–1990.

Economic Planning Agency of the Government of Japan. *Annual Report on National Income Statistics*. Tokyo, 1978.

Federal Reserve Board of the U.S. *Balance Sheets for the U.S. Economy, 1949–90*. Washington, DC, September 1991.

Hamilton, A. *Report of the Secretary of the Treasury of the United States, on the Subject of Manufactures*. Presented to the House of Representatives, U.S. Congress, 5 December 1791.

International Monetary Fund. *Balance of Payment Manual*, 4th edn. Washington, DC, 1977.

—— *Balance of Payments Manual*, 5th edn. Washington, DC, 1993.

Ministry of Finance of the Government of Japan. *Reported Outward and Inward Direct Investment*. Tokyo, May/June 1976–90.

Nourse, H., IDREC report: 6.

Organisation for Economic Co-operation and Development. Committee on International Investment and Multinational Enterprises. *Recent Trends in International Direct Investment*. Washington, DC, 1987.

—— *National Accounts, Detailed Tables*. Vol. 2. Washington, DC, 1979, 1980, 1981, 1982, 1984, 1985, 1987, 1990, 1992.

—— *International Direct Investment: Policies, Procedures and Practices in OECD Member Countries*. Paris, 1979.

—— *International Investment and Multinational Enterprises: Review of the 1976 Declaration and Decisions*. Paris, 1979.

—— *The 1984 Review of the 1976 Declaration and Decisions*. Paris, 1984.

—— *Surveillance of Structural Policies*. Paris, 1989.

—— *The OECD Declaration and Decision on International Investment and Multinational Enterprises: 1991 Review*. Paris, 1992.

—— *Code of Liberalization of Capital Movements: 1992 Edition*. Paris, 1992.

—— *International Direct Investment: Policies and Trends in the 1980s*. Paris, 1992.

—— *National Treatment for Foreign-Controlled Enterprises*. Paris, 1993.

U.S. Department of Commerce. *Factors Affecting the International Transfer of Technology Among Developed Countries*. Washington, DC: Government Printing Office, 1970.

—— Bureau of Economic Analysis. *Balance of Payment Manual*, 5th ed. Washington, DC, 1993.

—— —— *Foreign Direct Investment in the United States: Balance of Payments and Direct Investment Position Estimates, 1980–86*. Washington, DC, December 1990.

—— —— *National Income and Product Accounts of the United States*. Vol. 2. Washington, DC, 1959–1988, 1992.

—— —— *The Revised Detailed Benchmark Definition of Foreign Direct Investment*. Washington, DC, 3 February 1992.

—— —— *Selected Data on U.S. Direct Investment Abroad, 1950–76*. Washington, DC, February 1982.

—— —— *Survey of Current Business*. Washington, DC, August 1987 – July 1993.

—— —— *U.S. Direct Investment Abroad, 1977*. Washington, DC, April 1981.

—— —— *U.S. Direct Investment Abroad: 1982 Benchmark Survey Data*. Washington, DC, 1987.

—— —— *U.S. Direct Investment Abroad: Balance of Payments and Direct Investment Position Estimates, 1977–81*. Washington, DC, November 1986.

—— International Trade Administration. *Foreign Direct Investment in the United States, 1989 Transactions*. Washington, DC, June 1991.

—— Investment Trade Administration. *International Direct Investment: Global Trends and the U.S. Role*. Washington, DC, 1988.

—— —— *Recent Trends in International Direct Investment*. Washington, DC, August 1992.

U.S. Department of the Treasury. *National Treatment Study, 1979*. Washington, DC: Government Printing Office, 1979.

—— *National Treatment Study, 1984*. Washington, DC: Government Printing Office, 1984.

—— *National Treatment Study, 1986*. Washington, DC: Government Printing Office, 1986.

—— *National Treatment Study, 1990*. Washington, DC: Government Printing Office, 1990.

U.S. Trade Representative, *1993 National Trade Estimate Report on Foreign Trade Barriers*. Washington, DC: Government Printing Office, 1993.

Unpublished company reports and documents
(in company archives)

CB Commercial annual reports. Chicago, 1980–96.

Coldwell Banker annual reports. Los Angeles, 1970–9.

Cushman & Wakefield (US), international real estate market reports, 1989–91.

Dijkstra, F. "International Property Research: The New Dimension". *Comment '90*. Knight Frank & Rutley, London, 1990.

Deutsche Bank. "Deutsche Bank–A Brief History". Frankfurt am Main, December 1989.

Dr. Seebauer & Partner. "From East and West to Unified Germany: Real Estate Market and Real Estate Financing Market". Frankfurt, July 1991.

—— Statistisches Bundesamt. Frankfurt, 1991.

DTZ Debenham Thorpe. Corporate reports including, "Background to DTZ Debenham Thorpe", "DTZ Debenham Thorpe–A Brief History (1984–1994)", "DTZ–The Worldwide Operation", "DTZ Debenham Thorpe–International Statement", public company reports and prospectus documents, London, 1987–96.

Eastdil Realty. Corporate services brochure. New York, 1990–6.

Frank J. Russell Company. MCREIF Property Index. New York, 1975–91.

Giliberto, M. "Real Estate versus Financial Assets–An Updated Comparison of Returns in the United States and the United Kingdom". Salomon Brothers, New York, 16 February 1989.

Goldman Sachs & Co. Annual reports. New York, 1975–96.

Healey & Baker, international real estate market reports. London, 1989–96.

Hillier Parker. *The Hillier Parker Magazine*. Published corporate brochure. London, 1989.

——— *International Property Bulletin 1991*. London, 1991.

Hugill, P. "The International Investor Moves In". *Comment '90*. Knight Frank & Rutley, London, 1990.

Jones Lang Wootton. *A Guide for Foreign Investors in United Kingdom Real Estate*. London, October 1990.

——— International real estate market reports. London, 1980–96.

——— *JLWorld*, London, 1988–96.

Kaizai Chosa Kyoka, *Gaikoku Shihon no Tainichi Toshi: Gaikukuhen*, Tokyo, 1969, 1970, 1980, 1990.

Kalanik, L.M. "Mitsubishi Estate Company". Mitsubishi Estate Company, Tokyo, n.d.

Kenneth Leventhal & Co. "Japanese Capital Flows: Availability and Constraints". Los Angeles, 1992.

——— "1991 Japanese Investment in United States Real Estate". Los Angeles, 1992.

Knight Frank & Rutley. *Comment '90*, London, 1990.

Kostin, D.J. "An Initial Benchmark Portfolio for Global Office Building Investments". New York: Salomon Brothers, October 1989.

——— "German Real Estate Market: An Introduction for Non-German Investors". New York: Salomon Brothers, April 1991.

Landauer Associates. International real estate market reports. New York, 1985–96.

Louis Harris and Associates, Inc. "The Cushman Wakefield/Healey & Baker European Business Real Estate Monitor: American and European Businesses Rate Europe". New York, July–August 1990.

Merigo, E. and S. Potter, "Invisibles in the 1960s", Occasional Studies, *OECD Economic Outlook*, July 1970.

Morgan Stanley Realty. International real estate market reports. New York, 1985–96.

Nikkei Annual Corporation Reports (Kaisha nenkan) (Tokyo: Nihon Keizai Shinbunsha, 1960, 1970, 1980, 1990), which publishes financial statistics and annual stock and flow financial data, and a synopsis of investment activity in Japan by foreign companies.

Price Waterhouse. *Corporate Taxes: A Worldwide Summary*. New York: Price Waterhouse, 1987, 1991.

Prudential Real Estate Investors. Real estate market reports and brochures. Hartford, CT, 1985–90.

Richard Ellis. "Asian Property Market: Investment in the 1990s". London, 1990.

Salomon Brothers. "Real Estate versus Financial Assets–An Updated Comparison of Returns in the United States and the United Kingdom". New York, 15 February 1989.

Shima, Y. "Real Estate Industry Update: After the Land Boom". Goldman Sachs & Co., New York, 7 August 1991.

Shulman, D.G. "The End of the Global Property Boom". Salomon Brothers, New York: 11 December 1990.

—— "Will Rising Japanese Interest Rates Limit the 'Tokyo Takeout'?". Salomon Brothers, New York: 16 January 1990.

Weatherall, Green & Smith. *German Property Report 1990*. London, May 1990.

List of journals, periodicals and organizations

American Enterprise Institute for Public Research

Architecture

Bankers Magazine

Business and Economic History

Business History Review

Business International

Chartered Surveyor Weekly

Commercial Property News

Commission of the European Communities

The Economist

Estates Gazette

Euromoney

The European

European Affairs Journal

European Community Office of Official Publications.

European Economy

Federal Reserve Bank of the United States

Financial Times

Focus

Forbes

Harvard Business Review

Institutional Investor

International Economic Review

International Monetary Fund

Journal of Banking and Finance

Journal of International Business Studies

Journal of the Japanese and International Economies

Land Development Studies

London Trade Policy Research Centre

Mergers and Acquisitions

National Real Estate Investor

Organisation for Economic Co-operation and Development

Oxford Economic Papers

Pensions & Investments

Pensions & Investment Age

The Real Estate Finance Journal

Real Estate Forum

Real Estate Review

Salomon Brothers Center for the Study of Financial Institutions

Single Market Monitor

Site Selection

Site Selection Europe

UK Central Statistical Office

US Committee for Economic Development

US Council on Competitiveness

US Department of Agriculture

US Securities and Exchange Commission

The Wall Street Journal

The Washington Post

The World Economy

World Property

INDEX

247